Silence in the Second Language Classroom

Silence in the Second Language Classroom

Jim King
University of Leicester, UK

© Jim King 2013

All rights reserved. No reproduction, copy or transmission of this publication may be made without written permission.

No portion of this publication may be reproduced, copied or transmitted save with written permission or in accordance with the provisions of the Copyright, Designs and Patents Act 1988, or under the terms of any licence permitting limited copying issued by the Copyright Licensing Agency, Saffron House, 6–10 Kirby Street, London EC1N 8TS.

Any person who does any unauthorized act in relation to this publication may be liable to criminal prosecution and civil claims for damages.

The author has asserted his right to be identified as the author of this work in accordance with the Copyright, Designs and Patents Act 1988.

First published 2013 by
PALGRAVE MACMILLAN

Palgrave Macmillan in the UK is an imprint of Macmillan Publishers Limited, registered in England, company number 785998, of Houndmills, Basingstoke, Hampshire RG21 6XS.

Palgrave Macmillan in the US is a division of St Martin's Press LLC, 175 Fifth Avenue, New York, NY 10010.

Palgrave Macmillan is the global academic imprint of the above companies and has companies and representatives throughout the world.

Palgrave® and Macmillan® are registered trademarks in the United States, the United Kingdom, Europe and other countries

ISBN: 978–1–137–30147–5

This book is printed on paper suitable for recycling and made from fully managed and sustained forest sources. Logging, pulping and manufacturing processes are expected to conform to the environmental regulations of the country of origin.

A catalogue record for this book is available from the British Library.

A catalog record for this book is available from the Library of Congress.

For Hana,
whose first words are yet to come

When silence is prolonged over a certain period of time, it takes on new meaning.
– *Yukio Mishima*, Thirst for Love

Contents

Foreword by Zoltán Dörnyei	viii
Acknowledgements	x
List of acronyms	xi
Transcription conventions	xii
1 Introduction	1
2 Major theoretical frameworks of silence	12
3 An interdisciplinary overview of silence in Japan	32
4 A critical analysis of Japan's language education system	64
5 A structured observation study into L2 classroom silence	83
6 An interview study into learners' perspectives on L2 classroom silence	102
7 A naturalistic stimulated recall study of specific silence events	129
8 Summary and conclusions	151
References	170
Glossary of selected Japanese terms	187
Appendix 1: The COPS observation scheme	189
Appendix 2: The SOPIG interview guide	192
Appendix 3: The stimulated recall protocol	198
Author Index	203
Subject Index	208

Foreword

When I first heard about Jim King's research topic – silence – I was bemused but did not think that too much would come out of it. How wrong I was! Silence in the language classroom turned out to be a captivating, interdisciplinary subject, spanning a number of academic fields and producing surprising results. As I watched the project unfold, I was increasingly caught up in the fascinating realisation of how much we can learn about speech through silence.

I always thought that Japanese learners enjoy – or at least don't mind – being silent. Again I was wrong! They can find silence just as awkward as their Western counterparts, and yet we find disproportionately more silence in Japanese classrooms than probably anywhere else in the world. Why is this? Jim King's intriguing book offers a full investigation into this question. Drawing on complex dynamic systems theory as an organising framework, he presents rich quantitative and qualitative data to explain the widespread nature of the absence of student-initiated speech in Japanese language classrooms. Finding answers has not been easy. How do you observe silence in a structured way? How do you identify the multiple reasons underlying a student's lack of speech? And how do you collect verbal qualitative data from students whose main characteristic is that they do not speak?

Having lived in Japan for several years, Jim was in a good position to explore these issues. He knew the phenomenon well, since he encountered it on a daily basis, but he was also convinced that silence need not be an inevitable feature of Japanese language education. After all, he *was* able to get his learners to speak, and he was also aware of the fact that those Japanese undergraduates who did not open their mouths during a class could be positively verbose, even noisy, in the breaks after class! With this in mind, he set out on a journey of discovery: he had the patience, the sensitivity, the methodological know-how and the intellectual creativity to go beyond commonplaces and present a fresh picture. The result is a book that opens up several lesser-known layers of Japanese society and the educational system. This is a highly informative volume and – what I particularly appreciate – it is also a genuinely good read. Jim is a born story-teller even when presenting statistical data, and I am sure that readers will be engrossed in his narrative just as I was. How can I best sum up Jim's work on silence? Words fail me...

Zoltán Dörnyei
Professor of Psycholinguistics, University of Nottingham

Acknowledgements

My sincere thanks extend to all the staff and students in Japan who agreed to take part in the research on classroom silence which is presented in this book. In particular, I would like to say a big *'arigatō'* firstly to Atsuko Aono for the invaluable help she gave me in gaining access to research sites and participants, and secondly to Rodney Johnson for his cheerful hospitality on the Kansai legs of my fieldwork. I am deeply grateful to Zoltán Dörnyei in Nottingham for helping me to believe this book was possible and for sharing with me his exciting and innovative ideas about applied linguistics research and language learning. Thank you, Zoltán, for your expert guidance and infectious positivity! I would also like thank Olivia Middleton and Jill Lake at Palgrave for their expertise and support during the publishing process, and to thank Ana Jolly for her delightful artwork. The research presented here would also not have been possible had it not been for the unflagging support of my wife, Maiko. I cannot thank her enough for her unstinting encouragement and for all the help she gave me with translations and issues relating to the Japanese language.

The quotation by Yukio Mishima which appears on page vi comes from his novel *Thirst for Love* and is reproduced courtesy of Random House. Figure 1 'Interpretation of silence – Basic model' on page 16 is from *Discourse of Silence* by Dennis Kurzon (1998) and is reprinted here by kind permission of John Benjamins Publishing. Chapter 5 is a modified version of my paper: King, J. (2013) Silence in the second language classrooms of Japanese universities. *Applied Linguistics*, 34(3), 325–43. I am grateful to Oxford University Press for granting permission to reproduce the material here.

List of acronyms

ALT	Assistant Language Teacher
CLAIR	Council of Local Authorities for International Relations
CLT	Communicative Language Teaching
COLT	Communicative Orientation of Language Teaching (observation scheme)
COPS	Classroom Oral Participation Scheme (observation scheme)
DST	Dynamic Systems Theory
EFL	English as a Foreign Language
ESL	English as a Second Language
FLint	Foreign Language interaction analysis system (observation scheme)
FTA	Face Threatening Act
IRF	Initiation Response Feedback
JET	Japan Exchange and Teaching Programme
JTE	Japanese Teacher of English
L1	First language
L2	Foreign/Second language
MEXT	Ministry of Education, Culture, Sport, Science and Technology (Japan)
NS	Native Speaker
SLA	Second Language Acquisition
SOPIG	Silence and Oral Participation Interview Guide
TOEFL	Test of English as a Foreign Language
TRP	Transition Relevance Place
TTT	Teacher Talking Time
UCAS	Universities and Colleges Admissions Service (United Kingdom)
WTC	Willingness to Communicate

Transcription conventions

.	falling 'final' intonation	That'll do just fine.
,	continuing 'list' intonation	We saw larks, tits, finches and wrens
?	question intonation	Really?
!	animated talk	Super!
(..)	pause of about 0.5 second	But (..) it works anyway
(…)	pause of about 1 second	I think (…) it takes time
(2)	pause of about 2 seconds	Erm (2) let me see
(·hhh)	inhalations	(·hhh) That was close
(hhh)	aspirations	(hhh) It's been quite a day
((laughter))	other details	You're right ((spoken while laughing))
<u>Always</u>	emphasis	It'll take <u>forever</u>
:	lengthening of a sound	She al::::ways does that
(mist)	unsure transcription	I used to (skate) a lot
(xxx)	unable to transcribe	The (xxxxx) system is on now
-	abrupt cut off	He took- she took her time
CAPS	louder than surrounding talk	I never knew GEORGE could dance
°°	quieter than surrounding talk	I'm getting there °you know°

(adapted from Richards, 2003)

1
Introduction

This book explores the silent behaviour of learners studying English within Japanese university second language (L2) classrooms. The verbal unresponsiveness of undergraduates in this setting has been alluded to in a number of past works (e.g. Anderson, 1993; Korst, 1997) and there is much anecdotal evidence of Japanese students' propensity towards silence, and yet it seems strange that no major empirical research has been conducted positioning silence at the heart of its investigation whilst using Japanese tertiary education as its context. Why could this be? Perhaps it is because silence is a somewhat esoteric phenomenon that tends to exist on the edge of our consciousness. This lack of awareness, coupled to a relative scarcity of relevant literature dealing with the subject (when compared to spoken aspects of L2 learner discourse), means that silence simply does not seem to be on most educational researchers' radar. This in itself is odd because it is an issue that affects everybody who teaches; whether silencing the boisterous or encouraging the silent to contribute – both are part of educators' daily classroom realities. A further difficulty which might help to explain the lack of empirical studies in this area is that investigating silence presents a number of methodological challenges and interpretive conundrums that are not easily resolved. How can silence be effectively identified and measured within classrooms? How can accurate meanings be gleaned from something so multifaceted, ambiguous and highly dependent upon context for its significance? In answering these questions, the research presented here adopts a highly interdisciplinary perspective and draws upon multiple data types and sources in a bid to uncover the true complexity that lies beneath language learners' classroom silences.

1.1 My L2 pedagogical beliefs and assumptions

As the mixed-methods study of silence presented in this monograph involves a substantial qualitative element, it would be appropriate here to outline some of my own biases and personal beliefs about language learning in order to enhance the reflexive nature of my research. This is in line with Cohen, Manion and Morrison's (2007, p.172) conception that highly reflexive researchers are acutely aware of how their selectivity, perception and background help shape the research they conduct. It also acknowledges Dörnyei's (2007) assertion that qualitative research entails a co-constructed product made up of both the researcher's and the participants' perceptions, and as such, should involve reflexive discussion of the researcher's biases and assumptions.

While conceding that silence itself is certainly not an inherently negative phenomenon, indeed many is the time I have sought out its restorative or contemplative functions, I do believe that in the context of a foreign language classroom silence represents a significant threat to effective language learning when it is characterised by a lack of oral participation and verbal responsiveness on the part of students. Simply put, I believe that language learners have to communicate in order to acquire the target language they are studying. This position is partly informed by my many years of experience as a foreign language educator working in different countries around the world, but it is also a view well supported by what is a broad body of research into L2 learner interaction and output (e.g. de Bot, 1996; Ellis, 1999; Gass, 1997; Iwashita, 2003; Izumi, 2003; Mackey, 2002; Mackey, Gass & McDonough, 2000). Prominent within this canon is Swain's (1995) seminal work on language learner output which posits that production of the target language has three main functions that are worth setting out in more detail. They are: the noticing/trigger function whereby learners are prompted to consciously recognise their linguistic problems; the hypothesis testing function which sees learners use output to test whether their utterance is communicated successfully or whether it results in negative feedback and hence requires further modified output; and the metalinguistic function whereby output allows for reflection about the language produced by the self and others, this being a particularly useful function when learners are engaged in collaborative tasks (see Swain & Lapkin, 1998). A closely related study also worth mentioning here is Long's (1996) reworked version of the Interaction Hypothesis which suggests that conversational interaction promotes L2 development through the negotiation of meaning and 'connects input, internal learner capacities, particularly selective attention and output in productive ways' (pp. 451–2).

While it is true that not all classroom talk leads automatically to L2 development, few people would argue with the notion that opportunities for meaningful oral production in the target language do help students to achieve greater levels of spoken fluency. Through my own professional experiences I found this to be an issue particularly relevant to the Japanese L2 learning context. I spent a number of years as an English language lecturer within Japan's tertiary system and this experience reinforced my conviction that a premium has to be placed on maximising students' oral participation, particularly if their communicative competence (see Canale, 1983; Canale & Swain, 1980) is to be enhanced. While there were one or two notable exceptions, generally the undergraduates I encountered during my time in Japan possessed what could only be described as desultory L2 communication skills and appeared to have been very poorly served by a system of pre-tertiary foreign language education whose limited focus and restrictive practices neglected the development of the students' practical language abilities. In my role as a teacher trainer of Japanese teachers of English (JTEs), I was able to see at first hand how entrenched traditional grammar-translation instructional methods were amongst staff working in junior and senior high schools. Encouraging students to communicate in the target language simply was not a priority for these teachers. Although enthusiastic to learn about new task-based and communicative approaches to language learning, in private many JTEs freely admitted that pressure to achieve high examination scores, coupled to demands from senior staff to follow established institutional precedents and concerns about effectively managing learners' classroom behaviour, precluded them from ever being able to implement the communicative techniques they had learnt. The pedagogical position I endorsed on these courses acknowledged the importance of adopting a methodology appropriate to the social context (Holliday, 1994). This position is perhaps best summed up by Fotos (2005) when she points towards:

> an eclectic combination of methods and activities, with grammar, vocabulary, and translation activities retained and communicative activities added that contain abundant uses of target language structures and vocabulary, thus permitting exposure to target structures and providing opportunities for negotiated output in the target language. (p. 668)

I would further contend that classrooms which emphasise maximum cooperation between participants tend to be the ones in which successful learning is facilitated. While this applies to most learning contexts, I feel it is particularly relevant to university settings where learners ought to have reached a relative level of maturity. Cooperative learning in an L2 learning context (see Dörnyei, 1997; McCafferty, Jacobs & DaSilva Iddings, 2006; Oxford, 1997) can only take place when students engage in active, collaborative oral participation both with each other and with their instructor. This follows the belief by Johnson and Johnson (cited in Ehrman & Dörnyei, 1998) that, in addition to other factors, effective cooperation requires students to: ask for opinions; ask for help/clarification; justify their opinions; give full explanations; negotiate ideas; manage conflicts through discussion; encourage active participation by all; and give constructive feedback and criticism. Clearly these behaviours require overt verbalisation (whether in the students' own language or in the L2) and consequently learner silence is something which threatens the effective functioning of cooperation within a classroom.

I should note here that, in a bid to avoid influencing subject behaviour, throughout the various phases of data collection for this book I was careful not to reveal any of my pedagogical beliefs to those participating in the research. In interactions with the instructors whose classes I observed, I studiously avoided voicing support for any of the L2 instructional paradigms outlined above and was also meticulous in circumventing requests to provide feedback on the lessons I observed – at least until after data collection was completed. With the learners who participated in the study's various interviews, I endeavoured to maintain a strictly non-judgmental stance towards learner silence and reticence within L2 learning situations. Criticising such behaviour would not only have been detrimental to the interviewer–interviewee rapport I was keen to establish, it would most likely have resulted in the collection of rather limited and unreliable testimony.

My professional experiences in Japan proved to be not the only catalyst which stimulated a long-term academic interest in silence within social interactions. In my non-professional identity as a long-term resident of the country and keen student of the Japanese language who interacted with locals on a daily basis, I gradually became aware of what appeared to be a quite different disposition towards silence within interpersonal interactions than I had encountered previously. In naturalistic contexts it seemed that knowing when *not* to speak, and the ability to tolerate and interpret silence, particularly in more formal settings, were skills perhaps even more vital to successful interaction than being able to discourse on any given topic at length. This crystallising emic perception of appropriate Japanese paralinguistic behaviour proved important, as it enabled me to begin to view the verbal unresponsiveness of the L2 learners I was encountering in my professional life in a changed and slightly more sympathetic light.

1.2 The theoretical approach of this book

I have adopted an intentionally varied conceptual approach in this book in order to provide a thorough, yet cohesive examination of the wide-ranging and sometimes perplexing issue of silence. Helping to draw these interdisciplinary arguments together, I interpret the results of my research through the lens of dynamic systems theory (DST). At first glance DST can seem quite a daunting prospect for those who are new to the approach – it emanates from the hard sciences and is well known for having some rather difficult mathematics associated with it. However, the basic premise of the theory is really quite simple. Complex systems, which in the case of research on classroom silence might include, for example, an individual's classroom discourse system, have numerous interrelated and interacting components which work together to influence both directly and indirectly how the system develops. This means that it makes more sense to view a learner's oral behaviour as being shaped by multiple, connected factors whose influences wax and wane over time, than to explain the behaviour as being the result of a single variable.

A DST approach is very useful for silence researchers because it offers great flexibility. It provides an over-arching conceptual framework through which to view entrenched silent behaviour at individual, classroom, institutional and societal levels, whilst at the same time not precluding the use of other theoretical approaches to explain specific silence episodes. Silence is such an inherently ambiguous and varied phenomenon that its study necessitates the flexible, interdisciplinary approach which DST allows. Complementing the DST-orientated discussion with which I present my various research findings, in Chapter 5 I provide a more in-depth overview of the theory and introduce some key DST concepts and terminology relevant to the project.

1.3 The structure of this book

This book is organised in such a way as to provide an in-depth and inter-connecting critical exploration of the silence which exists in the

L2 classrooms of Japanese universities. Following on from this introductory chapter, Chapters 2 to 4 provide an overview of the various theoretical frameworks through which silence may be studied and also place the current research firmly within its Japanese context. The subsequent three chapters are presented as stand-alone studies. This approach makes a good deal of sense because each chapter employs a different primary research methodology, and when viewed in sequence they combine to form a natural progression from the general to the specific. In other words, the book progresses from research identifying general trends of silence within language classrooms, and then moves on to an individual-level analysis of students' fundamental beliefs about oral participation and classroom silence, and concludes with a detailed examination of learners' perceptions of event-specific silent episodes which occurred during their L2 lessons. This organisation provides the maximum coherence for what was an extensive multi-site, mixed-methods research project. In the following, I offer a more detailed outline of each chapter's contents.

Providing an overview of major studies which have to date sought to define and interpret the phenomenon of silence, Chapter 2 outlines a number of quite different conceptual frameworks dealing with people's silent behaviour. These works emanate from a range of academic fields and are intentionally eclectic in nature. This eclecticism is firstly a matter of necessity, due to the severe paucity of empirical research studies which place language learner silence at their heart, but more importantly, and as Jaworski (1997) rightly reminds us, silence is such a broad and diverse concept that only an interdisciplinary approach to its study can really do it justice. Hence the chapter draws from such varied disciplines as pragmatics, sociolinguistics, psychology, anthropology, educational theory, and conversation analysis, in an attempt to gain insights into the conundrum that is silence. One important theme to emerge here is that silence does not necessarily equate to a breakdown in communication. In a functional sense it may overlap with speech and, although sometimes misinterpreted (particularly in intercultural contexts), silence is often employed to convey a message. Another significant theme discussed in the chapter relates to the psychological and emotional aspects of a person's silent behaviour. That silence may reflect one's psychological inhibitions, and that it can be used as a very effective tool for emotional defence, are both concepts which become evident not just in this initial literature review chapter, but also throughout the book. A final fundamental idea to emerge in this section, supported in particular by insights gained from the ethnographic-orientated studies which I examine, is the merit of studying silence within a specific cultural context. As people's reactions to, and interpretations of, silence may vary significantly between cultures, it becomes vitally important to have a clear understanding of the relative value that particular speech communities place on silence in comparison to speech.

Chapter 3 seeks to extend the idea that valuable insights may be gained through a culture-specific study of silence by exploring how it is perceived and utilised within a Japanese sociocultural context. This wide-ranging and, once again, highly interdisciplinary chapter adopts a wide definition of silence (ranging from the micro-silence of pauses, through to the macro-silence of minimal verbalisation by a discourse community) in order to delve to the very roots of Japanese silent behaviour. I discuss how silence appears to be positively construed in many contexts, and how cultural concepts relating to hierarchical social relationships and the importance of group membership both provide helpful background knowledge for researchers hoping to understand Japanese silence more fully. After reflecting on how deep-seated cultural attitudes towards speech and silence are reflected in Japan's proverbs, poetry and literature, the chapter goes on to examine the assertion that the Japanese may in fact be socialised into a kind of silent, highly inferential communication style by specific child-rearing practices which tend to avoid overt verbalisation. I also consider the argument that Japanese children are encouraged from an early age to be sensitive to the thoughts and feelings of those around them, and that this sensitivity may eventually transmute into an ego-centric concern for how the self is presented which is manifested by a chronic silence-inducing inhibition that is especially evident within classroom situations. Linked to this is the idea that the avoidance of talk is an effective method of protecting one's own and others' face – this being an endeavour that is particularly important within Japanese society. I therefore draw on the work of researchers such as Sifianou (1997) to outline the various ways in which silence may be employed as a politeness strategy, before reflecting on the possible uses of silence by Japanese learners as a means of face protection. Chapter 3 concludes with an examination of silence from a linguistic perspective, and considers how cross-cultural differences in turn-taking styles may result in Japanese learners' prolonged pauses being misinterpreted during educational interactions.

I have to admit to being intrigued by language learners who, even though they possess the requisite L2 skills for oral communication in the target language, persist in remaining silent in class. Nevertheless, it should be acknowledged that for many Japanese students, their lack of talk has little to do with *choosing* to be silent but is primarily a consequence of significant deficiencies in their L2 abilities. With this in mind, Chapter 4 provides a wide-ranging critical analysis of how Japan's foreign language education system has persistently struggled to produce competent L2 users, despite the fact that English forms a compulsory component of every child's pre-tertiary education. Various top-down curricular reforms have been introduced over the years aimed at improving the situation, but these have proved to be poorly planned and ineffective, doing little to improve the nation's disappointing practical language skills. Part of the problem appears to be that the system places far too much emphasis on achieving high scores in university entrance examinations at the expense of developing students' basic L2 communicative competencies. I therefore provide a detailed overview of Japan's university entrance examinations and consider how these high-stakes tests may be related to the silence of its second language learners. Building upon this theme, the chapter subsequently addresses the issue of *yakudoku*, a common and deeply entrenched traditional pedagogical approach to L2 learning which appears to effectively silence learners whilst at the same time allowing instructors to avoid actually ever having to converse in the target language. One would think that the thousands of native speaker assistant language teachers (ALTs) who have historically been employed in Japan's schools would provide the perfect antidote to such an unproductive state of affairs. However, as we shall see in Chapter 4, for various reasons these generally inexperienced instructors have achieved relatively little success in helping learners improve their L2 communicative skills.

While there is plenty of anecdotal evidence concerning the taciturnity of Japanese language learners, large-scale, empirical studies aimed at measuring the extent of macro-level silence within Japanese university L2 classrooms are notably lacking. Chapter 5 responds to the gap in the literature by reporting on an extensive, multi-site study using a structured observation methodology to investigate the classroom behaviour of over 900 language learners across nine universities. In order to do this effectively, a classroom observation instrument called the Classroom Oral Participation Scheme (COPS) was specially developed for the task. Based on the in-time coding design of Spada and Fröhlich's (1995) Communicative Orientation of Language Teaching scheme (COLT) and the content categories of Moskowitz's (1971) Foreign Language interaction analysis system (FLint), the COPS provides a novel means of recording classroom events in real time, with an emphasis on the scrutiny of learners' oral production. Chapter 5 describes the scheme's various features in detail (see also the Appendix for a step-by-step guide to using the instrument) and outlines why the COPS is so efficient at collecting evidence of macro-level silences in language classrooms. 'The observer's paradox' (Labov, 1972) whereby the presence of a researcher influences subjects' linguistic behaviour is always a key concern in this type of research and so the chapter also discusses the range of measures I had to employ in order to ensure that reactivity amongst the teachers and students who were being observed was kept to an absolute minimum. In all, the phase of the project described in this chapter produced a total of 48 hours of data through a minute-by-minute sampling strategy. This data contained some startling results, especially concerning the negligible levels of initiated talk students were found to be responsible for within their classes. These results are interpreted through the lens of dynamic systems theory (DST), which suggests that silence emerges through multiple routes and has now formed a semi-permanent attractor state within Japan's L2 university classrooms.

Although systematic observation using a low-inference scheme provides a reliable methodology for identifying powerful attractor-governed phenomena within language classrooms, its cross-sectional approach of distinguishing general trends is not ideally suited to gaining an individual-level analysis of learners' silent behaviour. Therefore, complementing the quantitative findings of the observation phase of the study, Chapter 6 gives students a voice about their silences by drawing on over 70,000 words of transcribed data which I collected during a series of semi-structured interviews. This phase of the study was aimed at examining students' fundamental beliefs about silence and their individual attitudes towards oral participation in Japan's foreign language classrooms. It has to be said, though, that conducting a qualitative enquiry about classroom silence with learners who come from a society in which there is a marked tendency to avoid self-disclosure (Barnlund, 1974, 1989; Gudykunst & Nishida, 1993; Lebra, 1993) was a far from straightforward task. The chapter therefore describes the various interview-based research procedures that I had to implement in order to overcome the intriguing paradox of getting my interviewees to speak about not speaking. The testimony gained from a diverse sample of eight students demonstrates that silence has multiple forms and multiple functions within Japanese university L2 classes. These students reveal some of the principal and sometimes unexpected forces operating at learner, classroom and societal levels which help to shape their silent behaviour in educational contexts. The chapter also includes an interesting negative case example in which an undergraduate describes how her decision to leave a classroom clique of which she was a member, in conjunction with changes connected to a number of other key variables, resulted in the student becoming a more orally active language learner.

Chapter 7 adopts an event-specific focus on classroom silence. In order to uncover what students were actually thinking and feeling whilst silent episodes were in progress in language classes, I employed a stimulated recall methodology (Gass & Mackey, 2000) supported by empirical qualitative data gained from the observation phase of the project. While stimulated recall studies focusing on learners' oral interactions remain relatively rare, it is no exaggeration to say that retrospective research on language learner silence is even rarer. This chapter therefore provides a highly original attempt to acquire insights into why learners refrained from talk in particular L2 learning situations, how they perceived the task that was occurring at the moment the silence took place, and also how they perceived their co-participants. The students who took part in this phase of the research reflect well the wide range of L2 learning experiences on offer within Japanese universities. Included in the sample were both language and non-language majors whose levels of English language proficiency varied considerably. Gaining retrospective data from these students about the silent episodes they had produced was again no easy task and so I had to implement a number of procedural measures in order to facilitate the collection of sufficient and valid data. For example, the timing of the retrospective interviews (the sooner, the better after classroom events in order to avoid memory decay) and the language of the recall sessions (L1 to help subjects better verbalise their thoughts) were just two areas to which special attention was paid. Although the retrospective testimony elicited in this phase of the research could hardly be described as particularly eloquent, and it would be wrong to expect otherwise from highly reticent learners being asked to talk about their silent behaviour, the data presented in Chapter 7 do give important insights into what these students were actually thinking during specific silent episodes, particularly with regards to their feelings of anxiety when required to speak in the target language and their demotivation to study English at university.

Chapter 8 forms the conclusion to the book. The initial part of the chapter provides a summary of the study's main research findings and outlines how I overcame some of the major methodological challenges that were thrown up by a mixed-methods investigation. Following on from this, the subsequent section notes the project's limitations and discusses some possible future avenues for research into language learner silence. The final section of the conclusion presents a number of practical implications of the study. These implications cover both micro-level issues relating to pedagogical methodology and the macro-level issue of language education planning within Japan.

2
Major theoretical frameworks of silence

2.1 Introduction

How have researchers sought to define, interpret and understand silence? As a subject for study, this often-ignored phenomenon is both potentially fascinating and problematic in equal measure. Investigating something as intangible as silence, something that can be neither seen nor heard, poses real challenges for researchers, who must be creative and interpretively astute enough to capture silence's true essence. What follows then is a selective overview of major studies which have provided valuable insights into various theoretical aspects of people's silent behaviour. It will quickly become apparent to the reader that silence is not simply the absence of noise or merely the lack of communication. Indeed, the various studies reviewed below show that there are multiple ways to define silence and, concomitantly, multiple ways to go about the business of studying it. Even so, despite this seeming eclecticism, a number of major themes recur throughout the overview, for example, concerning how silence may be related to power, ambiguity, affect, and so on. Themes introduced in this initial outline will be referred to throughout the rest of the book.

The overview begins with an examination of two influential interpretive works that reach their theoretical conclusions by drawing on ideas from fields such as linguistics, sociology and, importantly, psychology. Ephratt (2008) notes that psychology has long been preoccupied with the study of silence (for a comprehensive review, see Lane, Koetting & Bishop, 2002), with the field having identified a variety of types and functions within the therapeutic discourse of psychoanalysis. With this in mind, the overview turns its attention to studies emphasising psychological and emotional aspects of silence, before considering how silence can be interpreted, often ethnocentrically, in either a positive or negative way. The importance of studying silence within a specific cultural context is then highlighted by a section detailing influential ethnographic-orientated works that have made silence the focal point for investigation. There exist a number of ethnographic studies which have investigated speech and silence norms within individual communities (e.g. Agyekum, 2002; Nwoye, 1985; Philips, 1976), but it is perhaps Basso's (1990) classic paper (originally appearing in 1972) on the silent behaviour of Western Apache American Indians that has been most significant, because it so effectively highlighted the roles that ambiguity and status inequality play in influencing whether a person decides to remain silent in a particular situation. I therefore outline the focal points of Basso's research, which complements the description I give of Saville-Troike's (1985) ethnographic framework through which silence may be viewed. As my research focuses on the silent behaviour of Japanese language learners, the final part of the overview concentrates on studies seeking to comprehend silences that occur specifically within educational contexts. I discuss both teachers' and students' attitudes and beliefs in relation to the differing ways in which they perform and construe classroom silence, and the reader will soon detect in this section an inherent tension resulting from dissimilar performances and interpretations.

2.2 Interpretive approaches

Jaworski's 'fuzzy categories'

One of the most important recent works contributing to our understanding of the theoretical aspects of silence is Jaworski's (1993) *The Power of Silence: Social and Pragmatic Perspectives.* Jaworski's interpretive work proposes that an essentialist approach to the study of silence in which one, true definition of silence can be reached, is untenable. He is particularly critical of Dauenhauer's (1980) essentialist study into the ontology of silence and questions the wisdom of trying to reach the essence of silence through a conclusive definition. According to Jaworski, this type of approach is a waste of time and inevitably leads to 'futile terminological disputes' (1993, p. 30). Indeed, he draws our attention to Dauenhauer's own telling admission that, in the end, 'no ontological interpretation of silence can be *definitively* established' (cited in Jaworski, 1993, p. 33). The rejection of this essentialist approach means that Jaworski is able to take up operational, working definitions which allow him flexibility in exploring the eclectic nature of silence in various communicative situations using various theoretical frameworks. Thus he is better able to reflect the true depth and complexity of silence using theories from fields such as psycholinguistics, semiotics, philosophy, pragmatics, literature, and, most notably, ethnography.

Jaworski rejects the notion of silence solely as an absolute signifying the breakdown of communication. Rather than being a negative category devoid of communicative properties, the construction of silence may be deemed a legitimate communicative act (see Bruneau, 1973). Indeed, silence can be construed semantically, is open to interpretation and may convey various meanings. This functional overlap with speech is emphasised by Jaworski's insistence that both speech and silence be treated as 'fuzzy, complementary categories' (1993, p. 48). He suggests that, 'silence and speech do not stand in total opposition to each other, but form a continuum of forms ranging from the most prototypical instances of silence to the most prototypical instances of speech' (Jaworski, 1993, p. 34). Given that the most prototypical concept of silence is a total lack of audible verbalisation, Jaworski's approach means that his working definition of silence can be extended to include a person failing to talk about a specific topic or to say what was expected. Thus someone may be speaking and making noise, but he/she may still be considered silent if a specific topic is avoided. Interestingly, Jaworski (1993, p. 71) draws on Verschueren to note that, unlike in Polish, Hungarian, or some other languages, the English language does not draw a lexical distinction between 'to be silent' in an acoustic sense and 'to be silent' in a pragmatic sense. The flexibility of this broad approach enables Jaworski to extend his discussion of silence to such areas as politics, literature and even the visual arts (see also Jaworski, 1997). Later empirical research he undertook into students' and teachers' attitudes to and beliefs about silence (Jaworski & Sachdev, 1998, 2004) will be discussed in more detail later.

Kurzon's model of intentionality

Following on in the interpretive vein, Kurzon's (1998) study examines silence within a broadly semiotic framework and recognises that its meaning is highly dependent upon context. As each society has its own tolerance range towards the length of a silence in conversation, Kurzon rightly suggests that the interpretation of silence has to be culture-specific. In the case of the current work, the focus is primarily on the Anglo-American context. Like Jaworski (1993), Kurzon draws on theories from a variety of fields, including psychology, sociology and linguistics and, in particular, draws on conversation analysis, to examine the silence that occurs in dyadic interactions. It is his ideas concerning the silent answer in question-answer adjacency pairs that are of most interest to the researcher investigating silence in educational settings because Kurzon highlights the key role that intentionality plays in the interpretation of silence.

Kurzon employs a modal interpretation of a person's silence to uncover their reason for not speaking, with 'knowledge' or 'ability to speak' as initial points for consideration. Regarding knowledge, he employs the following illustration.

> the silent addressee may know or not know the answer to the question s/he is being asked. If s/he knows, then there are two possible responses – verbal response as the cooperative way of responding to a question, or silence. Which is uncooperative, to say the least. If, on the other hand, the addressee does not know the answer, s/he has also the possibility of two ways of responding – by saying 'I don't know," or by keeping silent. I have claimed that since people are often embarrassed when they have to reveal their ignorance, they can hide this ignorance behind a wall of silence in situations where they are not forced to speak. A pupil sitting at the back of the class often plays this game. (Kurzon, 1998, p. 38)

It is interesting to note that in a Japanese educational setting, a silent response to mean 'I don't know' may not be deemed uncooperative at all by the addresser and is commonly employed by students in classroom situations.

Kurzon (1998, p. 38) goes on to suggest that the ability/inability to speak should also be taken into account when analysing silence. He divides a lack of ability to speak into two possibilities: lack of knowledge on the one hand and psychological disabilities, such as shyness or anxiety on the other. Thus, Kurzon considers silences derived from psychological inhibitions to be unintentional, characterised by an addressee having no control over his/her response and therefore lapsing into silence. Intentional silence, it is claimed however, results from, 'a genuine choice made by the addressee and may be verbalized through a speech act...e.g. "I will not talk"' (Kurzon, 1998, p. 36). This modal interpretation of silence appears to be a useful tool for uncovering a person's general reason for choosing to remain silent by not verbally responding to a question. The three possible modal interpretations of silence (Kurzon, 1998, p. 44) may be summarised as follows:

- Unintentional silence caused by psychological inhibitions – 'I cannot speak'.
- Intentional silence due to addressee's own choice – 'I will not/shall not speak'.
- Intentional silence due to an external source – 'I must not/may not speak'.

These modal interpretations can then be set into a basic model for interpreting silent answers, as set out in Figure 1. Note that 'presence' is signalled by the addressee either answering the question verbally or admitting explicitly that he/she does not know the answer. 'Non-presence', on the other hand, may be signalled by the addressee verbally stating a refusal to answer the question, or by remaining intentionally or unintentionally silent.

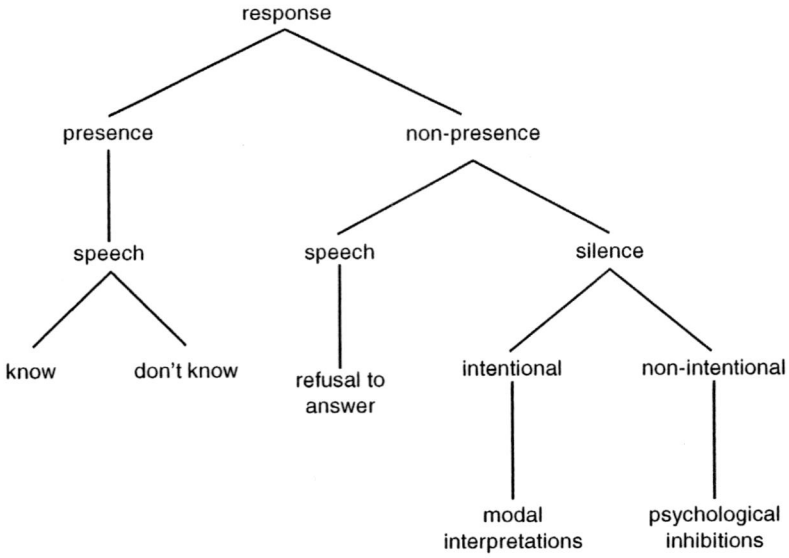

Figure 1 Interpretation of silence. Basic model (Kurzon, 1998, p. 45)

Though useful in focusing attention on the intentionality aspect of silent responses, Kurzon's framework for interpreting silences using a modal analysis does have some drawbacks. Firstly, modal verbs can only provide rather vague reasons for silent responses and are themselves sometimes ambiguous and open to interpretation. For example, 'cannot' refers to both ability and permission. In addition, Kurzon's model is best applied to interactions taking place within an institutional setting between two people and is biased towards cognitive factors in the creation of silence in formal settings. This is understandable though, considering the author's interest in how a defendant's silence may be misinterpreted in different legal systems around the world (see also Kurzon, 1995). In sum then, although like Jaworski (1993), Kurzon's contribution to our theoretical understanding of silence is not based on empirical evidence, his model is still useful in providing a broad interpretive framework for silent responses in dyadic interactions involving question-answer adjacency pairs occurring specifically in institutional settings.

2.3 Psychological aspects in the study of silence

Granger's psychoanalytic interpretation of the silent period

So far we have observed that the rich complexity of silence is best reflected in studies which are dynamic in their theoretical interpretations and interdisciplinary in nature. Granger's (2004) work continues this theme and takes the highly original stance that psychoanalytic theory provides the richest source of answers as to why learners may remain silent during the second language acquisition (SLA) process. This stance reaffirms Ehrman and Dörnyei's (1998, pp. 200–1) belief that insights from psychoanalysis can be of help to educators trying to make sense of seemingly irrational behaviour by learners in the classroom. Granger departs from the study of silence as a communicative strategy (c.f. Jaworski, 1993, 1997; Saville-Troike, 1985) and instead considers 'the silent period' as a manifestation of a learner's identity formation and re-formation during the early stages of acquiring a second language. Rather than a complete absence of sound, Granger interprets silence as being an absence of authentic, original and creative production of the second language. She describes this type of silence as being:

> ... not just of the vocal apparatus but of the *self*: a silence, that is, which may be symptomatic of a kind of suspension between two linguistic selves, occurring in a kind of moment that is both linguistic and psychical within the complex process (itself not merely linguistic, but also psychical) of moving from one language to another and,

simultaneously, from one linguistic self to another. (Granger, 2004, p. 21)

Granger draws upon ideas from the likes of Sigmund Freud and Donald Winnicott to establish how the four main concepts of psychoanalytic theory – anxiety, ambivalence, conflict and loss – relate to a language learner's changing self-concept within the early SLA process and how silence plays an integral role in such a process. Both Freudian ideas concerning melancholia and mourning, and Britzman's (1998) notion of the inherent conflict in learning (a conflict that consists of the self's struggle between the desire to learn and the desire to ignore learning due to the anxiety and loss of the familiar that such a process brings) are utilised by Granger to suggest that silence may be 'symptomatic of the loss, ambivalence and conflict that accompany the transition between two languages' (p. 62). Indeed, Granger claims that the silent period in some second language learners may therefore be a sort of 'psychical paralysis, a temporary freezing, a complex combination of an inability to articulate and a lowered self-regard' (p. 62) which results in the learner being suspended precariously between two selves, living unsteadily in a changed identity between two languages.

Although it de-emphasises the many socially and culturally grounded uses of silence, and only very briefly considers how identity is manifested differently in various cultures, Granger's study is of import to the researcher interested in silence in educational settings because it successfully illustrates that '"something of significance" is indeed happening, even when learners are silent' (Granger, 2004, p. 30) and disproves the myth that something of significance can only be taking place when learners are talking to each other. In addition, the study shows that the silent period is an ambiguous, difficult to define and dynamic phenomenon that repulses generalisations about learners' silences.

Crown and Feldstein's psychological correlates of silence in conversation

Moving away from an educational context, to which we will return later, I continue with the theme of psychology and silence by highlighting Crown and Feldstein's (1985) overview of studies focusing on the psychological correlates of silence and sound in conversational interaction. The silence in question here relates to micro-level silences found in the pauses of an interpersonal interaction. A number of psycholinguistic studies (e.g. Feldstein & Sloan, 1984; Feldstein, Alberti & BenDebba, 1979) have quantitatively measured speech tempo along with corresponding pauses in laboratory environments in order to investigate the relationship between silence and personality variables.

Taking into account self-attributed personality characteristics, Crown and Feldstein point out that 'longer pauses tend to be produced by individuals who can be described as distrustful, easily upset, worrying, shy, suspicious, troubled, fussy, and driven, but also self-sufficient and resourceful' (1985, p. 38). They claim it is not only the speaker's characteristics that influence the length of silences in interpersonal interactions – the listener's characteristics may also prove significant. Listeners eliciting longer pauses were described as being 'precise, sceptical, self-reliant, unsentimental, and practical, but also somewhat careless about social rules' (p. 38). Regarding switching pauses when the listener acquires the floor, people who speak slowly and employ longer, silent switching pauses are assessed by subjects as appearing 'aloof, rigid, and prone to sulk, but also as indolent, self-indulgent, and undependable' (p. 39). Conversation partners deemed to be reserved, timid, taciturn and detached elicited longer speaking turns than warm-hearted, cheerful, talkative partners (Crown & Feldstein, 1985, p. 39).

There are two reasons why I have included Crown and Feldstein's work in this review of sources taking silence as their main theme. Firstly, their study provides a good example of the acoustic paradigm in the study of silence, a paradigm that is characterised by chronometrical analysis of speech. This approach aims to make quantitative predictions on the ratio of speech and silence in conversation. Secondly, Crown and Feldstein's work perfectly illustrates an ethnocentric interpretation of silence as manifested by a discourse style characterised by extended silent pausing, slow speech tempo and long speaking turns. Note that in their study this style of discourse has virtually no positive personality qualities associated with it. Scollon (1985, p. 26) rightly points out that Crown and Feldstein's conclusions are only 'intuitively reasonable' if one considers a fast-paced, short-turn, short-pause style of conversation to be both typical and desirable (Scollon uses the metaphor of a humming machine to describe this type of interaction). The results are patently unreasonable however when one considers that not all cultures have an aversion to slow talk, long speaking turns and silence. Indeed, in cultures such as Japan that regard silence positively in many contexts (see Ishii & Bruneau, 1994; McDaniel, 2003; Lebra, 1987), 'talkative' could well be assessed as a negative attribution, whereas to be 'taciturn' would be a positive characteristic.

2.4 A linguistic approach

Tannen's theory of conversational style and the relativism of silence

Tannen (1985) sheds more light on this interpretive mismatch by providing an insightful theoretical discussion on the negative and positive valuation of silence, thus highlighting how differing assessments allude to the inherent ambiguity of silence as a communicative sign. In particular, Tannen points towards the positively valued silences of intimates who share an interpersonal bond:

> Silence is seen as positive when it is taken as evidence of the existence of something positive underlying — for example, proper respect; the silence of the telephone when it represents solitude for creative work; the silence of 'sweet silent thought'; and the silence of perfect rapport between intimates who do not have to exchange words. (1985, p. 94)

Here silence is non-threatening and provides a positive phatic function (see Ephratt, 2008, pp. 1923–24; Jaworski, 2000). In contrast, negative silence, silence which causes people to feel uncomfortable, 'hinges on whether or not participants feel something should be said, in which case silence is perceived as an omission' (Tannen, 1985, p. 96). What is crucial here is the *expectation of talk*, and this expectation varies across, and indeed within, cultures. Tannen points out that a failure to provide an appropriate formulaic expression is the clearest example of silence as omission, and that such an omission of expected talk during, for example, a greeting, is likely to result in a negative perception of both the silence and the person who employed it. Here again then, we are reminded that silence is not just a blank, it is not a communicative void. By choosing not to speak one actually sends a message (whether interpreted correctly or not) about oneself. As Sapir rightly states, 'We often form a judgment of what (a person) is by what he does not say, and we may be very wise to refuse to limit the evidence for judgment to the overt content of speech' (Sapir cited in Tannen, 1985, p. 96).

In addition to its value in highlighting the negative and positive aspects of silence, Tannen's work is of importance for the silence researcher because it also draws attention to variations *within* cultures of how silence is judged and tolerated. Tannen rightly treats the workings of conversational style as relative processes rather than objective behaviours, and she acknowledges that in different settings with different others, her participants' styles would appear very different (Tannen, 1984, p. 4). Through the use of an extended analysis of a conversation at a Thanksgiving Dinner she attended (Tannen, 1981, 1984, 1985), Tannen identified what she terms the 'high involvement' conversational style, as characterised by some New York Jews, in which interest is shown by asking rapid 'machine-gun questions', using fast, expressive speech in which overlap is tolerated and turns are not easily given up in the pursuit of personal topics for talk. It is an acute intolerance for silence which causes speakers of this high involvement system to toss out whatever enters their heads, and it is only through noisy, fast-paced conversation that a sense of rapport can be established amongst participants (Tannen, 1984, pp. 94–5). This frenetic style of interaction actually had the opposite effect intended on the non-New York Jewish participants (from California and England) who felt crowded and discomforted by it, and regarded its users as being aggressive and lacking in empathy. Consequently, these participants were assessed as slow talkers and highly tolerant of silence only *in comparison to* the New York Jewish participants. Lebra's (1993) observation that their behaviour closely corresponds to her expectation of how Japanese participants would have behaved in a similar situation, emphasises both the importance of treating discourse features related to silence as relative processes, and the importance of avoiding simplistic national stereotypes in the study of silence. Tannen's work clearly reminds us that the interpretation and valuation of silence depends heavily on context, speaker characteristics and their conversation styles.

2.5 Ethnographic works on silence

So far, I have provided examples of works which approach the study of silence from a variety of methodological angles, with Tannen's work providing a useful example of how discourse analysis can be effectively employed to discover more about silence in everyday interactions. Let us now turn our attention to another research paradigm that has provided a rich seam of data in the study of silence across cultures, namely the ethnographic approach.

Saville-Troike's framework of etic categories

In her attempt to develop an integrative theory of communication which incorporates both sound and silence, Saville-Troike (1985) sets up a broad ethnographic framework for understanding silence, thereby emphasising the importance of contextual clues. Arguing that silence 'is more context-embedded than speech, that is, more dependent on context for its interpretation' (Saville-Troike, 1985, p. 11), she highlights that it has enough illocutionary force to 'question, promise, deny, warn, threaten, insult, request, or command, as well as to carry out various kinds of ritual interaction' (1985, p. 6). Based on Hymes' (1964, 1974) ethnography of communication, Saville-Troike proposes a broad framework for the classification of silences relating to different levels of social action. The framework is significant because it aptly illustrates the complex nature of silence with its many forms and functions.

The following is therefore a detailed account of Saville-Troike's (1985, pp. 16–17) framework of etic categories through which we may view silence. The framework is initially divided into three broad types: institutionally-determined silence; group-determined silence; and individually-determined/negotiated silence. Each of these main types is then further broken down into sub-categories which are explained in more detail below:

1. *Institutionally-determined silences* may include the 'locational' silences of such places as temples or libraries; or the 'ritual' silences of religious services, legal proceedings, public performances, and so on. Institutionally-determined silences may also be associated with 'membership' of religious groups that have a vow of silence; they may be 'hierarchical/structural' when members of a society or organisation have less power/status than others; or they may be linked to 'taboos' when communication with persons of certain statuses is proscribed.
2. *Group-determined silences*, on the other hand, are categorised as situational, normative and symbolic. Group-determined 'situational' silences relate to when one's privilege to speak is allocated by a group decision (e.g. within legislative bodies or on committees). 'Normative' silences meanwhile encompass differential speaking privileges given to individuals or classes of individuals, including for example, the expectation that children should remain silent in certain situations, or the silence associated with shunning a person as a punishment.
3. *Individually-determined/negotiated silence* is the final category of Saville-Troike's framework, divided unequally between the larger category of 'interactive' silences and less wide-ranging 'non-interactive' silences (associated only with contemplative/meditative and inactive silences). Socio-contextual interactive silences may be 'role-indicative' (e.g. signifying the auditor in

conversation), 'status-indicative' by showing deference or superiority or 'situation-indicative' (e.g. denoting social control). These types of silence may also be 'tactical-symbolic/attitudinal' and can be associated with themes such as non-participation, anger, dislike, avoidance, concealment, and image manipulation. Saville-Troike also places the previously discussed 'phatic' silence as a sub-class of the interactive socio-contextual type. Still in the individually determined/negotiated silence category, but this time looking at linguistic aspects, three types of silence are identified: 'discursive' (e.g. when praying); 'propositional' (e.g. to denote such things as negation, consent, agreement, and so on); and 'didactic' (e.g. a teacher's silent pause allowing students to 'fill in the blank'). The third and final type of interactive, individually-determined or negotiated silence that Saville-Troike identifies is 'psychological' silence which has the uniformly negative associations of shyness, embarrassment, fear and neurosis connected to it.

Saville-Troike is careful to point out that the framework is 'far from exhaustive and is intended to be suggestive rather than a definitive proposal' (1985, p. 17). Even so, despite her reservations, Saville-Troike's theoretical contribution to the study of silence is of significance because the framework, which can be employed cross-culturally, clearly disproves the conventional notion of silence as inaction during communication, and emphasises its multiplicity of forms and functions. Rather than focusing on the more widely-studied micro-level type silences of pauses and hesitations, the framework focuses our attention on the existence of longer silences, which tend not to receive so much attention from researchers.

Basso's classic study on Western Apache silence

In his refreshingly lucid account of Western Apache silence, Basso (1990) provides us with an important example of empirical ethnographic research which seeks to understand how acts of silence in a specific culture are interpreted and understood to be appropriate by its participants. Like Saville-Troike's (1985) framework, Basso's study also takes Hymes' (1964) ethnography of communication as its theoretical foundation. It therefore pays particular attention to the specific settings of different social interactions and the differences in status between participants within these interactions, in order to gain insight into why some Western Apaches refrain from speaking for lengthy periods of time. Basso stresses the importance of research into silence within specific cultures with the pertinent observation that, 'For a stranger entering an alien society, a knowledge of when *not* to speak may be as basic to the production of culturally acceptable behaviour as a knowledge of what to say' (Basso, 1990, p. 305).

So when is it acceptable for Western Apaches 'to give up on words'? As we shall see in the following six situations that Basso identified, the answer to this question appears to involve heavily the themes of ambiguity, unpredictability and anxiety in social relationships.

1. *Meeting strangers.* Upon meeting a stranger, rather than engaging in small talk or relying on introductions, the Western Apache deem silence to be appropriate behaviour because 'verbal reticence with strangers is directly related to the conviction that the establishment of social relationships is a serious matter that calls for caution, careful judgement, and plenty of time' (1990, p. 308).
2. *Courting.* During the first stages of courtship, young Western Apache couples remain silent because they are intensely shy and self-conscious, complaining of '"not knowing what to do" in each other's presence and of the fear that whatever they say...will sound "dumb" or "stupid"' (p. 309). For women, silence during courtship is also interpreted as a sign of modesty.
3. *Children coming home.* Returning home from government-run boarding schools, Western Apache children are met in silence by parents who may remain silent for up to three days before engaging their child in conversation. This behaviour is predicated on the parent's fear that time spent away in an Anglo environment will have caused the child to see their parents as being 'ignorant, old-fashioned, and no longer deserving of respect' (p. 310).
4. *Getting cussed out.* Apt to occur in any setting because of its relationship to the consumption of alcohol, 'getting cussed out' occurs when a person vents his (Basso seems to only apply this category to men) anger on anyone who happens to be nearby. Fear of physical violence means that silence is the favoured strategy of people wishing to avoid attracting attention to themselves.
5. *Being with people who are sad.* The Western Apache consider it courteous not to engage a bereaved person in conversation and speech is deemed unnecessary to convey solace. In addition, it is assumed 'that a person suffering from "intense grief" is likely to be disturbed and unstable' (p. 313). Fear of conversation provoking an emotional or violent outburst means that, as in Situation 4, people will also remain silent to avoid confrontation with a grieving individual.

6. *Being with someone for whom they sing.* During night-long 'curing ceremonies', which take place in very restricted settings, patients are thought to acquire a kind of 'supernatural power' when chanted to by the medicine man. During the entire ceremony those in attendance must remain silent because the patients' 'newly acquired status places them in close proximity to the supernatural and, as such, carries with it a very real element of danger and uncertainty' (p. 315). Refraining from speech is therefore considered respectful and may avoid potentially hazardous consequences.

In each of the situations described above, silence indicates that the participant's interpersonal relationships are uncertain, unpredictable, and therefore potentially threatening. The status of focal participants can be deemed to be ambiguous, therefore making their role expectations unclear. In these circumstances, the predictability of normal social interaction is lost.

In light of these results, Basso theorised whether his conclusions about the Western Apache's silent behaviour could be applied to other cultures as well. This question was subsequently tackled by Braithwaite (1990) who confirmed and extended Basso's hypothesis by testing it cross-culturally in an examination of ethnographic accounts into the uses and meaning of silence within thirteen different speech communities. Braithwaite's analysis led him to conclude that in a number of other societies, (e.g. within Japanese and Japanese-Hawaiian contexts), silence is indeed associated with ambiguous and unpredictable social relationships. However, a more significant factor contributing to people's silent behaviour across cultures was found to be the existence of power differences amongst participants in an interaction. Silence, states Braithwaite, is 'a powerful communicative code to signal the presence of a differentiation in power' (1990, p. 325). The less power an individual holds, the more silent he/she is likely to be (c.f. Kurzon, 1992).

2.6 Silence in educational contexts

In the final section of this selected overview of studies contributing to our theoretical understanding of silence, I would like to turn our attention to research which focuses solely on the silences that occur within educational contexts. This final section will thus build upon my previous outline of Granger's (2004) work into the psychoanalytic aspects of learner silence by examining research concerned with the meaning and function of silent displays in the classroom, along with works that seek to uncover how students and teachers perceive silence in learning situations.

Gilmore's study on silence and sulking in the classroom

As Braithwaite's (1990) study is a timely reminder of the significant relationship between power disparities and silent behaviour, a logical study to examine next would be Perry Gilmore's (1985) 'Silence and sulking: Emotional Displays in the classroom'. This enquiry, which took place in a relatively deprived, inner-city African-American school, uncovers the ways in which teachers and students use silence differently to negotiate their unequal power relationships. The fact that Gilmore's study attempts to explain the silences of both students *and* teachers makes it of particular interest to the silence researcher.

After a commendably prolonged engagement with participants at the research site (she spent three years collecting data), Gilmore discovered that the teachers under her observation tended to employ silence as a means for controlling student behaviour. Often accompanied by marked shifts in the teacher's physical orientation, for example by 'looking up from a book, standing up, turning to or walking near an individual who is "breaking a rule"' (Gilmore, 1985, p. 145), silence was a favoured strategy to initiate, regain and maintain order in the classroom.

> The teacher's silence display appears to carry a mutually understood meaning for all classroom participants. It seems to mean 'pay attention to me' and/or 'what you're doing is not acceptable to me.' The appropriate student response is silence and attention. Usually the display is most effective as a transition device, a way to get attention and class cohesion for a new lesson or activity, marking the beginning of a new frame. (Gilmore, 1985, p. 147)

Lasting anywhere between a brief pause to over ten minutes, Gilmore interprets teacher silences as dramatic devices which seem to freeze time in the classroom. These silences, through which the teacher exerts his/her dominant status, keep the class waiting until the message contained within them is understood and the students' behaviour is consequently modified. Thus, refraining from speech provides the teacher with an effective method for controlling interactions within the classroom.

Much student silence within class is associated with fulfilling a cooperative listener role, which, Gilmore rather suspects, allows the majority of students to hide during most of the school day. Making it difficult for both researcher and teacher to notice them, this type of silence is employed by students in order to avoid attention and facilitate the discourse of the classroom (Gilmore, 1985, p. 148). More visible are the student silences which Gilmore terms *submissive subordinate* and *nonsubmissive subordinate*. Both are associated with teacher–student confrontations during which the student is being reprimanded and both illustrate the student's lack of power in such an interaction. Gilmore notes that submissive subordinate silence is 'only observed with interactions with the teacher or other adult authority, never with peers. This display is marked with body gestures such as a bowed head, quizzical expression around the eyes, a smile, even a giggle...' (1985, p. 148). Nonsubmissive subordinate silences, however, are examples of *stylized sulking* in front of peers during which the student, who is in a subordinate position, is able to save face by silently displaying his/her anger. Silence in this case becomes a tool for emotional management (see also Saunders, 1985) that allows for a passive expression of dissatisfaction. Employed by both girls and boys, nonsubmissive subordinate silences are accompanied by sex-particular physical adornments that are designed to attract, rather than repel, attention. Gilmore describes how boys and girls perform these silences differently:

> Girls will frequently pose with their chins up, closing their eyelids for elongated periods and casting downward side glances, and often markedly turning their heads sidewards as well as upwards... Striking or getting into the pose is usually with an abrupt movement that will sometimes be marked with a sound like the elbow striking the desk or a verbal marker like 'humpf'...
> Boys usually display somewhat differently. Their 'stylized sulking' is usually characterized by head downward, arms crossed at the chest, legs spread wide and usually desk pushed away. Often they will mark the silence by knocking over a chair or pushing loudly on their desk, assuring that others hear and see the performance. (1985, p.149)

Students perform the type of nonsubmissive subordinate silences described above as a defensive mechanism against the teacher's dominant status and do so highly aware of their peers' attention in the classroom. Gilmore (1985) rightly emphasises the role that saving face plays in these episodes with the observation that, 'Stylized silent sulking is frequently used as an ego-saving measure, and often turns the loss of face back to the teacher' (p. 155). Thus we can see that, on the whole, the classroom silences Gilmore observed had an almost uniformly negative interpretation because they were associated with defiance, conflict, anger, misbehaviour, and, in the case of students appearing to fulfil a listener role, deception. But does silence occurring within an educational context always have to be interpreted as such a negative phenomenon? Do staff and students sometimes interpret silent episodes differently? A good place to begin looking for some answers to these questions is Jaworski and Sachdev's (1998, 2004) research which investigated students' and teachers' beliefs and attitudes about silence in the classroom.

Jaworski and Sachdev's research on students' and teachers' beliefs about silence

One of my aims in this chapter is to illustrate the diverse ways in which researchers have pursued the study of silence. Jaworski and Sachdev (1998) contribute to this paradigmatic wealth with a rare quantitative study employing a questionnaire methodology to investigate beliefs about classroom silence. Following on from the work of Blimes (1994), Jaworski and Sachdev's survey considered student silence in the classroom to be the absence of relevant talk ('notable silence'), rather than the absence of noise ('absolute silence'). Influenced in particular by Sobkowiak's (1997) ideas regarding silence and markedness theory, Jaworski and Sachdev probed the beliefs and attitudes of Welsh secondary school pupils from varying socio-economic backgrounds to find out how they valued silence in their classrooms and in what situations they perceived silence to be marked or unmarked communicative behaviour. As we can see in the following extract, power disparities between participants in the classroom again appear to have a significant influence on the production and interpretation of silent behaviour:

> for pupils silence is the unmarked, underlying linguistic form in the classroom, while for teachers silence is marked and talk is unmarked. This discrepancy stems from the institutionalised power imbalance between teachers and pupils, teachers' right to control the discourse, privilege of self-nomination for another turn, granting speaking rights to pupils, demanding speaking turns from pupils and of allowing or demanding silence from them... (Jaworski & Sachdev, 1998, p. 283)

Interestingly, despite the power imbalances that Jaworski and Sachdev allude to above, their findings suggest that learners tend to view their own unmarked silence in the classroom positively, and consider it to be 'a facilitative device enabling students to gain access, organise and absorb new material' (1998, p. 286). In other words, those surveyed by Jaworski and Sachdev believed that by refraining from talk, they could improve the effectiveness of their learning. One wonders whether these results would be replicated if the questionnaire were to be distributed solely amongst language learners who need to be orally active in the target language in order to make progress with their second language (L2) development. This question is particularly intriguing in the context of my own study which focuses on the silence of Japanese language learners, because recent attempts to introduce communicative language learning in Japan have so far met with mixed results (see Hato, 2005; Guest, 2000; Mulligan, 2005; Poole, 2005; Sakui, 2004).

So far we have seen that within the three Welsh secondary schools Jaworski and Sachdev investigated, pupils believed they were more silent than their teachers in classroom situations and that their relatively unmarked silence had pedagogical merit because it facilitated learning. In an effort to find out whether teachers' attitudes towards quietness and silence differed from those of the students described above, Jaworski and Sachdev (2004) went on to analyse data collected from 178 University and Colleges Admissions System (UCAS) references written by teachers for applicants wishing to enter a British university's undergraduate programme. Applying a coding scheme that assumed a basic binary view of communication skills comprising of the categories *talk* and *silence*, the researchers found that teachers interpreted student silence as an overwhelmingly negative phenomenon when associated with academic matters. However, it should also be noted that silence was construed somewhat more positively when associated with students' personality traits, reflecting what Jaworski and Sachdev (2004) believe to be 'teachers' general, possibly stereotyped preference for "quiet" students implying submissiveness and obedience' (pp. 234–5). Even so, taken overall, Jaworski and Sachdev's (1998, 2004) findings suggest a conflict in students' and teachers' attitudes and beliefs about silence in the classroom, with students evaluating quiet, reticent behaviour positively, whilst many teachers deem it to be a portent of possible future academic failure.

2.7 Conclusion

In this overview of some of the major theories of silence I have attempted to achieve three things. One aim was to set out the studies' main focal points in a clear, unambiguous way so as to avoid the potential confusion that reviews focusing on multi-disciplinary approaches can sometimes give rise to. Following on from this, I wanted to show that although a diverse range of research methodologies has been utilised in the quest to understand and generate theoretical frameworks for silence, no single paradigm has been able to provide definitive answers to our questions about people's silent behaviour. The final objective was to begin the introduction of certain themes that I intend to return to throughout the book, as these themes are particularly salient to my study. The following is a summary of the major points that have emerged from the overview:

- Silence does not exist in complete opposition to speech. It can be viewed as a legitimate communicative act and forms part of a continuum where the functional aspects of silence and speech may overlap with each other.
- When studying silence, an important consideration for the researcher should be whether the silent act is intentional or not.
- If viewed from a psychoanalytic standpoint, the silent period of a second language learner, which is characterised by a lack of authentic, original L2 production, may be connected to the learner's changing self-concept during the early stages of the SLA process.
- Care must be taken not to interpret silence in conversation in an ethnocentric way when interacting cross-culturally. Extended silent pauses may be negatively construed in some cultures, but not in others.
- The silence researcher needs to be aware that interpretations and valuations of silent behaviour may differ not only between cultures, but also *within* cultures. Such appraisals depend heavily upon context, speakers' characteristics and their conversation styles.
- Ethnographic-orientated works emphasise the multiplicity of forms and functions that silence may take, and stress in particular the need to consider both the specific settings of social interactions and the precise nature of participants' interpersonal relationships when trying to reach an understanding of their silent behaviour.
- Uncertainty, unpredictability and ambiguity in interpersonal relationships play key roles in influencing whether someone decides to refrain from speaking. Moreover, the existence of power disparities between participants is a significant factor in people's silent behaviour, with those having less power being more likely to remain silent.
- In classroom situations, silent displays may be employed by students as an emotional defence against the teacher's authority and as a way of passively expressing negative emotions. In addition, teachers

often employ silence as a tool for classroom control. Both of these forms of silence are often accompanied by marked changes in physical orientation (e.g. teachers suddenly standing or walking towards a troublesome student).
- Teachers and students often interpret silence differently. Silence may have pedagogical merit in some situations because it facilitates learning, but when considered in relation to a student's academic performance, teachers appear to overwhelmingly rate it as a negative phenomenon.

What is certainly clear from the preceding discussion is that research into people's silent behaviour must be culture-specific and must carefully consider the relative value of speech versus silence within that culture. With this in mind, in the following chapter I turn my attention to silences that can be found specifically within a Japanese context, and attempt to outline some of the complex roots of silence within Japanese society, while drawing further attention to the multiplicity of ways in which silences may be defined.

3
An interdisciplinary overview of silence in Japan

3.1 Introduction

> To a natural man, another man's silence is not a reassuring factor, but, on the contrary, something alarming and dangerous. The stranger who cannot speak the language is to all savage tribesmen a natural enemy. To the primitive mind, whether among savages or our own uneducated classes, taciturnity means not only unfriendliness but directly bad character. (Malinowski cited in Jaworski, 2000, p. 110)

Malinowski's rather outdated and narrow understanding of silence as the mere negative absence of speech draws our attention to the fact that any proper examination of silence has to be culture-specific and must take into account specific speech communities' attitudes to and tolerance towards silence. As will become clear later, in Japanese society, silence may be positively regarded and welcomed whereas the overt verbalsation of talk is often viewed with suspicion and is seen as having the potential to cause great loss of face. Of course, much depends on the form of silence under consideration. This chapter adopts a wide definition of silence ranging from the tendency towards minimal verbalisation by a speech community, to the silence characterised by withdrawal from speech by a group of participants within a social interaction, to an individual's silence through non-participation in an interaction, to an individual's turn-constituting silent speech act, and finally to the shorter silences of intra- and inter-turn pauses and hesitations. I should admit here that I am more interested in the former macro-silences described above than the latter short, linguistic silences that tend to be the domain of conversation analysis. Even so, no overview of the potential roots of Japanese silence would be complete without an attempt to outline the nature of these micro-silences and the role that they play. In keeping with my wide-ranging definition of silence, I attempt to provide a broad sketch of its potential roots in Japanese interactions by drawing on literature emanating from a diverse range of sources.

I begin the chapter by delving into the deep philosophical roots of silence in Japan with a consideration of how Confucianism has influenced behavioural practices to create a communicative environment where, depending on context, silence may be encouraged and positively regarded. Despite Japan now being a post-Confucian society, I argue that an understanding of Confucian principles is still relevant today in order for the silence researcher to gain meaningful background knowledge, particularly when considering the role of hierarchical relationships and membership of in-groups. Section 3.2 raises some significant questions concerning the extent to which we may employ cultural explanations to interpret an individual's behaviour. Consequently, I address this issue whilst taking the opportunity to warn of the dangers that simple, dichotomous generalisations of national traits bring. I hope that this section will underline not only the need to consider contexts of culture when examining silence phenomena, but also the need to reflect on contexts of situation too.

After briefly considering how Japanese proverbs, poetry and literature reflect deep-seated cultural attitudes towards speech and silence, the chapter then looks at the claim that the Japanese may be socialised into the use of a kind of anticipatory, silent communication as a result of specific child-rearing practices, thus making them inclined towards inference. Discussion of the close mother–child relationship progresses into an examination of the possibility that empathy training by caregivers may result in children developing an inhibiting, silence-inducing tendency to excessively self-monitor when in the presence of others. This possibility is discussed in relation to the behaviour of Japanese learners in classroom contexts.

In Sections 3.7 and 3.8, I move into the areas of pragmatics and linguistics to try to further uncover more possible roots of Japanese silence. I outline how silence may be interpreted as a pragmatic politeness strategy and then illustrate how this concept could help to explain some of the silent episodes of Japanese learners and the resulting mismatch of pause expectations by non-Japanese instructors. The penultimate section focuses on the more micro-level silences that are to be found at turn-taking junctures. Here I outline cultural differences in turn-taking styles and tolerance of silent pauses, before considering how these issues are relevant to the Japanese language learning classroom.

The chapter ends with a short examination of the relationship between cognitive processing and the extended hesitations that Japanese language learners may display in an educational context.

3.2 The philosophical roots of Japanese silence

Japan as a post-Confucian society

In order to better appreciate the silence that may occur within human interactions in Japan, it would be pertinent to perform a brief examination of the philosophical influences that have historically shaped communication practices in that society. This reflects Yum's (1994) assumption that communication is a basic social process that can be affected by predominant value systems. A number of scholars point towards Confucianism as exerting a significant philosophical influence on behaviour in Japan (De Mente, 2004; Dollinger, 1988; Jandt, 2007; McDaniel, 2003; Stapleton, 1995; Yamada, 1997; Yum, 1994; Zimmerman, 1985). But how can this be? Surely in such a supposedly high-tech society which sees Shintoism and Buddhism as its principal religions, the impact of Confucian ethics should by now be minimal? Zimmerman (1985) draws on Reischauer to disagree:

> Confucianism probably has more influence on [the Japanese] than does any other of the traditional religions or philosophies. Any discussion of Japanese religions that overlooks this point would be seriously misleading. Behind the wholehearted Japanese acceptance of modern science, modern concepts of progress and growth, universalistic principles of ethics, and democratic ideals and values, strong Confucian traits still lurk beneath the surface... (Reischauer cited in Zimmerman, 1985, p. 21)

The Chinese scholar K'ung-Fu-tzu, whose name the Jesuits later Latinised to Confucius (Jandt, 2007, p. 28), lived in a time of great social turmoil in fifth-century China. It was during this period of feudal chaos that Confucius began advocating a more ordered social system based on proper, hierarchical relationships and a strict moral code encompassing the four principles of humanism, loyalty, propriety and wisdom (for a fuller discussion of these principles, see Yum, 1994). The first appearance of Confucianism in Japan coincided with the introduction of the Chinese logographic writing system between the sixth and ninth centuries A.D. (Stapleton, 1995) and the philosophy developed in such a way as to eventually lie at the heart of learning during the Tokugawa period, hence providing the moral foundation for the education system (Hane, 2000, p. 5). Despite the modernisation of the Meiji Restoration and subsequent pressure from Western influences, though today admittedly in a somewhat weakened state, the influence of Confucianism on Japanese communication patterns has remained ingrained and persistent.

Confucian influence on interpersonal communication

Yum (1994) draws our attention to five areas where Confucianism affects interpersonal communication, thereby providing useful background information on the phenomenon of silence in Japanese social interaction. The themes consist of particularism in relationships, long-term asymmetrical reciprocity, in-group/out-group distinction, the role of intermediaries, and overlap of personal and public relations. For our purposes, particularism in relationships and in-group/out-group distinction are themes of specific interest.

Status differences

A particularistic, rather than universalistic orientation towards relationships means that the nature of any interaction is heavily dependent on such differentiations as level of intimacy, social status, age, sex, and so on. This is revealed in the often highly elaborate honorific linguistic systems of East Asia which reinforce differences in status and therefore focus attention on correct propriety (for example, see Akasu & Asao, 1993 for more on Japanese honorific expressions, and Loveday, 1982, pp. 84–6 for a discussion on appropriate usage of Japanese name-suffixes when addressing specific interlocutors). McDaniel (2003) believes that Japan's superior–subordinate environment results in a situation where 'the junior is socially compelled to assume a passive role, awaiting and hopefully anticipating the senior's desires or actions. The senior, desiring to exemplify humility and avoid any social or personal discord, will endeavour to non-verbally ascertain the junior's expectations' (p. 54). This pattern is particularly relevant to Japan's universities, where students tend to observe a strict *senpai/kōhai* (senior/junior) distinction that is a key influence on their language and behaviour (see Lee-Cunin, 2005; McVeigh, 2002, pp. 220–4). The indirect, implicit style of communication which avoids overt verbalisation described by McDaniel can consequently be associated with Brown and Levinson's (1987) concept of face protection. Indeed, Yum (1994, p. 82) emphasises this point with the suggestion that it is the Confucian legacy of consideration for others and preoccupation with status that means Japan's less explicit communication style prevents embarrassment through rejection and avoids disagreement amongst partners. Indeed, silence is widely regarded as a useful politeness strategy which avoids the confrontation that a verbal expression might bring (Franks, 2000; Jaworski, 1993; Nakane, 2006, 2007; Sifianou, 1997; Tannen, 1985). It is clear that the connection between silence and politeness is noteworthy and therefore will be considered in more depth later on in the chapter. For now we must turn our attention to in-group/out-group distinction, the second relevant factor pointing towards Confucianism as a potential philosophical foundation of silence in Japanese communication.

Being one of the gang

The concept of *uchi/soto* (inside/outside) is a basic dichotomy that greatly influences Japanese language and behaviour (Akasu & Asao,1993; Jandt, 2007; Lebra, 1976, 1993; Loveday, 1982; McDaniel, 2003; Moeran, 1986; Nakane, 2006, 2007). *Uchi* denotes the idea of 'inside' or 'belonging to a particular group', whereas *soto* means 'outside' or 'of another group'. These distinctions are applicable to all spheres of Japanese life, from family membership, to classes in school, to companies, and even to the nation as a whole. Taylor (cited in Cathcart & Cathcart, 1994, p. 296) expands on this pervasive model:

> One of Japan's most prominent national characteristics is the individual's sense of the group. At every level of society the Japanese have a very strong sense of who is on the inside (*uchi*) and who is on the outside (*soto*). The group draws firm boundaries between "us" and "them" and, hierarchy is an essential guidepost to proper behaviour.

Depending on the context, particularly with regards to whether a situation is private or public, a Japanese person may feel at ease enough within the security of his/her in-group to be talkative and expressive. However, much less verbal interaction will take place in an out-group situation (Gudykunst & Nishida, 1993; McDaniel, 2003; Lebra, 1976, 1993), meaning there is a greater likelihood of silence occurring in these contexts. At its extreme, this is underlined by Jandt's (2007, p. 30) assertion that as Confucianism does not take into account relationships with strangers, such people may be silently ignored to the point of what some would consider rudeness. Lebra (1993) also makes the connection between *uchi/soto* distinctions and silent indifference. She refers to such behaviour as the 'anomic mode' in which the self moves out of the communicative circuit and treats those around indifferently, as if they do not exist (p. 56). It is indeed unfortunate for foreign language teachers in Japan hoping to improve their students' fluency that the official learning process in the classroom tends to be performed in the *soto* mode and is consequently characterised by learner silence and a resistance to speaking (Nakane, 2007, p. 55). Such reticence may not be solely the responsibility of Confucian values, as Stapleton (1995) somewhat exaggeratedly claims; the silences of Japanese students are certainly more shifting, complex and context-dependent than that. Nevertheless, knowledge of Confucianism's influence on Japanese communicative behaviour does provide helpful background information which contributes to our deeper understanding of the issue of silence in the Japanese language classroom.

3.3 Cultural representations as stereotypes

The *nihonjinron* approach

We have seen in the previous section how an appreciation of aspects of a culture's philosophical foundations provides an enlightening theoretical background when analysing certain communicative behaviours by its inhabitants. However, it is essential not to become too carried away by overly simplistic, stereotyping arguments in which all members of a specific culture are expected to behave in the same way. This is particularly true in the case of Japan, whose vast body of *nihonjinron* literature argues that the Japanese are a unique and homogenous people sharing a single history, language and lifestyle (c.f. Dale, 1986; Befu, 2001). *Nihonjinron*, translated variously as 'theories of the Japanese' (Kowner, 2002, p. 357), 'discussions of the Japanese' (Gudykunst & San Antonio, 1993, p. 24) or 'the Japanese way' (Cathcart & Cathcart, 1994, p. 294), attempts to draw a simplistic contrast between the so-called heterogeneous, individualistic, egalitarian West and homogenous, harmonious, hierarchical Japan. This theme extends to a dichotomous contrast of communication styles, as described by Gudykunst and San Antonio (1993):

> Communication in Japan is viewed as being based on a language that prizes reticence, sentiment, silence, ambivalence, emotions, subjectivity, situational logic, and particularity. Communication in the West, on the other hand, is viewed as being based on languages that value rhetoric, logic, talkativeness, rationality, objectivity, rigid principles, and universality. (p. 27)

This dichotomy is certainly not helpful if we view it as a static, context-free concept. Kramsch (1998) rightly reminds us that we should not equate one person or one culture with a single discourse style, as people are apt to display a range of styles depending on the situation. Certainly, outside of the classroom in a more relaxed environment, Japanese learners are quite capable of being as noisy and as talkative as any British or American students. Static cultural representations of Japanese students deny that the true Japanese self is socially contextualised (Lebra, 1993) and therefore in a state of constant flux, as was intimated in the previous discussion relating to particularity and how one's discourse style may change depending on the status of one's interlocutors.

Furthermore, by emphasising Japanese uniqueness, the *nihonjinron* approach draws attention away from the fact that silence in communication at social psychological, cognitive and linguistic levels is a phenomenon also to be found in supposedly verbose Western cultures too. For example, Saunders' (1985) study highlighting an Italian community's extensive use of silence as a tool for emotional management shows us that even so-called garrulous cultures can display a sophisticated use of silence in social interaction. The Japanese do not have a monopoly on avoiding talk. To underline this point we need only refer to Bernstein's (1971) theory of *restricted codes* amongst the British working class. Reflecting the social group which utilise them, restricted codes do not allow for elaboration and therefore involve non-complex talk that is relatively predictable (see Littlejohn & Foss, 2005, pp. 303–5 for a more comprehensive critical overview). Dale (1986) provides us with a convincing examination of the argument that Bernstein's ideas clearly parallel the *nihonjinron* concept of Japan being a homogenous, collectivist-orientated society whose members' shared experiences and assumptions result in a discourse style that does not require elaboration.

Scratching the surface of *nihonjinron* themes

Although some *nihonjinron* writing can be pseudo-sociological, pseudo-psychological babble of the worst kind (e.g, Tsunoda's widely de-bunked 1985 book, *The Japanese Brain*), and its extreme relativism is unhelpful, we must not be blinded to the fact that the genre has isolated numerous concepts that are useful to both the study of the use of silence in society and how students behave in the foreign language classroom. For example, on the issue of homogeneity engendering non-verbal, implicit communication, Japan is obviously not an entirely homogenous society (see Weiner, 1997), although it is certainly more homogenous than the United Kingdom or the United States, and, as McPake and Powney (1998, p. 178) remind us, the myth of homogeneity is widely believed by the Japanese – therefore making it an important cultural concept.

In addition, just because *nihonjinron* writers refer to a collectivistic society with a preoccupation for group harmony (see Barnlund, 1974), as was alluded to in the previous discussion of the *soto/uchi* concept, we should not dismiss the notion of the group exerting a significant influence over the behaviour and communication practices of the Japanese. It is true that recent writing in cross-cultural psychology (e.g. Bond, 2002; Oyserman, Coon & Kemmelmeier, 2002) has challenged long-held assumptions on the bi-polar dimensions of Hofstede's (1980) famous individualism-collectivism construct regarding Japan and the United States. Bond (2002, p. 75) rightly points out that the pattern of correlations Hofstede found at the national level is not replicated at the individual level and Japanese people are quite capable of scoring highly on individualism ratings. Indeed, Woodring (cited in Jandt, 2007, p. 163) discovered just such a result by applying Hofstede's original questionnaires to a sample of Japanese college students. Even so, to deny that the group plays little role in Japanese society would be preposterous. An important point to bear in mind is that the group and the individual are not diametrically opposed entities, particularly when we consider the aforementioned dynamism of the Japanese contextualised self. Hendry (1986) takes up this idea when she considers the case of Japanese pre-schoolers, who receive extensive training in kindergarten on how to act in unison as a group and how get along with others in their peer group:

> ...it should be reiterated that a child does not disappear as an individual into this new collective entity... As Durkheim pointed out long ago in *L'Education Morale*, 'the attachment to social groups... far from checking individual initiative...enriches personality'. (pp. 171-2)

Befu (cited in Gudykunst & San Antonio, 1993) reinforces this argument with the claim that 'behind the appearance of group solidarity one will find each member is being motivated more by personal ambitions than by his (or her) blind loyalty to the group...Japanese are loyal to their groups because it pays to be loyal' (p. 30). Thus while it is appropriate to consider the influence of the group when studying the silence of Japanese learners, individual differences should not be overlooked.

What the above discussions concerning homogeneity and collectivism illustrate is that once one scratches the surface of widely-held assumptions concerning Japanese society, one finds a much more dynamic and complex reality than at first supposed. Certainly, *nihonjinron* literature needs to be approached with caution as it does over-emphasise the uniqueness of the Japanese experience and it can be based on false nationalistic assumptions. However, it is still useful as a source of relevant themes for the study of silence and non-participation of students in the Japanese foreign language classroom.

The benefits of the middle ground

While cautioning against the *nihonjinron* tenet's extreme relativism as a source for the perpetuation of national stereotypes, I would also like to briefly discuss the concomitant dangers of an excessively universalistic approach. A number of writers have challenged the cultural stereotype of the silent, passive Asian learner who relies on rote learning (Cheng, 2000; Guest, 2002; Kember & Gow, 1991; Kubota, 1999; Littlewood, 2000). While I applaud these attempts to move away from monolithic cultural constructs and simplistic dichotomising binaries that do not reflect the complexity of reality, universalistic arguments for sameness can at best be described as 'confused post-modernist thinking'. In an effort to fashionably myth-bust, it is easy to ignore that cultural differences patently do exist and, to a degree in conjunction with other variables, they can certainly influence learner behaviour. To argue for complete universalism is as misguided as arguing for complete relativism. Therefore the only reasonable approach is to take a pragmatic stance away from both ends of the spectrum, while employing reliable, empirical research to reach conclusions. Specifically regarding the silence of Japanese learners, Nakane (2007) provides us with a good illustration of this sensible approach. Nakane's rigorous mixed-methods research has allowed her to identify that Japanese students are indeed likely to be, and be perceived by others as, non-vocal, and that cultural and linguistic factors do indeed play a role in this; however, the reasons for and types of silences students display differ amongst participants and most importantly across *specific classroom contexts*.

3.4 Sociocultural clues to attitudes towards silence

To say nothing is a flower

Cultural values and beliefs concerning the relative benefits of silence and talk have a profound impact on a person's communicative behaviour (see Hall, 1981; Jandt, 2007; Kramsch, 1998). The rules, attitudes and norms of one's culture play a pivotal role in shaping assumptions concerning such things as politeness, topic choice, body language, eye contact, use of silence, and so on. Culture, defined as 'socially acquired knowledge' (Hudson, 1980, p. 76; Yule, 2006, p. 216), may be primarily learnt unconsciously from interaction with others, but there is also an array of other ways to acquire this knowledge. One such means is through proverbs, maxims or adages which, as Samovar and Porter (2003, p. 9) point out, can be repeated with such regularity from childhood that they become part of one's belief system. Although it is questionable whether such axioms are as powerfully influential as Samovar and Porter suggest, they can provide a good starting point for examining a society's traditional beliefs about speech and silence. Saville-Troike (1985, p. 10) concurs with this notion when she highlights the fact that in addition to their helping to locate the relative value of speech versus silence within a speech community, proverbs also provide 'clues to culturally defined connotative meanings of silence...' However, Jaworski and Sachdev (1998) certainly have a valid criticism that merely surveying a plethora of popular sayings leads only to simplistic rules about the functioning of silence across cultures. Silence does indeed warrant a much more in-depth, sophisticated analysis to be fully understood, but even so, as a starting point for examining attitudes within a particular speech community, proverbs do provide an enlightening insight. This is particularly true in the case of Japan, where proverbs (*kotowaza*) are renowned for their traditional use in controlling deviations from social norms and for reflecting values concerning appropriate communicative behaviour (Fischer & Yoshida, 1968; Ishii & Bruneau, 1994).

The apparent Japanese mistrust of overt verbalisation and supposed preference for a more silence-orientated, implicit communication is clearly illustrated in the sheer number of proverbs which point towards this attitude. Katayama (cited in Ishii & Bruneau, 1994, pp. 247–9) analysed 504 Japanese proverbs and found that 320 (63 per cent) had negative values; while only 124 (25 per cent) were positively orientated towards language; and the rest were neutral. Katayama's findings are reflected in Fischer & Yoshida's (1968) systematic and comprehensive analysis of Japan's traditional *kotowaza* which resulted in their stark conclusion that 'basically, the most ubiquitous lesson about speech in Japanese proverbs is "Shut up"' (p. 36). The following examples from Fischer and Yoshida's (1968, pp. 36–9) taxonomy are indicative of this traditional Japanese scepticism towards speech:

Regarding the mouth as a source of talk and therefore trouble:

Kuchi o mamoru kame no gotoku su. (One treats one's mouth like a guarded jar.)

Kuchi wa motte kuubeshi, motte iu bekarazu. (Mouths are to eat with, not to speak with.)

Concerning excessive self-disclosure and the danger of speaking too much:

Kotoba ookereba haji ooshi. (If there are many words there will be much shame.)

Kuchi no tora mi o yaburu. (The tiger in one's mouth destroys oneself.)

These two proverbs reflect another saying well known by those connected to English language teaching in Japan, a saying that points toward students' silences in class resulting from their sensitivity to the group and fear of standing out, namely: *Deru kui wa utareru.* (The nail that sticks up gets hammered down.) For more discussion concerning this famous adage, strangely missing from Fischer and Yoshida's extensive survey, refer to Anderson (1993).

Speaking too much signifies coarseness and ignorance:

Kotoba ooki wa hin sukunashi. (A person of many words has little refinement.)

Shiru mono wa iwazu, iu mono wa shirazu. (Those who know do not speak, those who speak do not know.)

Iwanu ga hana. (To say nothing is a flower.)

Many of the proverbs allude to an implicit, indirect style of communication which relies heavily on the listener to interpret meaning, rather than on the speaker to directly state the message. The following is said of somebody good at making inferences:

Ichi o kiite juu o shiru. (On hearing one s/he knows ten.)

And finally, a distrust of spoken eloquence is amply reflected in:

Kuchi ni mitsu ari, hara ni ken ari. (Honey in the mouth, a sword in the belly.)

These examples amply reflect the traditional notion that those who do not speak much are positively regarded, for being both wise and cultured. People are expected to think carefully before they speak and are reminded that excessive verbalisation may lead to shame and possible disaster. Naturally, there do exist some Japanese proverbs that reflect an opposite viewpoint to this, as Rose (1996) and Susser (1998) in particular have attempted to remind us. But Fischer and Yoshida (1968, p. 36) are quite right in pointing out that it is the sheer degree to which the vast majority of Japanese proverbs provide a logically consistent view of the functions of speech which provides us with such useful background information on that discourse community. Proverbs are certainly not a direct research tool, but they do help to set the scene for anybody wishing to undertake a study of Japanese attitudes towards silence.

". . . . ."

We can see that the deep-seated cultural attitudes towards speech and silence displayed in traditional proverbs are also reflected in Japanese poetry and literature. For example, regarding silence in written form, meaningful silent pauses play an integral part in the minimal verbalisation of the traditional three-line *haiku* (see Gilbert & Yoneoka, 2000), whilst the use of punctuation to denote silent markers in Japanese novels is common practice.

Jaworski (1993) appears to contradict Saville-Troike's (1985) assertion that the non-verbal dimension of written language, as reflected by spacing and punctuation, has received inadequate attention from scholars. In his analysis of the social and pragmatic perspectives of silence, Jaworski (1993, pp. 24–7) demonstrates that a number of studies, for example, Rovine (1987) or Tannen (1990), have focused on the role of silence in literature, most notably from an ethnography of communication standpoint. Even so, it seems that Saville-Troike (1985, p. 5) is right to suggest that it is perhaps Japanese literature which displays the most highly developed use of the silence marker '. . . . .'. Hokari underlines this belief by drawing our attention to Tatsuo Hori's employment of '. . . . .' 173 times in 103 pages of his novel *Kazetachinu /The wind has risen*, and by pointing out that Kobo Abe used the marker as frequently as 15 times per page in *Kigadomei/The starving unions* (Hokari cited in Saville-Troike, 1985, p. 5). (I actually counted up to 24 occurrences per page in my copy of Abe's novel.) This practice of using silence markers in writing complements the Japanese conviction that once something is expressed in words, its true essence and, perhaps, beauty is lost.

> When parents die, when the son passes the entrance examination to a university, and when we see something extremely beautiful, there should be silence. There is a well-known poem which starts 'Oh, Matsushima (name of an island in Japan)...', but because the poet

was so impressed by its beauty he could not continue; this poem is considered one of his masterpieces. (Williams cited in Saville-Troike, 1985, p. 8)

As with the prevalence of proverbs that consistently assess overt verbalisation negatively, such extensive use of silence markers in Japanese literature helps to point towards a society that is at ease with and accepting of quietude and hence treats silence as a relatively unmarked phenomenon. We have seen that culture in the shape of literature and art does play a role in reflecting values and beliefs regarding silence and talk in specific speech communities, but now we will turn our attention to an examination of the Japanese mother–child relationship in order to gain a better understanding of how such attitudes might possibly be transmitted from generation to generation.

3.5 Socialisation and silence

The cradle of Japanese silent behaviour?

A number of scholars claim that the Japanese proclivity for silence appears to be related to child-rearing practices (Clancy 1990; Hendry 1986; Ishii & Bruneau, 1994; Pritchard, 1995; Yamada, 1997); in particular, the extent to which the primary care-giver verbally interacts with the infant appears to be of significance. It seems that the cultural experience of children who are less vocal about their needs includes early caregivers spending extended periods of time in close physical proximity to them, along with the expectation that adults or siblings will provide care without verbalisation being necessary (Saville-Troike, 1989). Yamada (1997) rightly points out that the more private context of the home plays a crucial first role in socialising discourse norms before the public arena of the school exerts its influence on how one communicates. The process includes not only acquiring knowledge of the structure and use of language to become communicatively competent, but also the values and patterns of silent interaction (Ishii & Bruneau, 1994, p. 248).

Although it is apparent that, due to an inability to cope with ambiguity, a child's capacity to produce and correctly interpret meaningful silences is only honed relatively late in communicative development (Jaworski, 1993; Sobkowiak, 1997), there is compelling evidence that by as early as 3 to 4 months of age culturally-specific child-rearing practices may influence the amount of silent behaviour an infant displays. Studies examining the acquisition of silence in infanthood, as opposed to the acquisition of language, are notably lacking, but this is somewhat made up for by Caudill and Weinstein's (1969) seminal paper on comparative child-rearing practices in Japan and the United States. Through the use of a systematic, long-term observational methodology coupled with comprehensive quantitative statistical analysis, Caudill's (the chief researcher) investigation suggests that the Japanese may be socialised into less verbally active, implicit communicative behaviour from a very early age.

Caudill selected a matched sample of thirty Japanese and thirty American firstborn 3- to 4-month-old infants from intact middle-class families living in urban locations and observed the behaviour of both infants and mothers in their homes over a period of three years. The general findings of the study showed that there was a pronounced difference in styles of care-giving between the two cultures. The American mother appeared to have a much livelier and stimulating approach to her baby, for example by looking at, positioning and, most importantly, chatting to the infant significantly more. This correlated in increased 'positive vocalisations' on the part of the infant. In contrast, the Japanese mother seemed to have a more soothing and lulling approach, while being physically in close proximity to the infant for extended periods (Caudill & Weinstein, 1969, p. 30). Consequently the Japanese baby appeared relatively passive, subdued, with occasional 'unhappy vocalisations' as his/her mother communicated through physical rather than vocal means. From Caudill's work we can see that by the tender age of only 4 months, Japanese infants are already developing a pattern of silent togetherness with their mothers. (It does seem to still be the mother who performs the role of primary caregiver despite recent shifting gender balances – see Nakatani, 2006). Perhaps the reason why effective use of silence is seldom mastered in a second language context is because so much non-verbal competence is acquired in early childhood and therefore operates at an unconscious level (Saville-Troike, 1989, p. 245).

Even though Caudill's findings and conclusions are very attractive for anyone wishing to get to the roots of Japanese silence, we must be careful about attaching too much importance to a solitary study, and one that could hardly be described as contemporary. Even so, it is interesting to note that additional research in sociology by Vogel (1963), and in developmental psychology by Camras *et al.* (1998), and Fogel, Toda and Kawai (1988) seems to support Caudill's assertion that Japanese caregivers tend not to be overtly vocal, thus providing initial implicit lessons on silent interdependent communication. For instance, Vogel's study, which focused on Japanese mothers in a Tokyo suburb, found that immediately after birth, mothers would try to find out under what specific circumstances their babies cried and then tried to minimize this vocalisation to just a few seconds. Pritchard (1995) concurs with Vogel's claim that although Japanese mothers used less verbal communication, they were still intensely involved with their infants, 'to the extent that their beings were almost merged' (p. 260). This deeply close relationship provides the context for a style of communication that relies little on overt verbal messages from the sender and more on empathetic, anticipatory understanding by the listener. To better understand this concept in the Japanese context we must next examine a key term from Japanese psychology called *amae*.

Amae and silent dependency

The theory of *amae* was first proposed by the psychoanalyst Doi (1973) to describe the interdependent state of Japanese social relationships. Doi (1988) defines the term thus:

> ...*amae*, the noun form of *amaeru*, an intransitive verb that means "to depend and presume upon another's benevolence." This word has the same root as *amai*, an adjective that means "sweet." *Amaeru* has a distinct feeling of sweetness and is generally used to describe a child's attitude or behaviour toward his parents, particularly his mother. (p. 20)

Hendry (1986, p. 18) claims that this 'dependency', which is obviously essential in infanthood, is encouraged to persist in adult life in Japan, while in contrast, the Western approach tends to encourage independence from an early age. *Amae* begins in the close mother–child relationship and later transfers to peers, the child's teachers and other people in authority, therefore making an understanding of the concept crucial for teachers working with Japanese students (for more on transference and the role of the teacher as parent, see Ehrman & Dörnyei, 1998, pp. 223–5). This transference supposedly means that *amae* provides an emotional undertone for all interpersonal communication in Japanese society, particularly where formal relationships are concerned. The concept links in closely with the Confucian philosophy that dependency is a necessary part of all human relationships and should be accepted and not looked down upon (Yum, 1994).

Doi (1974, pp. 19–20) believes that the frequent silences found in Japanese interactions provide participants with an opportunity to feel each other out, assess the situation, and reassure themselves of a mutual understanding based on *amae*. Clearly such an indirect and intuitive system of communication is only possible in a society that is characterised by an expectation of empathy. Clancy (1990, p. 27) points out that ideal interaction in Japan is therefore not one where the speaker expresses his/her needs, wants and opinions clearly, with the addressee understanding and complying. Rather, it is one where both parties understand and anticipate each other and fulfil any needs before verbal communication becomes necessary. Yamada (1997) provides an illustration of this type of implicit communication that stresses the value imparted on silence between two intimates. She points out the traditional Japanese belief in which:

> ... only the belly speaks the truth. The best communication is without words in *haragei* (literally, belly art), silent communication. Such visceral communication is thought of as occurring between an ideal couple in Japan through *a-un no kokyuu* (literally, ah-hm breathing): If a husband says, "Ah," a wife would immediately understand. Ideal communication is communication without talk. (p. 17)

The problem is that such implicit messages are inherently ambiguous and consequently prone to misinterpretation, particularly when employed in a cross-cultural communication context where interlocutors have little shared experience. Indeed, within the English as a foreign language (EFL) classroom an expectation of indulgent, wordless empathy by the learner towards the teacher is hardly conducive to an active and dynamic classroom discourse. Furthermore, it should be noted that due to understatement and ambiguity, the Japanese themselves often have trouble negotiating meaning when communicating with each other. A good example of this can be found in Befu (1986) in which, after much internal dialogue, the author struggles to ascertain whether a subtle, implied invitation to dinner from an acquaintance in Kyoto is genuine or not. Even after attending the dinner he is still not certain! Such difficulties are also apparent in Yohena's (2003) interactional sociolinguistic study of ellipsis in Japanese conversations which provides empirical examples of how silence can lead to miscommunication when Japanese couples interact.

It was with slight hesitation that I decided to highlight the relationship between *amae* and the silence of the Japanese. Doi's theory is, after all, fairly unfashionable now and has recently come in for some criticism, most notably from Dale (1986), who lambasts Doi's psychoanalytic theories as being merely *nihonjinron*, nationalistic rhetoric that profits from crypto-linguistic assumptions. Certainly, Doi's industrious, if misguided, attempts to stretch the theory of *amae* to explain such disparate phenomena as trade union unrest and the maintenance of the Imperial Emperor system were unwise, and, consequently, *amae's* credibility has not benefitted greatly from these theoretical over-extensions. Nevertheless, I do believe, despite Dale's misgivings, that by limiting its scope to the initial mother–child relationship, and subsequent transferral to the student–teacher relationship, an understanding of the concept of *amae* is conducive to a better appreciation of the roots of silence in the Japanese foreign language classroom. Furthermore, in addition to apparently encouraging implicit communication through an indulgent expectation of empathy, *amae* also seems to play a key role in engendering shyness (Doyon, 2000; Sakuragi, 2004). According to Zimbardo (cited in Doyon, 2000, p. 14), 'the more you foster dependence in a child (or anyone else for that matter), the more you foster shyness'. It would be easy to dismiss shyness as being an overly simplistic explanation as to why so many Japanese students are verbally reticent when learning a foreign language. I would contend that many learners are actually socialised into a state of hyper-sensitivity to those around them from a very early age and this excessive awareness of others does indeed lead to verbal reticence in public situations. But how is this silence-inducing meta-awareness of others possibly inculcated during the child's preschool years?

Empathy training and *sasshi*

Clancy's (1990) research into the discourse of Japanese mothers and their 2-year-old children provides us with a good insight into how the Japanese are taught to compulsively become aware of others, and to engage in a communicative style that does not require overt verbalisation. Complementing Caudill and Weinstein's (1969) findings on younger children, Clancy's data reveal that 'Japanese mothers teach their children to pay attention to the speech of others, to intuit and empathize with their feelings, to anticipate their needs, and to understand and comply with their requests, even when these are made indirectly' (Clancy, 1990, p. 28). Children are habitually trained to perform the listener role well, a role that requires them to competently respond to subtle, indirect, and cautious intimations from the speaker (Lebra, 1993, p. 71). Furthermore, they are expected to perform this role even when nobody has spoken. During her research, Clancy found that mothers routinely attributed speech to silent third parties and even inanimate objects to indicate to the child what they might be feeling or thinking (Clancy, 1990, p. 30). Such empathy training continues throughout the child's development (Yamada, 1997) and ideally results in an ability to perform the anticipatory guesswork needed to understand another's under-elaborated communication. This skill is known in Japanese as *sasshi*, '... meaning conjecture, surmise or guessing what someone means. In its verb form (*sassuru*), its meaning is expanded to include imagine, suppose, or empathise with, and make allowances for others' (Nishida, cited in Gudykunst & Nishida, 1993, p. 151). Miyanaga (cited in Gudykunst & Nishida, 1993, pp. 155–6) points out that a person who is not skilled at *sasshi*, an unreceptive person who fails to pick up on cues, is considered dull, impolite or *gaijin mitai* (like a foreigner). High receptivity is greatly admired as it implies one is able to guess the true intention of others. The expectation of *sasshi* effort is clearly linked to the notion of *amae*. A word of warning though: we must not be blinded too much by Japanese terminology into thinking that *sasshi* is a uniquely Japanese phenomenon. Inference is, after all, a pragmatic skill that may be observed across cultures.

3.6 Socio-psychological silence

A silence-inducing hyper-sensitivity to others

Clancy (1990, pp. 31–2) claims that Japanese mothers often use appeals to the child's empathy as a control strategy. Indeed, training in empathy (*omoiyari*) does help to develop a sensitivity to the needs of others and, therefore, *sasshi* ability, but it also teaches children to fear the criticism and disapproval of those around them too. Children are often taught from an early age that their behaviour is being constantly monitored by the disapproving gaze of 'others' (Greer, 2000; Lebra, 1976, 1993; Yamada, 1997). But what is meant by the concept of 'other' in the Japanese context? Kuwayama (cited in Greer, 2000, p. 191) details three concentric levels with the self at the centre: *seken* (society); *hito* (person or people at large); and *mawari* (people around). Fear of embarrassment or shame at the hands of these monitors of behaviour can produce an egocentric concern for presenting the self in an acceptable light. Lebra (1993) expands on this notion:

> In self's view, *seken* consists of an unbounded group of people, visible and invisible, who surround and watch self's conduct. The self-centeredness of the *seken* concept may be underscored by substituting

mawari or *shui* (sic) for it, both meaning 'surrounding' and equivalent to *seken*. The point is that these terms, while indicative of each person's self-centered orientation, connote the oppressiveness, at the same time, of the surrounding social environment equipped with its eyes, ears, and mouth. The Japanese sensitivity to the *seken's* sharp eyes and the *mawari's* whisper entails both an egocentric concern for self-esteem and an allocentric readiness for conformity like two sides of a sheet of paper. (pp. 74–5)

Fear of others in the classroom

As Ehrman and Dörnyei (1998, pp. 119–22) rightly argue, shame and embarrassment are factors which can have a powerful effect on the defensive behaviour of students in the classroom. If we consider these two malevolent influences, coupled to the Japanese enculturated notion of an ever-watching 'other', we can begin to understand why the Japanese EFL classroom can often be characterised by learners unwilling to engage in the potentially embarrassing behaviour of active oral participation. Silence as a defensive strategy for the socially anxious is the much preferred option. This is well illustrated by Greer's (2000, pp. 183–4) account of why some of his students in a Japanese university language class remained silently unresponsive. Using the students' own writings, Greer identified the following reasons why they were unwilling to speak out: another student might not understand and that would cause trouble; concern that other students might disagree if an opinion is expressed; fear that the conversation might stop because of lack of English ability; unease that their topic might be thought of as 'insignificant' by others; apprehension that their pronunciation might be perceived as strange; and concern with speaking in English whilst others remained speaking in Japanese. These factors seem to suggest that the students' hyper-sensitivity to how they were perceived by the group resulted in a silence-inducing resistance to the communicative learning approach.

This theme of excessive self-monitoring is reflected by McVeigh (2002), who squarely lays the blame for unresponsive students on *seken*, which he translates as 'the official gaze'. 'Once deeply internalized beyond conscious awareness, the official gaze is transmuted into a horizontal gaze (i.e., among peers), thereby encouraging a conspiracy of deafening silence in the *daigaku* [university] classroom' (McVeigh, 2002, p. 197). It is telling that McVeigh's students disclosed to him on a number of occasions their dislike of small classes, the reason being that such groups fail to afford the same protective anonymity of a large class – protection not only from the instructor, but also from other students in the group.

Of course, not all Japanese students are silenced by the disapproving stare of *seken* or the eyes of *hito*. Some are prepared to take the risk of speaking out in a foreign language in front of others. When this does happen, we should applaud their courage in overcoming a very real culturally ingrained fear of shame and embarrassment in front of their peers. Furthermore, we must make every attempt to create and maintain a supportive classroom atmosphere, thereby encouraging more students to take a similar risk of social exposure. By paying closer attention to group dynamics, we can perhaps avoid the *norm of mediocrity* (see Dörnyei, 2005, p. 89) characterised by a lack of participation and student silence.

Lessons about silence from psychoanalysis

Kurzon (1998, p. 35) draws attention to the fact that the link between shyness, shame, embarrassment and silence is often mentioned in psychoanalytical literature. Even though much of the writing tends to examine case studies of extreme examples of neuroses, Kurzon believes such reports can help us to better understand the silent episodes of people who do not have a psychiatric illness. For example, he cites the illuminating case of a 20-year-old woman experiencing severe chronic detachment and psychotic breaks who was embarrassed by her weakness and afraid that people would laugh at her. As her ideal self-image was at risk if she spoke, she therefore withdrew into silence as a way of regaining power, self-control and control of her situation. This notion of using silence to wrest control back in a potentially embarrassing or shameful situation invites parallels with the silent-strategy of students in the Japanese EFL classroom who are hyper-sensitive to those around them.

At its most extreme this sensitivity to others, inculcated in early childhood by empathy training and the use of shame as a control strategy, may lead to a social anxiety variant known as *taijin-kyoufu* (delusional social phobia). Miyake and Yamazaki (cited in Sakuragi, 2004, p. 806) suggest that this fear of interpersonal relations (sometimes termed *taijin kyofusho* – see Essau, Sasagawa, Chen, & Sakano, 2012; Kleinknecht, Dinnel & Kleinknecht, 1997) is characterised by an incomplete separation between mother and child, overprotective parents and a resulting excessive display of *amae* by the child. The view is supported by Kasahara (1986), who proposes that Japanese child-rearing practices, which habitually refer to children being watched censoriously by others, could contribute to a fear of eye-to-eye confrontation among young adults. A typical sufferer of this sub-type fear of interpersonal relations describes the dread of being watched thus:

> In the presence of others, I become tense and feel ill at ease. I am self-conscious of being looked at by others. At the same time, I am embarrassed as to where to direct my eyes...Meanwhile, my looks lose their naturalness and I end up by staring into others' eyes with piercing looks...my unnatural piercing look hurts others by making them feel unpleasant. This is not merely imagination; it is indeed a fact for me. The reason I can insist on this is because I know intuitively by the way others behave towards me. Others look away from me, become restless, make grimaces, or leave their seat abruptly. It is psychologically so painful for me to embarrass people in this way that I end up avoiding people as much as possible. (Kasahara, 1986, p. 380)

Although McDaniel (2003) believes the traditional Japanese notion of prolonged eye contact with a superior being interpreted as a threat or sign of rudeness seems to be on the wane, Harumi (cited in Nakane, 2007, p. 170) found that, in contrast to home students, the Japanese sojourners she observed at a British university tended not to direct their eye gaze towards the teacher during their in-class silences, thus increasing the ambiguity of the silence. From my own experience teaching in Japanese universities, I have taught a number of students who were completely unable or unwilling to make any direct eye contact with me or others in the group. Invariably, such students would remain silent for the entire class period, or would speak minimally and in such a voice as to be barely audible. It seems that high school and university students are susceptible to this inhibiting disorder for a number of reasons. According to Kasahara (1986, pp. 380–1): the syndrome first manifests itself in puberty, but becomes rare by the age of 30; it is induced in situations where the sufferer comes into contact with people of intermediate familiarity, who are neither close, nor strangers; and finally, the sufferer is most susceptible when in a small mixed-sex group of several people who share a similar age and background. It is certainly not my intention to suggest that there exists an overwhelming number of students who remain silent in their classes because they are acutely neurotic; but I do think that, as with Kurzon's (1998) previously described case study which informs us about the potential use of silence by the disempowered, an awareness of the fear of eye-to-eye confrontation disorder provides us with useful background information relating to some of the more potentially deep-rooted socio-psychological causes of silences on the part of Japanese learners, in particular their hyper-sensitivity to being watched whilst speaking in a foreign language. As one of Greer's (2000) students ominously described, when speaking in front of her classmates, *'yappari, mawari no me wa kowai*; lit., the eyes around me are frightening' (p. 184).

3.7 Silence as a pragmatic function

Silence and politeness strategies

The preceding discussion about the inhibiting effect of a heightened awareness of those around one leads us nicely to the related topic of silence as a politeness strategy. Although some speech communities consider the absence of talk in social interactions as being something profoundly negative and slightly disturbing (see Jaworski, 2000), it would be quite wrong to view silence purely from this single, static perspective. Aided by its inherent ambiguity, silence can actually be an extremely effective tool for somebody wishing to avoid conflict or the potential imposition that a verbal utterance might cause (Jaworski, 1993; Sifianou, 1997; Tannen, 1985). Although extended silent pauses at turn-taking junctures are associated with a polite discourse style in many cultures (e.g., see Enninger, 1991; Scollon & Scollon, 1981, 1990; refer also to section 3.8 of this book), the silence I will discuss here in relation to politeness focuses on what Saville-Troike (1985, p. 6) describes as 'silent communicative acts which are entirely dependent on adjacent vocalizations for interpretation, and which carry their own illocutionary force'. An example of this type of silence would be a conscious decision not to verbally contribute to an on-going interaction, or a deliberate silence in response a question or request.

In her seminal paper on silence and politeness, Sifianou (1997) highlights that politeness-orientated silences can best be understood by extending Brown and Levinson's (1987) concept of negative and positive politeness, this extension being necessary because Brown and Levinson's work is more concerned with overt verbalisation and only very briefly touches upon the issue of politeness encoded in silence. Brown and Levinson's theory in turn is dependent on the notion of face (Goffman, 1967), meaning the public self-image claimed by a person. Face is either positive – the need to be connected and involved with the group, or negative – the need to be independent and free from imposition.

Brown and Levinson propose that most communicative acts pose a risk to face and can therefore be considered face-threatening acts (FTAs). The five main strategies for dealing with FTAs (1 – do the FTA on record; 2 – do the FTA on record with positive politeness; 3 – do the FTA on record with negative politeness; 4 – do the FTA off record; and 5 – don't do the FTA) are supposedly gradable with the higher the number posing the greater the risk to face (c.f. Scollon & Scollon, 1981).

Hence, according to Brown and Levinson's (1987) theory, we can see that by choosing the strategy 'Don't do the FTA', the speaker has decided upon the option of not speaking and therefore avoids any potential threat to face through the employment of silence. Sifianou (1997) extends the theory by proposing that silence may be used both as an effective positive politeness strategy, and an effective negative politeness strategy, and can also be associated with off-record politeness (not forgetting that silence additionally has the potential to be impolite and face-threatening). Positive politeness manifests itself through the use of silence to build rapport and solidarity, and is based on the idea that rather than coming through words, understanding emanates from 'shared perspective, experience and intimacy' (Tannen, 1985, p. 97). Silence as a negative politeness FTA, however, can be used as a distancing tactic which displays deference for older or socially superior people, or can serve to protect speakers from potential intrusions (Sifianou, 1997, p. 72). Finally, it is possible to use silence as an off-record politeness strategy when it operates as an indirect speech act. As Tannen (1985) explains, 'silence is the extreme manifestation of indirectness. If indirectness is a matter of saying one thing and meaning another, silence can be a matter of saying nothing and meaning something' (p. 97). Even so, Blum-Kulka (cited in Sifianou, 1997, p. 73) warns that off-record strategies have the potential to be the least polite forms due to their ambiguity and the inferential burden they place on the listener.

Japanese students' silence as a politeness strategy

Certainly the link between silence, indirectness and politeness is particularly relevant to the Japanese context when one considers the great importance placed on saving face (one's own and one's addressees') and the avoidance of conflict in Japan (see Gudykunst & Nishida, 1993). Franks (2000) underlines the notion of silence as a means to obtain social approval and avoid social penalty:

> Face-saving is crucial to the Japanese way of life, and through the culture's tremendous value of face-saving (or saving the dignity of

both the speaker and the listener) silence is encouraged. During communication interactions, therefore, silence together with indirect language is used to save embarrassment, to ease tension, and to respect the feelings of the speaker. The rationale here is that what you don't say cannot hurt anyone. (p. 6)

Brown and Levinson's (1987) assertion that Japan's culture can be classed as having a negative politeness orientation perhaps detracts from the fact that members of any cultural group need to maintain both negative *and* positive face during social interactions (Kramsch, 1998). Within an EFL context a learner may remain silent not only out of a desire to protect his/her positive face, but also to save the teacher's negative face which may be threatened by asking for repetitions or explanations. Regarding Japanese learners in an English-speaking study abroad context, Nakane (2006, 2007) found that the students she observed tended to remain silent more as a strategy to protect their own positive face than as a negative politeness strategy aimed at not interrupting the flow of the lesson. Silence as a strategy to maintain positive face appeared to emanate from learners' second language anxiety and their preoccupation with providing 'correct' answers. We can see that this strategy is closely related to the previous discussion concerning the inhibiting effects of excessive self-monitoring and how a fear of being judged negatively by others results in a student's non-participation in speaking activities. Students also used silence as a 'Don't do the FTA' politeness strategy by not expressing their disagreement with the instructor and adopting a more deferential attitude than their native-English speaking peers. Nakane identified instances where Japanese learners used off-record politeness silence in response to being nominated in class 'as an indirect way of communicating "I don't know the answer" or "I have no idea" or "I'm not quite sure I understood the question"' (2006, p. 1826). The use of silence in this situation is common in Japanese classrooms but is open to misinterpretation from those unaccustomed to it and therefore may be seen as a threat to the teacher's face. This rather ambiguous strategy reflects the student's indulgent expectation of an anticipatory understanding of meaning by the instructor and is characterised by the anticipation of empathy.

One final consideration that does not seem to be covered in the literature, is the possibility of students remaining silent in order to reflect a positive politeness strategy aimed at maintaining solidarity and building rapport with other class members. For this situation to come about, the class would have had to have slipped into a norm of mediocrity characterised by non-participation and non-response to questions and cues by the teacher. Even perfectly able students might choose to remain silent so as to be considered an accepted member of the *uchi* in-group. It is questionable though whether such silence is motivated by a sense of wanting to make a conscious effort to be polite to other non-participating students. In my opinion such silence is much more likely to emanate from the student's fear of being judged negatively by peers and the desire to protect his/her own positive face.

3.8 Silence as a linguistic phenomenon

Cultural differences in turn-taking styles

In order to provide a fully comprehensive overview of the roots of Japanese silence, I would now like briefly to examine the more micro-level silence of pausing within and at the end of conversational turns. In their seminal paper on dyadic turn-taking, Sacks, Schegloff and Jefferson (1974) found that most transitions between speakers occur with little or no gap between turns, and extended silence at these junctures is therefore an indication that the interaction is not progressing smoothly. Jefferson (cited in Watts, 1997, p. 93) claims that inter-turn silences of more than 1.5 seconds lead to a perception of dysfluency in interactions, whereas inter-turn silences of less than this length appear not to be registered as unusual and therefore do not affect perception of fluent discourse. Watts (1997) suggests an inter-turn silence of 1.5 seconds to be the central point in a continuum of 1.3 to 1.7 seconds where anything more than this becomes marked and can affect the discourse status of participants. Drawing on Levinson, the range of potential non-verbalisations at turn-taking junctures is neatly summarised by Jaworski (1993, p. 17) as follows:

1. A *gap* before the current speaker who terminates his or her turn assigns the next speaker, before another party in the interaction self-selects to be the next speaker, or before the current speaker claims further right to the floor in the conversation.
2. A *lapse* when the current speaker does not nominate the next speaker but stops speaking, when the next speaker nominated by the current speaker fails to claim the floor, or when another party does not self-select to be the next speaker in the interaction and the current speaker does not resume speaking.
3. A selected next speaker's *significant* (or *attributable*) silence after the next speaker is nominated by the current speaker who has stopped speaking.

Although it is important to note again that we should not equate one style of interaction with one culture or person, as people are able to adopt a number of different styles depending on context, it does seem that people tend to prefer one discourse style over another in any given situation. This is underlined by a number of writers who point to the culturally specific nature of turn-taking pauses within particular cultural groups (Jaworski, 1993, 2000; Scollon & Scollon, 1981, 1990; Sifianou, 1997; Tannen, 1981, 1984; Trompenaars, 1993). Sato's (1982) observation study which analysed the turn-taking behaviours of learners in her own English as a Second Language (ESL) class provides sound empirical evidence of differences in how turns at talk are taken. Sato found her East Asian students (from countries such as Japan and Korea) took significantly fewer turns at talk than their non-Asian counterparts because they tended to bid for fewer turns and were nominated less by their teacher.

Difficulties may occur when two interlocutors have different ideas about what is an appropriate length of pause between or during turns, and this notion of appropriateness will partly be informed by the prevailing attitude towards silence in one's discourse community. Trompenaars (1993, p. 68) has suggested a quite broad framework which considers turn-taking patterns and informs us about potential differences in attitudes to pause length. Though useful, it should be noted again that Trompenaars' model is rather static and does not reflect the dynamic and shifting nature of an individual's discourse style. The model consists of: the 'Latin' style, in which turn-taking does occur but with a lot of overlapping employed to show interest in what others are saying; 'Anglo' style, in which people switch turns with no perceptible pausing, tend not to interrupt each other and find silence uncomfortable; and finally, 'Oriental' style, which is characterised by turn-taking with marked pauses at transition relevance places (TRP), thereby indicating respect for the speaker and comprehension by the listener. Considering the last of these styles, which would be relevant to Japan, Trompenaars fails to point out that such a style would likely not be as pronounced in informal interactions and is more relevant to formal or public interactions, such as in a classroom, where power differences among participants exist.

Tolerance to silent pauses at turn-taking junctures

It is unfortunate that there appears to be a lack of empirical, quantitative studies measuring cross-cultural differences in tolerance of silence at TRPs. Even so, Yamada (1997, p. 77) provides us with an interesting example of the silent pauses of two Japanese and American business meetings that seems to confirm Trompenaars' model and supports the notion that the Japanese have a high tolerance for silence at turn-taking junctures. Yamada found an average of 5.15 seconds silence per minute in the Japanese meeting she analysed compared to just 0.74 seconds in the American one. The longest pause of 8.5 seconds in the Japanese meeting was almost double that of the American meeting at 4.6 seconds. Although Yamada's observations were rather limited and we are given scant information about the participants, her results do suggest that marked pausing may be acceptable for Japanese in more formal, public interactions and that this silent pausing does not necessarily lead to communication breakdown. Yamada claims that rather than being hollow lulls in the interaction, such silences are in fact periods of intense cognitive activity during which participants engage in *sasshi* (guesswork), asking such questions as, '"Is everyone getting this?" "Do we need/want to keep talking on this topic?" or, "Should we move on to something else?"' (Yamada, 1997, p. 77).

Enninger's (1991) account of the silences occurring at TRPs in a 40-minute conversation between three adult Amish underlines the notion that we should always bear in mind that tolerance to silence can vary not only between national cultures, but also between subgroups within a culture. Enninger (1991, p. 17) found that there were '...no fewer than eleven between-turn silences longer than twenty seconds, the longest being fifty-six seconds' within the Amish conversation he observed. He found no evidence to suggest that these extended silences between turns resulted in communication breakdown, and in post-conversation interviews the participants deemed the interaction to have run smoothly, refuting the idea that time had been wasted by not filling the silences with talk. However, when members of US-mainstream culture and the Amish interact Enninger observes '...the obligatory and the optional quality of the rules governing the tolerable length of between-turn silences may produce cross-cultural pragmatic failure with concomitant attributions' (1991, p. 18).

Keeping the focus on North America, this time considering the interactions between Native American Athabaskans and Anglo-Americans, Scollon and Scollon (1990) provide us with a timely account of how communication breakdown may occur when interlocutors fail to share common notions of appropriate turn-taking pauses:

> ...Athabaskans allow a slightly longer pause between sentences than do English speakers. The difference is probably not more than half a

second in length, but it has an important effect on interethnic communication. When an English speaker pauses he waits for the regular length of time (around one second or less), that is, his regular length of time, and if the Athabaskan does not say anything, the English speaker feels he is free to go on and say anything else he likes. At the same time the Athabaskan has been waiting his regular length of time before coming in. He does not want to interrupt the English speaker. This length of time we think is around one and one-half seconds. It is just enough longer that by the time the Athabaskan is ready to speak the English speaker is already speaking again. (p. 273)

As was mentioned at the beginning of the section, it is interesting to note that Scollon and Scollon also deem around 1.5 seconds after a turn has been taken to be a key point when participants might start to make (mis)interpretations about the meaning of the silence they are experiencing. Misapprehensions and, consequently, stereotyping can occur when two speakers with an ethnocentric understanding of silent pauses and topic control interact with each other, as can be seen when the Athebaskan's turn-internal rhetorical pause is mistakenly read as a turn-surrendering silence. Indeed, the Anglo-Americans' ethnocentric perception of the longer switching pauses resulted in them branding the Athebaskans as "'passive', 'sullen', 'withdrawn', 'unresponsive'. 'lazy', 'backward', 'destructive', 'hostile', 'uncooperative', 'antisocial', and 'stupid'" (Scollon, 1985, p. 24). In contrast, the Anglo-Americans were deemed to talk far too much and were considered impolite (Scollon & Scollon, 1981, p. 36). Note that even though both sides were perfectly fluent in English, miscommunication often still ensued.

TRP pausing and the Japanese foreign language classroom

The lack of understanding shown by the Athebaskans and the Anglo-Americans about each other's discourse norms has the potential to be mirrored in the Japanese EFL classroom when students interact with non-Japanese instructors from so-called 'talkative' English-speaking cultures. Certainly the negative labels assigned to the Athebaskans do seem to correlate to the stereotypical notion of the silent, passive, non-cooperative Asian student (c.f. Cheng, 2000; Kubota, 1999; Littlewood, 2000). This seems to be supported by Harumi's (2006) study in which Japanese and English informants were shown a video extract featuring a Japanese student employing prolonged silences in response to her native English teacher's questions. The informants were then asked to comment on how they interpreted the situation. The Japanese informants talked about the student's silence as an indication of waiting for the teacher's help and wanting the teacher to understand without the student having to speak (an example of an expectation of indulgent *amae*?), whereas the English informants interpreted the student's silence as rudeness, boredom and laziness as 'she does not try to understand and when she finally answers, she says, I don't know (an easy option)' (Harumi, 2006, p. 3). This type of prolonged pausing at TRPs in cross-cultural learning situations may indeed lead to mutual stereotyping because of misinterpretations of extended pauses which turn into silent responses. An additional problem occurs when the teacher mistakenly believes an inter-turn pause has become a silent response. With a teacher's failure to be aware of localised norms for extended pauses in turn-taking comes the danger of instructors jumping in and interrupting the student during one-to-one encounters before the student has a chance to produce a response. In an account of her own teaching experiences in Japan, Thorp (1991, p. 114) relates how she had to 'adapt to Japanese ideas concerning what was an acceptable pause length between speaker turns, and between question and answer.' Cross-cultural differences in inter-turn pause lengths may be further exacerbated by Japanese students' tendency to produce a falling intonation as an accompaniment to their silence, resulting in their losing the floor (Lawrie, 2006). Rogerson and Gilbert (cited in Lawrie, 2006, p. 6) point out that rising intonation usually indicates an utterance will continue, whereas falling intonation is normally interpreted as signifying the end of an utterance and an opportunity for the hearer to take a turn. To fully understand turn-taking within a classroom group context, we need to look closely at participant structures and the role of teacher wait-time. These concepts will be discussed in relation to the Japanese educational context in more detail in the following chapter, but, suffice to say here, there does seem to be evidence that extending teacher wait-time can significantly improve classroom communication and the learning experience of students (Shrum, 1984, 1985).

3.9 Silence and cognition

Hesitation for cognitive processing at TRPs

No examination into the possible roots of Japanese L2 learners' silence would be complete without a short examination of the relationship between cognition and silence. This concerns the inter- and intra-turn hesitations that are related to silent thinking time during interactions. Chafe (1985, pp. 79–80) points out that hesitations caused by cognitive activity may occur not only when speakers are deciding on *what to* talk about next, but also when they are deciding on *how to* talk about something. Drawing his conclusions from a study which involved participants recounting the events they had seen in a short film, Chafe claims that hesitations in deciding what to talk about next tended to 'occur between phrases and clauses which express the foci of consciousness' (1985, p. 87). This is in contrast to predominantly intra-turn hesitations which occurred as a result of speakers encountering difficult to categorise, low codability items. Unsurprisingly, Chafe reached the conclusion that pause length is correlated with the degree of difficulty in coding objects whilst one is speaking.

According to Nakane's (2007) investigation into the silences of Japanese sojourners studying at an Australian university, cognitive factors play a key role in contributing to longer pausing. As students have to interact in learning situations using a second language, deficiencies in English ability may lead to their requiring longer pauses in order to decode previous speakers' utterances and then to formulate appropriately grammatical sentences in response. Putting linguistic factors aside, Nakane (2007, pp. 91–2) speculates whether Japanese students may need more time for cognitive processing as, unlike Australian students, they have not been trained to react rapidly to questions and cues in the classroom. An inability to deal with the quicker reaction times expected in the Australian classroom, coupled with a lack of familiarity with turn-taking procedures, relevant knowledge schema and discussion topics, resulted in Nakane's subjects experiencing pronounced difficulties coming up with ideas, organising their thoughts coherently and producing relevant verbal responses. One interviewee described her experience thus:

> When I am asked a question, it takes a while for me to think about it. So, while I am thinking about the question, other people say various things, and the lecturer makes the final remark, moving on like 'Okay, next.' It's like that. They finish and move on. (Nakane, 2007, p. 91)

Rather than just being a blank, passive, non-participatory silence, we can see that the student's extended pause after she has been asked a question is actually a period of involved cognitive activity. Even so, it is extremely difficult to determine the exact cause of the student's silence. Perhaps she needed a longer cognitive processing time because of linguistic deficiencies in English grammar or vocabulary in comparison to her Australian peers, or maybe second language factors played no significant role in the creation of her silence and all that she needed was more time to organise her thoughts before participating. What all this hypothesising shows us is that it is incredibly difficult to determine the exact causes of individual students' silences in the cognitive domain. This is especially true when we consider that cognitive causal factors may overlap with other factors relating to anxiety, embarrassment, notions of appropriate student behaviour, lack of knowledge concerning turn-taking or participant structures, and so on.

3.10 Conclusion

In this chapter, I have illustrated how silence has many faces – from the rejection of talk by a whole discourse community, to the briefest of hesitations while an individual's brain kicks into gear. In order to truly understand a learner's silent episode we must first consider the underlying attitudes and beliefs towards the relative merits of speech versus silence in his/her culture, whilst at the same time paying close attention to the context in which the silences occur. It also appears that the learner's individual sense of self plays a crucial role in the production of silences. Even so, factors involved in the creation of silence are varied and it is no easy task to gauge whether there are sociocultural, psychological or linguistic reasons for the silence. Indeed, its ambiguity, coupled to its context-dependent character, means that silence is often a source of frustration and misunderstanding, particularly when those who do not share a discourse style meet. By presenting a wide range of issues connected to silence in Japanese society, this chapter has helped to realise the sophisticated and complicated nature of silence in the Japanese EFL classroom. The following is a summary of some of the main points I have discussed:

- Despite its status as a post-Confucian society, Confucianism in Japan still provides an underlying philosophical background in which silences may be positively regarded and may be shaped by particularistic relationships and attention to group membership.
- Simplistic stereotypes of the silent Japanese are best avoided, but the nationalistic literature of the *nihonjinron* approach does provide some useful themes (if extended) for the study of Japanese silence.
- Clues to Japan's orientation towards non-vocalisation and its positive interpretation of silence can be observed in the culture's proverbs, poetry and literature.

- The close mother–child relationship which does not rely on vocalisation is potentially a source for the socialisation of infants into a less vocal, more implicit style of communication. However, more up-to-date, empirical evidence is needed to confirm this point.
- Much literature focusing on Japanese communication posits that ideal communicative exchanges take place without words and rely on empathetic understanding. Hence children are trained to perform the listener role well.
- Excessive self-monitoring and a hyper-sensitivity to others can lead to inhibitive silences in public situations. Japanese learners talk about a fear of being watched as one reason why they do not participate orally in class.
- Psychoanalytic theory can provide us with some potential clues as to the causes of some silences, particularly regarding feelings of disempowerment. It suggests that silence may be a place of relative safety into which disempowered people may retreat.
- Silence may be employed as any one of Brown and Levinson's (1987) politeness strategies, though Japanese learners tend to use it for their own positive face protection.
- The link between silence and politeness is particularly relevant for the Japanese context because of the great importance placed on saving face in that society.
- Pauses of over approximately 1.5 seconds at turn-taking junctures appear to indicate that communication is not flowing smoothly in certain cultures.
- Differences in turn-taking styles exist across cultures and disparities in tolerance to silence may lead to communication breakdown and mutual stereotyping.
- Silence caused by cognitive processing may signal a learner's difficulty in organising his/her thoughts coherently and may be due to a lack of foreign language proficiency.

Concerning the last point, in this chapter I have only briefly touched upon silence which finds its roots in a person's lack of foreign language ability. An investigation into the aims and nature of a society's education system, including its attitudes to and provision for foreign language learning, is crucial for the better understanding of language learner silence. The following chapter will therefore critically analyse the stunning failure of the Japanese education system to consistently produce competent English language speakers.

4
A critical analysis of Japan's language education system

4.1 Introduction

Why does Japan's education system appear unable to produce learners who can actually converse in a language which they have been compelled to study for at least of six years? What situational factors have contributed to classroom environments where silent language learners appear to be the norm rather than the exception? In this chapter I attempt to answer these questions by offering a critical analysis of Japan's dysfunctional language education system. After providing a general overview of education in Japan, I will discuss how recent language learning reforms by The Ministry of Education, Culture, Sport, Science and Technology (MEXT) have been met with widespread scepticism by an EFL community who believe the ministry's plans are unfeasible and fail to take into account the reality of language teaching in Japan's schools today. It is clear that a key element in why students appear unable to develop L2 communicative competence is the continued dominance of university entrance examinations within the system. These tests remain hugely influential at the pre-tertiary level, despite demographic changes meaning competition for university places is not quite as fierce as it once was (see Kamiya, 2009; Kinmonth, 2005), and they continue to shape which aspects of a foreign language are taught and how these aspects are studied. This leads me to the issue of *yakudoku* (a grammar-translation approach) which remains a deeply entrenched instructional method popular amongst Japanese teachers of English (JTEs). After exploring how this approach in effect silences students who are unfortunate enough to be exposed to it, I will outline some of the issues surrounding the presence of native speaker assistant language teachers in Japanese schools and consider why these instructors have proved relatively unsuccessful in developing learners' linguistic skills. The chapter concludes with an appraisal of how the disturbing issues of bullying (*ijime*) and nationalism contribute to a learning context which is far from conducive to encouraging L2 fluency amongst Japan's legions of language learners.

4.2 An overview of the system

Based on the United States' 6-3-3 model, Japan's education system was established in the years following the end of World War Two. The system comprises of six years of compulsory elementary schooling from the age of 6, followed by three more obligatory years at junior high school, and culminates in an optional further three years at senior high. Although in theory students may end their schooling at the age of 15, in reality the vast majority – 97.9 per cent in 2009 (MEXT, 2010, p. 55) – continue on to upper secondary education, and this process usually involves having to sit an entrance examination in order to gain admission to the senior high school of one's choice. While most elementary and junior high schools tend to be run by local municipal authorities, the number of private institutions increases dramatically at senior high level. In 2009 just over a quarter of these schools were privately run, fee paying institutions (MEXT, 2010, p. 57). The large proportion of private schools in this sector, coupled with a relaxation of catchment area rules at upper secondary level (for more on catchment area reforms, see Cave, 2003, pp. 94–6), means that there is intense competition for places at the best senior highs.

At the other end of the pre-tertiary spectrum, we should not ignore the widespread provision of education that is available to Japanese children prior to the commencement of their nine years of compulsory schooling. Nursery schools (known as *yōchien*) provide the first steps on the transition from home to formal schooling for children from the age of 3 years upwards. Over 60 per cent of the 13,500 nursery schools in Japan are private organisations (MEXT, 2010, p. 44) and it is not unheard of for the most prestigious ones to subject toddlers to entrance exams in order to gain admission – this being an excessively early taste of the academic rat race which is to come later on. According to Hendry (1989), some kindergartens feel that examining 3-year-old children is potentially too problematic and therefore opt to test the children's mothers instead! Much of the literature examining nursery schools points to the essential role they play in socialising children into becoming 'good Japanese' by introducing the concepts of group-mindedness, cooperation and self-discipline within the curriculum (e.g. Hendry,

1986; Kotloff, 1996; Lewis, 1984; Peak, 1989). Although curriculum activities vary tremendously from nursery to nursery, some schools do offer English language instruction for their pupils, particularly when children must prepare for exams to enter elite private elementary schools. Interestingly, it appears that little major research has been carried out on the learning of English within Japan's nursery schools, and what studies there are tend to be found in only local-level journals (e.g. Terao, Suzuki, Nasukawa & Takahashi, 2010; Yokoyama, 1999).

Operating in the shadow of the formal schooling system is a massive cram school (*juku*) and private tutoring industry which provides tuition in all subjects for students of all ages and abilities. It is difficult to overstate how massive this industry is, but one estimate for 1994 calculated its annual turnover at 1.4 trillion yen (Ukai Russell cited in Aspinall, 2005, p. 209). *Juku* are particularly ruthless in their focus on examination preparation activities, so much so that it is common for learners to feel they do not need to pay attention to lessons in regular school because these classes are so far behind what they may have already learnt at cram school (see Steger, 2006). The existence of Japan's huge shadow system of education is evidence of the failure of formal schooling to provide learners with an adequate standard of education. What is more, *juku* perpetuate inequality in an already inequitable system as families seek to pay for the examination success of their children.

4.3 Pre-tertiary language education

'Foreign language activities' in elementary schools

Following revisions to official curriculum guidelines by MEXT in 2008, from the beginning of the 2011 academic year a controversial new policy was adopted throughout Japan's public elementary schools which saw the introduction of mandatory 'foreign language activities' for all fifth- and sixth-year students. These activities consist of one period (approximately 45 minutes) of L2 instruction per week and, while not explicitly stated in the main description of MEXT's policy document, it is understood that English should be the language taught during these new lessons. MEXT (2011, p. 1) claim their objectives are:

> To form the foundation of pupils' communication abilities through foreign languages while developing the understanding of languages and cultures through various experiences, fostering a positive attitude towards communication, and familiarizing pupils with the sounds and basic expressions of foreign languages.

It appears though that MEXT's admirable stated intentions are likely to be compromised by classroom realities at the local level, and as we shall see later, this appears to be a recurring theme where the ministry's reforms are concerned. A lack of funding means that rather than being taught by L2 specialists, general homeroom teachers not qualified in foreign language instruction must take responsibility for the new English classes. Research carried out by Fennelly and Luxton (2011) has shown that many of these instructors feel they have received too little training and lack confidence both in their ability to use English and to teach it. Furthermore, it seems there is widespread confusion amongst Japan's pre-secondary teaching profession about the goals of MEXT's new course of study.

Along with growing provision for L2 instruction in nursery schools, the introduction of compulsory English lessons into elementary schools is part of a wider trend in Japan towards ever younger language learning. The popular belief of 'the younger the better', which tends to go unquestioned by non-specialists, fails to take into account compelling research into the age effect on second language acquisition (for an overview see Nikolov & Djigunovič, 2006) that suggests learning a language in a formal context at a younger age may in fact prove detrimental to a student's L2 linguistic progress. Contrasting formal and naturalistic learning contexts, Dörnyei (2009) points out that among other variables, the quantity and quality of instruction are key factors in determining whether instruction at an early age might prove successful. When we consider that over the course of the academic year, elementary school students will receive just 35 compulsory lessons, each of less than one-hour duration, and these classes will be led by unqualified, under-trained teachers who lack both L2 confidence and proficiency, it becomes apparent that learners are likely to experience a significant poverty in both the quantity and the quality of their L2 input. Initially, children tend to be very positive and excited about learning a new foreign language. Let us hope that classroom realities shaped by a lack of resources in Japan's pre-secondary sector do not merely serve to hasten the onset of the demotivation to study English which currently blights learners throughout Japan's junior and senior high schools (see Falout & Maruyama, 2004).

Secondary level reforms: the gap between policy and practice

MEXT has been well aware for some time that the language education system in Japan's secondary schools is consistently struggling to produce proficient L2 users able to communicate in the target language. A number of ineffective curricular reforms have been introduced over the years to try to remedy the situation, culminating in 2003 with the *Action Plan to Cultivate 'Japanese with English Abilities'*. Although an in-depth examination of the Plan's contents is beyond the scope of this chapter (for comprehensive summaries, see Butler & Iino, 2005; Tanabe, 2004), it suffices to say that MEXT's proposals place a much greater emphasis on developing students' practical English skills, with the expectation that 'On graduating from junior high school and senior high school, graduates can communicate in English' (MEXT, 2003). However, the Action Plan has come in for considerable criticism from scholars concerned about its unrealistic, top-down reforms which fail to take into account a host of situational constraints. These include severe shortfalls in CLT training provision, a chronic lack of available instruction time, deficiencies in teachers' L2 proficiency and deeply entrenched traditional teaching methodologies (Hato, 2005; Nishino, 2008; Nishino & Watanabe, 2008; O'Donnell, 2005; Sakui, 2004; Taguchi 2005). At the heart of Japan's L2 communicative malaise, though, lies the fact that Japan's secondary school system is still geared almost exclusively towards preparing students for success in university entrance examinations. These high-stakes exams focus primarily on receptive language skills and consequently there exists very little incentive for students to develop their L2 communicative competence, or for teachers to use up precious class time attempting to do so. As we shall see, the effects of these entrance examinations permeate deep down into the education system and they play a hugely significant role in silencing Japan's second language learners.

4.4 University entrance exams

An overview of university entrance examinations

Even though alternative routes into tertiary education do exist, usually involving some form of recommendation from a candidate's high school (see Kinmonth, 2005, p. 120 for a fuller description), most potential entrants opt to sit examinations in order to gain admission to university (Guest, 2008; Lee-Cunin, 2005). Japan's university entrance examinations can be classified into two types: *Daigaku Nyūshi Sentā Shiken* (the National Center Test for University Admissions, often referred to as 'the Center Test' for short) and *Niji Shiken* (which translates as the Second Tests). The Center Test takes place over two days in January and is a nation-wide, standardised examination administered by the National Center for University Entrance Examinations. The majority of students hoping to gain a place in tertiary education sit the multi-choice exam, with more than half a million candidates having done so in 2010 (National Center for University Entrance Examinations, 2010). MEXT introduced the test in its present form in 1990 with the aim of increasing freedom and variety in the system by allowing individual universities to choose the subjects their applicants must study for entry (Aspinall, 2005; Guest, 2008). The exam itself is comprised of up to six subjects, with English being a core component. Other foreign language options are available but are very rarely taken. This is borne out by the fact that in 2010, a massive 99.84 per cent of candidates chose to be examined on the English component, compared to only 0.03 per cent opting for Korean, the language of Japan's nearest neighbour (National Center for University Entrance Exams, 2010). The Center Test is employed by universities as a means of initially screening candidates prior to the subsequent round of examinations, known as *Niji Shiken*, which usually take place in February and March.

Individual faculties within universities set and administer their own *Niji Shiken* to candidates who have been guided where to apply based on their Center Test score. Candidates often sit these exams at more than one institution in order to ensure entry to a university should they fail to be accepted by their first choice. Some, particularly those hoping to enter one of the more prestigious universities, may concentrate on only one institution, thereby taking the risk of becoming a *rōnin* (literally, a 'masterless samurai') – a failed candidate no longer of high school age who is condemned to wait until the following year to retake an entrance exam. Most universities are happy to allow candidates to take their entrance tests more than once because the fees generated provide an important source of revenue (Kinmonth, 2005). Indeed, it appears that one of the primary functions of entrance exams is to generate income for universities, often at great cost to applicants. Brown (2002, p. 95) underlines this point with an account of how a colleague's son sat (and failed) eight tests over one entrance exam season at a cost of up to forty thousand yen per test. Top universities can make several million pounds from just a few days of examinations (see Murphey, 2004, p. 707).

As individual universities and their departments have control over *Niji Shiken*, there is some variety of form – for example, in addition to the multiple-choice style questions of the Center Test, they may have detailed translation exercises, open-ended questions and occasionally even a listening component in their English sections. Even so, the tests do still tend to conform to the traditional Japanese notion of what an examination should be by emphasising the memorisation of factual information and 'correct answers', with a focus on receptive rather than productive knowledge. Unsurprisingly, these tests have a reputation for being fiendishly difficult, with reading passages in some English sections challenging enough to trouble Anglophones (Brown & Yamashita, 1995; Kikuchi, 2006).

The negative impact of the examination system

So what impact do entrance examinations have on Japan's students and how might these tests have affected teaching and learning at the pre-tertiary level of schooling? McVeigh (1997, p. 97) draws on Dore to describe how the effects from university entrance exams permeate not only into senior high schools, whose curricula have been devastated through a preoccupation with preparing students for the tests, but also to junior high schools who are themselves preoccupied with entrance exams for senior high schools with the best records for getting students into prestigious universities. McVeigh suggests there is further washback (see below) into primary schools, with the ripple effects of such a competitive system eventually even reaching down to nursery schools. Indeed, preparation for getting into a good university is not limited to the final years of high school. It is a process that begins much earlier and sees children from an early age concentrating their efforts on studying the vast amounts of detailed factual information needed to pass exams in Japan (Aspinall, 2005). Negishi (cited in Doyon, 2001, p. 448) proposes that, over time, this approach to learning has a profoundly damaging effect on the thinking and behaviour of modern university students who:

> ...have since childhood, for a long time, lived in an environment based on manuals and textbooks geared to an entrance examination course classified by *hensachi* (deviation scores). In other words, they have never had the time or room to attempt anything but the instructions offered in manuals and, hence, no room for exercising their creativity. Due to this situation, when they finish their formal education, these students have no individual autonomy (*shutaisei*) in their business or even their daily lives; and there has been ingrained in them a tendency to always habitually seek instructions or manuals.

Certainly Japan's education system is not one where the rewards for initiative and creative thinking are particularly high. On the contrary, it reserves its greatest rewards for those students who are best able to memorise and regurgitate the mass of prescribed knowledge that has been spoon-fed to them in teacher-centred classrooms. Schooling in Japan therefore represents 'an enormously elaborated, very expensive testing system with some educational spin-offs, rather than the other way around' (Dore cited in Goodman, 2005, p. 9). Students within this 'examocracy' (McVeigh, 2006) appear to be fully aware that most of what they learn in school through mindless repetition will be of little use except in passing exams (Aspinall, 2005; Yoneyama, 1999) and are consequently alienated by an education system notable for the tedium of its pedagogy. In a school system which is increasingly characterised by absenteeism and declining scholastic levels, many students simply cannot keep up with the academic demands imposed on them and consequently fall by the wayside. Murphey (2001, p. 37) sums up the situation well with his forthright view that the entrance exam system is responsible for 'bleeding the life out of the youth of Japan'.

Entrance examination washback

Could the Japanese education system's preoccupation with testing and ranking contribute in some way to the silent behaviour of language students who are a product of it? Certainly, it would appear that these exams have done little to encourage communicative language teaching in Japanese schools. Indeed, why focus valuable time and resources on improving students' speaking abilities when oral skills are superfluous to the requirements of the Center Test and most universities' *Niji Shiken*? Helgesen (1993, p. 38) is representative of the widespread belief amongst many language practitioners in Japan that the 'wall of silence' meeting most teachers in university classrooms exists because students are simply not taught to speak in English throughout their time at junior and senior high school. Helgesen's intuitively appealing position leads us to the issue of washback, which may be defined simply as 'the effect of external testing on the teaching and learning processes in language classrooms' (Brown, 2000, p. 3). (For a more extensive discussion of various washback definitions, see Spratt, 2005, p. 8.) Research into the washback effects of exam-orientated language instruction has shown that such classes can result in less pairwork, more teacher talking time (TTT) and reduced opportunities for students to speak (Alderson & Hamp-Lyons, 1996). Although there are some studies questioning the extent or even existence of entrance exam washback in Japan's schools (e.g. Mulvey, 1999, 2001; Watanabe, 1996), it is apparent that entrance exams are a major factor in why the Japanese education system does not appear to be well suited to producing competent speakers of English.

Ryan (2009, p. 4) underlines this observation by making the pertinent point that the English taught in pre-tertiary classrooms is predominantly *juken eigo* (English for exams), a form of English far removed from the language used for communication outside of the classroom (see also McVeigh, 2002, pp. 153–4). As an academic subject rather than a tool for real life, *juken eigo* stresses the importance of detailed linguistic knowledge over communicative performance. The students themselves are well aware of *juken eigo*'s lack of practical applicability. Citing a large-scale survey of high school students by a major Japanese educational company, Kobayashi (2001, p. 69) reveals that a startling 93 per cent believed the English education they were receiving would not enable them to actually speak the language. This depressing statistic illustrates how the dominant grammar-translation methodology found within pre-tertiary classrooms essentially has a silencing effect on language learners. The prevalence of this grammar-translation approach, known as *yakudoku*, within English education in Japan is such that I will next explore it in more detail.

4.5 Traditional language teaching methods

Yakudoku: an enduring instructional method

Yakudoku has a long history in Japan. Its origins can be traced back over a thousand years to the Nara and Heian periods when Japanese Buddhist scholars, unconcerned with developing their oral proficiency, studied and read Chinese scripts by translating the target language word-for-word into Japanese before reordering and recoding the translation to match Japanese syntax (Henrichsen, 1989; Hino, 1988). Despite recent curriculum reforms, it would appear that not much has changed since those ancient times, as this non-oral approach to language learning remains the dominant way in which students are taught English (Gorsuch, 1998, 2002; O'Donnell, 2005; Nishino & Watanabe, 2008; Poole, 2005). Typically, language teachers in Japan can still be found standing at the front of classes picking English sentences apart 'as if they were abstract equations' (Aspinall, 2003, p. 106).

In addition to the important precedent set by tradition (which is difficult to overstate in the Japanese context), Hino (1988) suggests one possible reason why *yakudoku* is so persistently practised in schools is because it lessens the demands on teachers. The method 'requires little professional training, and also little preparation is needed for each class. Anyone who has studied English through *yakudoku* is able to teach it in the same way without much effort' (pp. 50–1). When one considers the lack of pre- and in-service teacher training (Browne & Wada, 1998; Nishino & Watanabe, 2008; O'Donnell, 2005), together with the severe time constraints many teachers are under at the pre-tertiary level (see Hato, 2005; Nishino, 2008; Sakui, 2004), the appeal of the *yakudoku* approach becomes all the more understandable.

The silencing effects of *yakudoku*

As *yakudoku* primarily involves the verbatim translation of English texts into Japanese, the method effectively silences students by severely limiting their chances to vocalise English. The only time many learners may be able to actually speak the language is during rigidly structured drill practices involving the repetition of sentences read out by the teacher. Thus students are silenced not only in the pre-tertiary classroom, but also it would seem in their later lives, as their generally poor English oral/aural skills are so greatly hindered by such archaic pedagogical practices. In describing interactions with university students trained in the *yakudoku* method, Mulligan (2005) illustrates how ill-equipped such learners are for conversing in English and highlights the concomitant silences of their extended cognitive processing:

> ...translation or *yakudoku* does not facilitate understanding or acquisition of a language, but it does create bad language habits. When eliciting a response from a student, how many of us have observed the agonizing period of silence, the long pause, the language conversion process of translating what has been said into Japanese and then going through the same process when answering. (p. 33)

In addition to limiting students' opportunities to vocalise English, *yakudoku* appears to focus learner attention more on the Japanese translations of texts than on the foreign language itself (Gorsuch, 1998; Law, 1995). Hino (1988, p. 47) observes that Japanese students of English tend to consider reading a foreign language text and translating it as synonymous actions. The goal is to render texts into a Japanese version with no consideration as to the value of the original. If recoding has not taken place, 'reading' is not considered to have occurred. Understanding only takes place in Japanese, not in English. Law (1995) goes as far as to suggest that the hidden purpose of *yakudoku* is actually indirect teaching of the mother tongue, noting that:

> the focus of attention is only initially on the codes of the foreign language; most of the productive energy of the method is directed

towards the recoded Japanese version. At the end of the translation class, students are left with a text in their native language to contemplate and review. Preparation of the translation exam will often come down to memorization of this recoded version; the original alien code will have largely been displaced from view. (p. 216)

Students have a very limited engagement with the English they come across in texts, and what little engagement there is tends to take place below the sentence level, with only individual lexical meanings being derived directly from the texts. Hino (1988) is quite right in his assessment that any possible benefits of *yakudoku*, such as a supposed improvement in mental discipline or increased syntactical knowledge, are far outweighed by the deleterious effects the approach has on students' listening, speaking and writing skills.

The language of instruction: setting a good example?

Clearly, *yakudoku* remains a dominant methodology in Japan's English education system in part because of the washback effect of university entrance exams. Even so, perhaps an even stronger factor is the role played by teachers' own attitudes and beliefs about their subject and the very nature of learning (Gorsuch, 1998, 2000; Watanabe, 1996). One area where this is particularly true relates to the language used by instructors in the classroom. Backing up Gorsuch's (1998) observation that instruction in translation-orientated classrooms takes place overwhelmingly in Japanese, Taguchi (2005, p. 5) discovered that only 7 per cent of the 92 high school teachers she surveyed reported using English as an instructional medium. This finding may actually be quite high, as Taguchi's results come from a postal survey where more than two-thirds of teachers failed to respond. Further evidence of instructors' reluctance to speak the language they teach comes from a recent MEXT survey which reported only 3.9 per cent of language teachers from junior highs and a mere 1.1 per cent from senior high schools conducted their classes mostly in English (*Sensei ga chikara busokuja...* cited in Miyazato, 2009, p. 41).

Isa, the protagonist in Nobuo Kojima's post-war short story *The American School*, is a fictional JTE emblematic of many high school instructors content to hide amongst intricate explanations of non-generative grammatical points but unable or unwilling to use English as a practical tool for communication in their classrooms:

> he had never had a single conversation in English; occasional attempts at practical application of the language in the classroom

had left him tingling with embarrassment; and when word came that the Americans would soon be visiting his school he had feigned illness... Listening to these mellifluous English voices, he could not account for the fear and horror which the language had always inspired in him. (Kojima cited in Kowner, 2003, pp. 129–30)

Although the example of Isa may appear extreme, his behaviour does allude to the significant role that face protection (see Brown & Levinson, 1987; Goffman, 2006) plays within Japanese society as a whole and within the public sphere of educational settings in particular. A teacher may indeed be orally active in the classroom but if this speech is only in the L1 with English being avoided, we may consider him/her to be metaphorically silent (see Jaworski, 1993; Knapp, 2000; Kurzon, 1998) – this being the face-saving silence of absence or evasion. As Mulligan (2005, p. 35) rightly points out, by remaining in their mother tongue and conforming to the status quo, language teachers may avoid the castigation (from both colleagues and students) reserved for those supposedly arrogant enough to dare to use English in their classrooms. Because of their cultural knowledge, JTEs have much to offer their students (see Miyazato, 2009), but with so many teachers unwilling to use English, is it any wonder that Japanese learners remain disinclined to do so also?

4.6 The Japanese Exchange and Teaching Programme

The missed opportunities of the JET Programme

The Japan Exchange and Teaching (JET) Programme was set up in 1987 as a means of fostering international exchange at a grassroots-level in Japan, while at the same time boosting foreign language education within the nation's pre-tertiary school system. Administered by The Council of Local Authorities for International Relations (CLAIR) with the support of three government ministries (Education, Home Affairs and Foreign Affairs) and various local government organisations, each year the JET Programme sends large numbers of young non-Japanese graduates into schools around the country to act as Assistant Language Teachers (ALTs). In 2010 there were nearly four thousand ALTs working in prefectures throughout Japan, with the majority of participants (over two thousand) coming from the United States (CLAIR, 2010). Very few ALTs possess any formal qualifications in language teaching (McConnell, 2000) and most only receive a few days' cursory training upon arrival in Japan. Their unqualified, non-permanent, outsider status is not lost on the JTEs with whom the ALTs are expected to share team-teaching duties in lessons focused specifically on developing students' L2 communicative abilities. Stories abound of JET Programme participants being ignored and left to their own devices for large parts of the school day by teaching staff resentful of the extra work that hosting these inexperienced and sometimes culturally insensitive interlopers entails.

Miyazato (2009) points out that the team-teaching aspect of the programme has been dogged by controversy because of problems in team teachers' relationships. JTEs have found it difficult to give up sole authority in their classrooms, particularly as ALTs lack any credible professional status. Although one of the aims of the programme is to expose JTEs to communicative language teaching (CLT) methods and authentic English through interaction with a native speaker (Gorsuch, 2002; Wada & Cominos, 1994; Samimy & Kobayashi, 2004), McConnell (1996, p. 452) notes that many JTEs minimise opportunities for such spontaneous interaction within their classrooms either by using ALTs as 'human tape recorders' whose job it is merely to read out sections of the approved English textbook, or by conceptually and logistically dividing up lessons into ALT-led conversation activities and JTE-led exam-related study. Inevitably, in a system geared exclusively towards achieving success in entrance examinations, classroom activities aimed at improving learners' communicative abilities are deemed by JTEs to be irrelevant and a waste of valuable class time. The discord in team teachers' methodological approaches and L2 teaching objectives is well summed up by the experience of one ALT (quoted in McVeigh, 2002, p. 157) who recounts:

> I was told by my team teacher that I wasn't needed on a certain day because he was going to 'teach, teach, teach,' meaning that my time in class did not equate to teaching but something less — more like fun and not considered serious and academic. The Japanese teachers would say they have to teach English so the students can pass exams but my role is to basically entertain them and try to get them interested in English.

Despite widespread confusion and the incongruous perceptions of team-teaching roles held by JTEs and ALTs (Mahoney, 2004), it is generally agreed (e.g. McConnell 1996, 2000) that although the JET Programme may have done little to improve Japanese language learners' L2 communicative skills, the presence of non-Japanese ALTs in schools' language classrooms has acted as a motivational stimulus for some students – at least in the short term. We should remember though that the JET Programme, a scheme born during US–Japan trade tensions of the 1980s' economic bubble years, was instigated primarily as an exercise in 'soft diplomacy' with the dual aims of deflecting criticism of Japan's economic protectionism and increasing goodwill and understanding of Japan abroad (Lincicome, 1993; McConnell 1996, 2000; Miyazato, 2009). While it may have been successful in achieving its political goals, one cannot help feeling that, as the largest and best-funded cultural exchange scheme in the world, the JET Programme has proved to be somewhat of a missed opportunity where improving the nation's foreign language skills are concerned.

The emerging threat of outsourcing

A further concern is that the recent changes in Japan's financial climate are having a negative impact not only on the size of the JET Programme, which has declined from a peak of over six thousand participants in 2002 (CLAIR, 2003), but also on the quality of existing language education in Japan's pre-tertiary system. As local Boards of Education attempt to save money, they are increasingly turning away from the JET Programme and are instead recruiting ALTs from private outsourcing companies (Flynn, 2009). The relatively poor terms and conditions offered by these companies, coupled with the transient nature of the work they provide, means teacher turnover is high (Aspinall, 2008; Flynn, 2009), leading to inconsistency in the classroom for students. Furthermore, Sekeres (2010) claims that some outsourcing companies actively discourage their employees from engaging in team-teaching activities with their JTE counterparts, presumably in order to protect their teaching materials and lesson ideas. It is indeed unfortunate that such financially driven developments within Japan's school system will do little to ameliorate the quality of students' language learning experiences.

4.7 Contextual challenges for language learners

Ijime: bullying students into silence

Bullying, termed *ijime* in Japanese, is a serious and widespread problem in Japan's authoritarian and hierarchical education system. Although often hidden from view by administrators, teaching staff or even the students themselves, the extent of the problem within the country's schools is such that Naito and Gielen (2005, p. 169) draw on

Takatoku to point out that between 1985 and 1998, over 1,200 papers and more than 400 books were published on this subject alone. In her examination of Japanese high schools, Yoneyama (1999) suggests that intense social pressure to conform combines with excessive academic pressure to perform well in the cauldron-like atmosphere of Japan's classrooms, making *ijime* a pervasive phenomenon. She asserts that bullying is used primarily by students to police non-conformity and ruthlessly stamp out any instances of individualism or difference. It therefore tends to be a collective endeavour directed towards individuals (see also Maeda, 1999), and while taking many forms, often involves the insidious psychological tactic of silently ignoring victims in order to ensure their social isolation. While bullies may use silence to inflict psychological harm on their targets, students quickly learn to not to be vocal at school in order to avoid also becoming a target. Silence is not just the prerogative of students alone though. Surrounding the whole issue of *ijime* is what Yoneyama (1999, p. 179) calls a 'pact of silence' acting to serve the vested interests of teachers, schools and MEXT, who all hope to benefit from the downplay of bullying incidents.

It is therefore of little wonder that so many learners have an overriding dread of making mistakes and are simply not prepared to take the risk of standing out by speaking up in the target language in their L2 classes. Certainly it appears to take very little for a student to become conspicuous in the conformity-ridden atmosphere of Japan's schools. As the writer Sakamaki (cited in Kerr, 2001, pp. 291–2) explains:

> An odd nuance of speech or appearance is enough to invite ostracism, and in a society where conformity is everything, no stigma weighs heavier than the curse of being different. Too fat or too short, too smart or too slow – all make inviting targets. Many Japanese children who have lived abroad deliberately perform poorly in, say, English classes so as not to stand out.

Indeed, Kanno (2003) confirms that even though the wider society is gradually beginning to view returnee students (known as *kikokushijo* in Japanese) as a valuable resource due to their English proficiency, at the classroom level there has been a disproportionate amount of bullying directed towards these learners. The same also appears to be true for students of mixed Japanese-foreign ethnicity whose physical traits and linguistic abilities can also set them apart from their peers (see

Daulton, 2002; Daulton & Seki, 2000; Kamada, 2010). Currently marginalised and positioned as *hāfu* (from the English word 'half') or as *gaijin* (the pejorative term for foreigner) within schools, such students – in common with their returnee counterparts – will only gain the confidence to openly display their L2 skills once a more supportive and facilitative learning atmosphere, that tolerates difference, is established within Japan's classrooms. Perhaps once this is achieved these students can emerge from their silence and begin to act as models rather than as targets for their peers.

Nationalism and English language learning

As attitudes towards *kikokushijo* and *hāfu* are intrinsically linked to predominant false notions of a monolithic, homogenous national identity, an apposite moment presents itself to consider the debate surrounding Japanese nationalism and the learning of English. Central to this debate is the view that, as Yamada (1997, p. 140) explains, 'You are Japanese because you speak Japanese, and if you speak Japanese, you do not – indeed you cannot speak a foreign language fluently'. It follows that achieving fluency in English is therefore seen to present a threat not only to one's own personal identity, but could also cumulatively threaten the identity of the nation as a whole. Befu (cited in Seargeant, 2008, p. 133) goes as far as to suggest, 'It is as if the ineptitude of foreign language instruction and learning is maintained (though, needless to say, unconsciously) for the very purpose of convincing millions of Japanese of their separateness.' Failure to be able to communicate in a foreign language hence becomes something of a matter of pride as it is proof positive one is truly Japanese.

Although it is difficult to assess how widely held such views are, the issue of foreign language education has been used by a number of academics to warn against the dangers of English linguistic imperialism and its potentially detrimental effects on both the national language (*kokugo*) and the behaviour of Japan's youth. Aspinall (2003) provides an enlightening overview of the nationalist position on English language education in his examination of the work of two influential scholars: the social linguist Takao Suzuki and Yukio Tsuda, a professor of international communication. Both believe Japan is suffering from a kind of illness in the form of 'English worship' (*eigo shinkō*) which 'goes hand in hand with an inferiority complex towards one's own language and culture' (Aspinall, 2003, p. 109). Drawing in part on Tsuda's (2000) revealingly titled book *'A Recommendation for Bad English'*, Aspinall (pp. 109–10) outlines a range of proposals for foreign language education reform from the nationalist utilitarian perspective, based on Suzuki and Tsuda's ideas. These suggestions include:

- Changing the primary aim of foreign language education from its current emphasis on learning *from* non-Japanese. Instead, learners should study foreign languages in order to express their ideas *to* non-Japanese.
- Due to an over-reliance on English as a source of information about the world, other languages should be given much more emphasis in the foreign language curriculum.
- In English language classes, learning about the history and culture of other countries should be replaced by an emphasis on talking about the history and culture of Japan.
- English should become an optional subject. Only those learners who choose to should have to study the language.
- The massive job losses that these reforms would bring about would supposedly be offset by retraining JTEs to become Japanese language teachers. University students should be encouraged to study their L1 instead of English.

Even though one needs to approach the nationalist agenda with caution, particularly as many of the premises underlying it are based on the spurious logic of *nihonjinron* theory (see Chapter 3), the suggestion that Japan's L2 education system should give prominence to other languages in addition to English and the idea that English language study should not have to form a compulsory component of all learners' tertiary education do both appear to be eminently reasonable proposals. Certainly, the former proposition is well supported by Kubota and McKay (2009) whose critical ethnography of a small Japanese town's changing linguistic ecology suggests that, in reality on the ground, English has little relevance in local communities which are more likely to see their foreign residents made up of non-English-speaking immigrants from countries such as Brazil, China and Korea. (This also begs the question: how useful is English to the thousands of undergraduates who are forced to study the language for an extra two years at university?) It is difficult to object to resistance against the spread of the English language when it emphasises the growing multilingualism and cosmopolitan pluralism to be found in Japan today. The danger is, of course, that historically such resistance has primarily taken the form of a nationalist discourse that emphasises an essentialist version of Japanese identity.

4.8 Conclusion

In this chapter I have explored the aims and character of Japan's language education system in order to better understand why such a large proportion of the country's learners do not possess the requisite linguistic proficiency to communicate in the second language they have spent so many years studying. Not only have these learners been socialised into classroom participation structures which severely inhibit active oral participation, they have not been well served by a language education system which is preoccupied with achieving good test results at the expense students' communicative abilities. The following points summarise the main arguments to emerge in this chapter's critical examination of the country's ineffective approach to the study of foreign languages:

- Encouraged by private enterprise in the education sector, there is a strong trend towards ever-younger language education in Japan. This trend ignores compelling arguments surrounding the current critical period debate surrounding a piecemeal approach to language learning for children may in fact prove detrimental to their L2 development in later years.
- MEXT's recent attempts to reform foreign language teaching in Japan's schools by introducing compulsory English lessons for all elementary students and by recommending a more communicative approach in junior and senior high schools are an acknowledgement that there appears to be dissatisfaction within the current system. However, it is apparent that a rather large gap exists between the ministry's vision for language education and what actually happens in Japan's classrooms.
- Part of this classroom reality is that entrance examinations still play an incredibly influential role in shaping the language education students receive. As a consequence, a focus on English as an academic subject (*juken eigo*) rather than as a practical tool for real life means that teachers are unwilling to invest valuable class time developing students' oral competencies.
- Grammar-translation (*yakudoku*) remains a deeply entrenched pedagogical approach in Japan's schools. This method of language learning severely restricts learners' opportunities to vocalise in the target language and tends to emphasise the importance of the recoded Japanese version of a text, rather than the L2 original.
- Many Japanese teachers of English are either unable or disinclined to speak in the target language whilst teaching. Teachers' attitudes

towards English and their beliefs about learning play central roles in their reluctance to converse in the L2, as does the desire to avoid loss of face by making a mistake in the public setting of the classroom.
- The JET Programme has enabled thousands of unqualified native speakers to teach in Japan's schools. While the scheme may have been successful as an instrument in 'soft diplomacy', it seems to have done little to improve the nation's L2 communicative proficiency. Difficulties in team teaching relationships between JTEs and ALTs have meant JET participants have not always been used to best effect.
- The pervasiveness of bullying (*ijime*) within the education system has created an unconstructive school environment where students are loath to stand out by vocalising in the L2 during lessons. While bullies may use silence to psychologically isolate their victims, it seems the sensitive issue of *ijime* in Japanese schools is surrounded by silence as stakeholders attempt to downplay the phenomenon.
- Nationalistic arguments which posit that one's Japanese identity may be threatened if one becomes proficient in a foreign language are unhelpful in the quest to achieve L2 fluency for the country's language learners. Even though nationalist scholars may base their objections to English language education on ethnocentric beliefs, there is some validity in the contention that English has little relevance in the daily lives of most Japanese people.

5
A structured observation study into L2 classroom silence

5.1 Introduction

Although a small number of works (e.g. Li, 2001; Reda, 2009) do assign silence in certain general education contexts a quite positive valuation, student silence in the classroom is more widely perceived to be a serious problem for many educators. As I outlined in Chapter 1, this is particularly so in second language learning contexts, as a large body of literature has illustrated how oral interaction and production of the target language can significantly aid L2 development (e.g. de Bot, 1996; Ellis, 1999; Gass, 1997; Iwashita, 2003; Izumi 2003; Long, 1996; Mackey, 2002; Mackey, Gass & McDonough, 2000; Swain, 2005). Yet the curious fact is that very little research has targeted the issue of silence, particularly within the Japanese university language class setting. The problem I faced prior to embarking on this project was that although there seemed to be tacit agreement amongst many inside (and outside) Japan's L2 teaching community that learners' levels of oral production were perhaps not what they should be, reliable empirical evidence proving the existence of classroom silence strangely did not exist. I therefore set about considering how best I could investigate this intangible phenomenon on a large enough scale and decided that some sort of observational approach would be necessary. While it is true that ethnographic approaches (e.g. Agyekum, 2002; Basso, 1990; Philips, 1976) relying on unstructured observation to investigate silence within specific speech communities have been particularly fruitful in producing a rich seam of data, this research paradigm is not ideally suited to investigating general trends of silence. A quantitative study using a systematic observational method presented itself as a much more productive option and there was the added benefit that silence-orientated structured observation studies appear to be notably lacking from the literature.

The research presented in this chapter therefore helps to fill this gap by applying a systematic, structured observation methodology in a large-scale, multi-site investigation focusing on the silent behaviour of over 900 Japanese university language learners. An original classroom observation instrument, the Classroom Oral Participation Scheme (COPS), employing a real-time coding approach, was developed specifically for the study. The evidence produced by the COPS, in the form of empirical, statistically based data, suggests there is a strong, national trend towards silence in Japan's second language classrooms. Characterised by reluctance, inability or lack of opportunity to speak, the silence uncovered over the course of the study's 48 hours of structured observation is interpreted from a dynamic systems perspective. Although not suited to measuring the extent to which relevant variables are interconnected or how their influence may shift over time (both key characteristics of a dynamic system), structured observation does provide an ideal methodology for identifying seemingly fossilised attractor states in the form of core trends related to learners' classroom behaviour.

An overview of dynamic systems theory (DST)

Originating from a branch of mathematics and well-established in the natural and social sciences (de Bot, Lowie & Verspoor, 2007), dynamic systems theory has only relatively recently come to the fore as an exciting theoretical framework within the field of applied linguistics. Led by Larsen-Freeman (1997) with her seminal work on chaos theory and SLA, an increasing number of researchers (e.g. de Bot, Lowie & Verspoor, 2005; Dörnyei 2009; Ellis 2007; Larsen-Freeman & Cameron, 2008; van Geert, 2008) have begun to look to DST and the closely related strand of complexity theory as a move away from traditional linear, cause–effect explanations of language production and language learner behaviour. A DST framework reflects the complexity of real life in that it recognises that human behaviour is continuously influenced by multiple, interrelated variables which are constantly changing over time.

One important feature of dynamic systems particularly relevant to the present study is that, as systems develop, a period of relative stability may be achieved due to the influence of *attractors* and their ensuing *attractor states*. Dörnyei points out that attractor states are like powerful magnets which may be internal (e.g. connected to the learner's cognition) or external (e.g. related to the sociocultural environment) and that they act 'as "safe islands" towards which the system gravitates in its inherent search for equilibrium' (2010, p. 3). Another good analogy common to the literature is that of a ball rolling over a surface covered in holes of various sizes, some of which are gathered together in basins. As the ball (representing, say, a learner's discourse) rolls along, it is pulled towards a hole (signifying an attractor). An attractor state is apparent when the ball becomes firmly ensconced within a hole. Attractors of certain behaviours – including the behaviour of remaining silent in a language classroom – may vary in their individual strength, but once a system (in our case, a classroom discourse system consisting of learner's classroom talk sub-systems) has organised itself into a settled attractor state, force is needed to push the system out of its equilibrium (Larsen-Freeman & Cameron, 2008). Therefore, the stronger and more numerous the attractors drawing a learner's discourse activity towards the state of saying nothing, the more energy is needed to push the system into a state of flux whereby the learner talks. Attractor states may initially be apparent at the level of the individual but have the potential to operate at group, institutional or societal levels depending on the strength of the behaviour trend.

The research presented in this chapter offers an empirical examination of the extent of this phenomenon, and reflects on the value of adopting a DST perspective to interpret its results. It should be noted though that the data presented here are primarily cross-sectional in nature and therefore do not allow one to go beyond what is essentially recognition of similarities and resonances with DST. To fully illustrate the evolution of silence, research using in-depth qualitative interviews and retrospection is needed and this is provided in subsequent chapters.

5.2 Method

Participants

Japan's tertiary education sector is made up of three basic types of university: national (run by the state), municipal (run by local authorities) and private. As of 2009, when this study began, a total of 773 universities were operating in Japan of which 86 were national, 92 were municipal and a massive 595 (77.0 per cent) were private (MEXT, 2010, p. 85). To reflect this variety of tertiary institutions the project employed a dimensional sampling strategy which resulted in a multi-site study comprising nine universities. Data were collected from one municipal, two national and six private universities located in rural, urban and metropolitan sites across Japan's main island of Honshu. Although any assessment of the quality of a university is subjective up to a certain point (for more on the ranking of Japanese universities see Doyon, 2001, p. 445; McVeigh, 2002, pp. 29–33), the establishments included in this study ranged in standard from what could best be described as provincial and average, through to some of the most prestigious institutions in the country.

When selecting classes for observation, the primary aim was to obtain a sample that was as large and diverse as possible. Such a heterogeneous class sample provided the potential to identify core trends and behaviours more relevant generally to Japan's varied tertiary education system. Access was therefore gained to 30 different classes with an overall student population of more than 900. These classes focused primarily on improving students' practical English language abilities and included activities practising all four skills, in addition to instruction on such things as communication theory, translation techniques, and so on. Twenty of the classes were for first years; seven were for second years; one was a third-year class; one contained postgraduates; while another was made up of a combination of students from years one to four. Thirteen of the classes were for English-related majors; students from other faculties, such as law, economics and engineering, made up a further 16 classes (English tends to be a compulsory subject at university regardless of one's field); and one group included a mixture of both English and non-English majors. Class sizes ranged from just nine students to 103 (the latter being a huge communicative English class which the instructor handled with aplomb), with a mean attendance of 28.73 per group. The student sample (N 924) achieved a reasonable gender distribution – 52.92 per cent were male and 47.08 per cent female. In order to avoid the assumption that any silence encountered during the study would purely be down to a deficiency in students' L2 abilities, the sampling strategy ensured learners of varying proficiencies were observed. At a minimum, the cohort had received the compulsory six years of English language education that is a requirement for all Japanese entering junior high school at age 11. In the end, the student sample provided an excellent mix of levels, and this was well illustrated by participants, who were clearly from both ends of the L2 aptitude spectrum. Although some learners were at a level where, despite their years of compulsory L2 schooling, they could barely comprehend and respond to the most basic of English language greetings, yet others were of near native-like proficiency following a number of years living in English-speaking countries during childhood.

The COPS instrument

To obtain reliable quantitative data on the extent of student silence in classes, the study employed a systematic observation approach using a low-inference scheme. Inspired by the design of Spada and Fröhlich's (1995) COLT and the content categories of Moskowitz's (1971) FLint, the present study stayed true to observation researchers' penchant for acronyms to produce the Classroom Oral Participation Scheme (COPS). This structured observation scheme (see Appendix 1) was developed specifically so that a minute-by-minute picture of classroom events could be recorded in real time, with emphasis on the scrutiny of oral participation throughout the lesson. The COPS consists of two sections, both of which are divided into 60 one-minute segments – this hour-long timeframe was found to be ideal for ensuring a standardised length of observation throughout the study, thus mitigating late lesson starts and early finishes. Two things ensured the validity of the instrument. Firstly, it was designed to be a highly structured scheme of the low-inference type requiring the observer to tally rather than infer classroom events. In this, the COPS fully follows Part A of the COLT's reliable method of real-time coding. The second point is that the author paid special attention to piloting (see below) so that use of the scheme became an almost automatic, routine undertaking. As such, the instrument offered an almost foolproof method of recording classroom events.

The first section of the COPS concentrates on the overall participant organisation of oral interaction within the class. Using an *exclusive focus* coding approach (see Spada & Fröhlich 1995, pp. 31–2) in nine categories, this part of the scheme measures who is speaking within the classroom and how the interaction is organised. Hence, by obtaining data on who is talking and how this talk is arranged, we can conversely learn much about those who remain silent during the course of a lesson. The first section's categories are as follows:

Teacher (initiated): Talk, in the form of asking questions, presenting information, providing feedback, giving task instructions, and so on, which is initiated by the teacher and to which the majority of students are exposed.

Teacher (response): Talk in which the teacher responds to questions or solicits posed by students.

Student (initiated): A student produces an unsolicited turn at talk to which the majority of class members are exposed. The learner initiates oral interaction through an unexpected question or statement.

Student (response): Talk in which a student responds to a question or prompt by the teacher. The interaction may be either a self-selected turn or a response to being individually nominated. Talk in this category includes students giving presentations after having previously been invited to do so by the teacher.

Students in a pair/group (single): Talk involving a single pair or single group of students, usually modelling an exchange, to which the rest of the class is exposed.

Students in a pair/group (multiple): The whole class is organised into pairs or groups in order to perform speaking tasks such as discussion, role play, and so on.

Choral: Talk in the form of a choral speaking drill during which the class repeats after the teacher or in response to another source, such as a tape recorder.

Off-task melee: The majority of the class are no longer on-task, but are instead involved in raucous L1 chatting with peers, often involving much laughter.

Silence: No oral interaction on the part of participants. Included in this category may be the periods when audio/audio-visual equipment (recorded as 'A' or 'AV' instead of a tick on the observation schedule) is playing. Each extended silence is briefly further described in the *Task outline/Notes* section in the borderless right-hand column of the instrument.

The second section of the COPS aims to provide a more in-depth analysis by focusing on the modality of three individual students within each class. As with the first, this section follows a one-minute time sampling format, thereby allowing a chronological representation of each student's modality to be constructed over the course of a class period. As the present study is primarily concerned with the extent of oral participation by students in foreign language classes, coding within this section is weighted towards how talk performed by the students is organised. Thus, *talk* is coded into four categories reflecting those found in the first section of the scheme. These four categories code whether the individual student's talk is a response or an initiated interaction that the rest of the class are exposed to; whether the interaction takes place within a pair/group; or whether the talk is part of a choral exercise. Helping to uncover where oral input is coming from, the COPS then divides *listening* into three categories: listening to the teacher; listening to a student or students; and listening to audio equipment. The next skill of *reading* comprises of two modes: reading aloud and silent reading. The final two categories are *writing* and *off-task*. The latter category covers such popular student activities as sleeping, playing with a mobile phone, and so on.

Obviously a student may perform a combination of skills at any one time or successively within the minute-long observation segment. Where this occurs, the COPS employs a primary focus coding convention (Spada & Fröhlich, 1995) whereby the skill deemed to be the most significant and which takes up the majority of the segment is the one noted on the observation scheme. As with any structured observation scheme, there is always the danger that a restricted set of predetermined categories may not accurately reflect the rich variety of events which can occur within classrooms. Even so, constructing a list of all the potential behaviours undertaken by participants would indeed be a somewhat Sisyphean task (see Adams cited in Richards 2003, pp. 146–7 for an apt illustration). The COPS avoids the unworkable confusion of endless coding categories by limiting its focus to low-inference classroom activities and participant behaviours which are related to the research question and which have been identified during a process of careful piloting. A final feature of the scheme which further offsets the potential drawbacks of restricted coding categories is the inclusion of space for the observer to make brief notes in parallel to the in-time sampling data. Although of necessity these notes have to be extremely concise, it was found over the course of the study that they were invaluable in providing extra contextual detail to events recorded on the scheme.

Procedures

The instrument and research procedures were thoroughly piloted prior to the main study. A series of full-length pilot sessions resulted in modifications to the COPS which refined its coding categories and thus enhanced the instrument's validity and general ease of use. Initially the scheme attempted to code the individual modality of five students. However, this proved unmanageable for a single observer and so, following further testing, it was found that the optimum number of individual learners who could be reliably monitored was three. This phase of the project proved essential in confirming that a methodology using structured observation was indeed appropriate to both the study's context and research aims. In addition, piloting the instrument provided the researcher with valuable practice at achieving speed and consistency at data entry.

The main study consisted of two phases of data collection culminating in a total of 48 classroom observations, all of which were carried out by the author. The initial phase of research took place over two months during the second semester of the 2009/2010 Japanese academic year. This timeframe, during November and December, was chosen specifically to avoid examination periods and the beginning of the academic year – a time when the inhibiting, silence-inducing effects of attending an unfamiliar, new class may be at their height. During this initial collection phase, multiple observations of the same class were employed in order to enhance the reliability of findings. Nine classes were therefore observed on three separate occasions, producing 27 hours of data. While such an approach allowed for each class to be studied with relative depth, the second, follow-up phase of observations provided an element of breadth to the study. During this secondary stage, which was initiated in an attempt to discover whether the surprising findings of the first phase would be replicated more broadly within Japan's varied tertiary system, single observations of a further 21 classes took place in the latter half of the 2010/2011 academic year's first semester.

As Allwright and Bailey (1991) rightly note, anxiety caused by the presence of an outside observer in a classroom may have a profound effect on both teachers' and learners' performances. The study therefore employed a number of measures to combat reactivity amongst participants during the data gathering process. Where timetabling demands allowed, pre-observation meetings were set up with participant teachers in order to establish rapport, explain the research procedures, and reiterate the confidential nature of the study. The creation of these pre-observation dialogues, whether in person or by electronic means, stressing the non-threatening and non-judgmental nature of the study and the need to avoid 'show lessons', was crucial in helping mitigate the tendency amongst many teachers to view classroom observation purely as a menacing tool for supervision and performance appraisal (King, 2005). Other strategies for reducing reactivity concerned the students themselves. During the piloting stage it was found that by not introducing myself, I aroused increased levels of curiosity amongst students that initially distracted them from the lesson content and therefore led to out-of-the-ordinary behaviour. Consequently, at the beginning of each new observation within the main study, I very briefly introduced myself to the class, light-heartedly reassured the students I was not a spy sent by the administration (for a discussion of the delicate balance between spying and collecting research data, see Mitchell, 1993) and emphasised my presence was indeed benign. Their curiosity satisfied, students invariably complied with the request to continue with their lesson as if the observer were 'invisible', and were aided in this task by further reducing my presence by taking up a non-intrusive seating position from which to observe proceedings. In an additional attempt to 'blend into the woodwork' (Murphy, 1992, p. 224) and thus augment the study's data validity, throughout the observation period, no interactions were initiated with participants. On the handful of occasions that questions or statements from either learners or teachers were directed towards me, I kept my responses to a polite but absolute minimum.

As part of the study's attempt to build up a picture of how student modality impacts upon oral participation, at the beginning of observations three individual students were chosen from each class group for closer scrutiny so that minute-by-minute accounts of their actions could be recorded over the class period. A partially stratified sampling strategy, based on sex, seating position and whether there was a clear line of vision for the researcher was employed when selecting these students, who remained unaware they were being observed, in order to preserve natural behaviour. During the initial data collection phase involving multiple observations of single classes, the same three students were monitored for each of the three one-hour observation periods. It is perhaps a testament to the great emphasis placed on attendance as the primary means of passing university courses in Japan (see Clayton, 1993; McVeigh, 2002, pp. 130–2), that only two from a cohort of 27 individually observed students had a whole-class absence during this first data gathering phase. In all, the modality of 90 individual students was coded over the course of the entire study.

All coding on the COPS was performed in real time during the study's 48 one-hour observation periods. Using interval recording, whereby the researcher placed ticks in appropriate categories to record what had happened during the preceding minute, a chronological representation of classroom events, from both a whole-class and individual perspective, was systematically generated. As I was ever careful to maintain a non-intrusive, passive role within the classrooms I visited, I opted to audio record lessons for later analysis rather than videotape them because of the potential for video cameras to be highly distracting for participants and their tendency to encourage atypical behaviour (see Dörnyei, 2007, pp. 184–5; Zuengler, Ford & Fassnacht, 1998).

5.3 Results

The tally marks in each variable column on the COPS sheets were added together so as to provide the total number of minutes that a particular behaviour or activity had occurred during each observed lesson. From these totals it was then possible to calculate the mean average time each observed data variable occurred over the course of the study, with the unit of analysis being one lesson. Table 1 illustrates tally mark totals (i.e. minutes) and average percentages of observation time coded for the COPS's first section of nine categories focusing on oral participation at a whole-class level. From these results we can see that the instructors in the sample clearly dominated classroom talk, with approaching half of all lesson time having been taken up by teacher-initiated discourse. Interestingly, the medium of instruction appears to have had little effect on the incidence of student-initiated talk. Whether the instructor spoke in English, in Japanese or in a mixture of both languages seems to have made little difference here. Of course, it is hardly surprising that teachers should dominate classroom discourse when we consider their institutional role and the silence-inducing power imbalances which exist between staff and students (see Gilmore, 1985; Jaworski & Sachdev, 1998), but the contrast with the incredibly low incidence of student-initiated talk is startling. With less than a quarter of 1 per cent of lesson time in the study consisting of students producing self-selected turns at talk in front of their peers, a picture emerges of Japanese university language learners who are profoundly silent and orally passive whilst lessons are in progress.

Of the seven coded incidences of student-initiated talk over 48 hours of observation, three were produced by learners already highly proficient at English – one came from a so-called *kikokushijo* (returnee) (see Kanno, 2003) who had received his secondary education in the United States' school system, while postgraduate students at one of the country's top national universities attending an intimate seminar-style English class which included two non-Japanese East Asian learners provided a further two instances. Though limited, these examples suggest that enhanced opportunities for intercultural communication encounters may encourage learners to initiate discourse in the target language (see Yashima, 2002, 2010).

The results concerning individual student modality serve to back up the COPS's findings on oral participation from a whole-class perspective. Table 2 shows a remarkably low mean average incidence of student-initiated talk amongst the 90 students who were individually monitored

Table 1 Whole-class oral participation results

	T initiated	T response	S initiated	S response	Ss pair/group single	Ss pair/group multiple	Choral	Off-task melee	Silence	Total
Phase 1: Obs 1–27	759	4	4	88	34	188	49	24	470	1620
Phase 2: Obs 28–48	538	2	3	62	27	278	48	48	254	1260
Totals (mins)	1297	6	7	150	61	466	97	72	724	2880
Mean per class	45.03%	.21%	.24%	5.21%	2.12%	16.18%	3.37%	2.50%	25.14%	100.00%

T – teacher; S – student; Ss – students; Obs – observations

Table 2 Individual student modality results

	Talk response	Talk initiate	Talk pair/group	Talk choral	Reading aloud	Reading silent	Writing	Listening to T	Listening to S/Ss	Listening to audio	Off-task	Total
Phase 1: Obs 1–27	30	2	263	75	47	307	486	1676	305	362	1158	4711
Phase 2: Obs 28–48	10	1	325	37	28	275	278	1494	407	351	574	3780
Totals (mins)	40	3	588	112	75	582	764	3170	712	713	1732	8491
Mean per class	.47%	.04%	6.92%	1.32%	.88%	6.85%	9.00%	37.33%	8.39%	8.40%	20.40%	100.00%

on a minute-by-minute basis throughout observation periods. While spending less than one twentieth of a single per cent of their time initiating discourse, these students actually spent the vast majority of the class time (37.33 per cent) listening to the teacher talk. In an incident which aptly illustrates the rarity of student-initiated discourse within the Japanese tertiary context, at the conclusion of one observed class for language majors preparing for study abroad, the teacher, unprompted by the researcher, expressed great surprise that a student had asked her the simple unsolicited question, 'What is the date today?' in English.

Table 1 further reveals that oral participation in the form of a single pair or single group of students talking, usually modelling exchanges to peers, made up just over 2 per cent of class time. As with the student-initiated talk and student response talk categories, it is important to note that even though these interactions do involve students speaking, while they are in progress the vast majority of class members remain resoundingly silent. Nevertheless, we can see that in comparison, oral participation by multiple pairs/groups is a relatively more common phenomenon in Japanese university language classrooms. This was particularly so during the second phase of data collection which involved an increased number of observations of classes for foreign language majors where a more communicative approach held sway (the ratio of non-language to language majors in the first phase of observations was 2:1; whereas in the follow up phase there was an equal ratio, with one additional mixed group). The relatively unstructured nature of such multiple pair and group work appears to make off-task melees more likely, and this seems to be borne out by the increase in such incidents during the second phase of the study. If we consider silence from a pragmatic rather than an acoustic perspective (Jaworski, 1993), even though such melees may be periods of intense noise, the concomitant lack of relevant target language talk on the part of students means they are also periods of learner L2 silence.

Even though the observed use of oral practice in multiple pairs/groups reflects a movement away from conservative teacher-centred methods of instruction that has been steadily growing in Japan since the 1970s (Poole, 2005), the amount of class time spent on these communication-orientated activities was far exceeded by the number of coded episodes in which no oral participation took place whatsoever. Table 1 shows that over a quarter of class time in the study was characterised by silent behaviour by *all* participants, both staff and students alike. Furthermore, as revealed in Table 2, for more than half of their class time, student participants were engaged in the task of listening – either to the teacher, to other students or to audio equipment. Coupled to the fact that over 20 per cent of students' time was consumed by being off-task and disengaged from the learning process, we can see there only remains a thoroughly condensed opportunity, which appears to be rarely taken, for learners to orally participate in class.

5.4 Discussion

Clearly then, with its microperspective focus on both whole-class and individual activity, the COPS has provided empirical quantitative evidence of a robust nation-wide trend, with minimal variation, towards silence within Japanese university foreign language classrooms. To date, there have been various attempts to explain the silent reticence of East Asian learners based on such factors as: their inherent shyness (Doyon, 2000); difficulties in bidding and turn-taking behaviours (e.g. Sato, 1982); the washback university entrance exams have on speaking skills (see Brown & Yamashita, 1995); resistance to a repressive education system (Yoneyama, 1999); or a general lack of L2 sociolinguistic ability (e.g. Jones, 1999; Korst, 1997). However, when there is such a powerful pattern of silence across such a diverse sample, as is evident in the current study, a single-cause explanation for students' oral reticence is unlikely. Clearly the general state of silence found in Japan's L2 classrooms is built on many pillars. This is, in fact, almost exactly what a dynamic systems theory (DST) perspective would suggest, as the paradigm rejects traditional linear, cause-effect explanations of language production and language learner behaviour.

DST provides a useful theoretical framework from which to interpret the silence found in this study because it acknowledges that human behaviour is constantly shaped by numerous, interconnected variables. We should view silence as a phenomenon emerging through a number of routes, termed 'attractors' in DST, which exert an influence at a variety of different levels, for example at individual, classroom, institutional and societal levels. Indeed, these attractors appear to be so numerous and powerful within Japanese university L2 classrooms that silence has now fossilised there into a semi-permanent and relatively predictable attractor state. In order to illustrate some key agents attracting students' silent behaviour, below are five conceptions of silence which became apparent during the study:

The silence of disengagement. The manifestation of boredom, apathy and inattention, the silence emerging through this route is often found lurking in large, teacher-centred, lecture-style language classrooms. This type of silence was possibly the most prevalent within the study, and was unquestionably dominant within compulsory English language classes for non-language majors. Of the students whose individual modality was observed during the study, perhaps ST20 (M) personifies this type of silence best. During the three hours that his behaviour was coded in a second year English class for non-language majors, ST20 spent 73.89 per cent of the time asleep. Within the class, this was not particularly out-of-the-ordinary behaviour, reflecting an acceptance of sleeping within Japan's wider education system (King & Lind, 2007; Steger, 2006). On the two occasions ST20 did orally participate during the lesson, both instances consisted solely of him uttering *'hai'* (yes) in a rather drowsy response to being nominated by the teacher. Each time, unable or unwilling to answer the teacher's question further, ST20 remained unfalteringly silent until eventually the storm passed and another unfortunate victim was called upon.

The silence of teacher-centred methods. This type of silence is inexorably linked to the silence of disengagement. The decisions that teachers make concerning the pedagogical technique they employ with a class, in addition to their choice of lesson materials and task activities, can have a profound effect on whether classroom discourse systems are pulled towards a pattern of non-participation. It became apparent over the course of observations that a strong trend exists within Japan's university L2 classrooms, particularly where compulsory English classes for non-language majors are concerned, for lessons to be dominated by a rigid Initiation Response Feedback (IRF) pattern (Sinclair & Coulthard, 1975; see also Larsen-Freeman & Cameron 2008, pp. 179–82) which requires only minimal or single-word responses from learners. Indeed, open-class solicits almost inevitably resulted in no learner response at all. Teachers' attitudes and beliefs about language learning play an important role here. As I discussed in Chapter 4, in the Japanese context, *yakudoku* (a grammar-translation approach), remains a deeply entrenched teacher-centred instructional method (see Gorsuch, 1998; Hino, 1988) which silences learners exposed to it by severely limiting their opportunities to vocalise in English.

The silence of non-verbal activities. For extended periods of class time students were on-task and engaged in activities which did not require talk and during which it would have been either difficult or inappropriate to speak. For example, referring to Table 1, of the 25.14 per cent of lesson time in the study when there was no oral participation by any participants, 10.73 per cent was absorbed by students listening to audio equipment (the *Listening audio* figure is slightly lower in Table 2 due to coded off-task behaviour amongst the individually tracked students). Aural activities aside, according to Table 2, around 15 per cent of students' time was spent either writing or silently reading. The silent behaviour of learners here does not necessarily present a threat to their general L2 development but it does illustrate the narrowing of an already limited opportunity to speak in the target language in class. This silence reflects McCarthy's (2000, p. 91) notion, based on data from the CANCODE corpus, that there exists an intimate relationship between language and action which means that tolerance of silence during a period of activity becomes longer than would be acceptable during casual conversation.

The silence of confusion. The very first observation of the main study provided a good example of a scenario during which silence through confusion emerged. During the lesson it was observed that most learners within the group, upon encountering even the most basic L2 input, required time in order to decode utterances and then to formulate an appropriate response. The COPS does not record such hesitations unless they develop to become the most significant phenomenon within the coding interval. Even so, this silence as cognitive processing time (see Chafe, 1985; Nakane, 2007, pp. 91–2) may, of course, eventually extend into the silence of confusion. Lack of L2 ability, unfamiliarity with topics/tasks, problems with the delivery of the teacher's talk, and so on may all lead to the failure of learners to orally respond because of confusion. During this first observation an instance of this type occurred at a whole-class level – there was prolonged silence after students failed to begin a speaking activity following some rather convoluted task instructions by the teacher. It should be noted though that not all confusion within the language classroom is genuine. McVeigh (2002) points out that some university students in Japan may feign confusion and 'play dumb' as a strategy for passively resisting an education system in which they feel virtually powerless.

The silence of salient cliques. A familiarity with the principles of group dynamics (see Dörnyei & Murphey, 2003) can give the silence researcher a head start in understanding the potential sources of many classroom silences. Certainly, few things will inhibit and silence students more than the presence of one or two dominant cliques within a classroom. This phenomenon was apparent within one class in particular during the first phase of the study. Consisting solely of all-male sports science majors, this large, second year class was made up of members of the university's various sports teams. The centre of the sportsmen's classroom was the domain of the baseball squad, to their right sat the football team, and towards the back were the university's budding tennis stars (for an account of the important role sports clubs play within the Japanese education system see Cave, 2004). Members of these groups tended to arrive together, *always* voluntarily sat together, and would drift away together at the conclusion of each lesson. Clearly then, this class could be characterised as having cliques, who appear to have played a part in influencing oral interaction patterns within the classroom. Interestingly, in addition to absolutely no recorded instances of student-initiated talk, little or no inter-group oral interaction was observed over three hours of coded behaviour within lessons. To better understand why this was, an awareness of the Japanese concept of *uchi/soto*, which was touched upon in Chapter 3, may be useful. *Uchi* (inside) relates to the idea of belonging to a particular group – be it at a family, club, institutional, company or national level, while *soto* (outside) denotes membership of another group. The privacy and familiarity of an *uchi* context means that people tend to be much more expressive and vocal when within in-group settings. *Soto* contexts, or out-group situations, conversely result in more circumspect vocal behaviour and therefore in less vocal interaction (Gudykunst & Nishida, 1993; Lebra, 1976, 1993; McDaniel, 2003). As classrooms are deemed to be public settings in Japan, interactions within them tend to be performed in the *soto* mode (Nakane, 2007). The silence which emerges in classrooms containing dominant cliques is of course intimately linked, in true dynamic fashion, to learner-internal issues of inhibition, embarrassment and the desire for face protection.

Although the above examples are far from an exhaustive taxonomy of forces attracting silent behaviour in language classrooms, they are salient and typical ones and they do serve the task perfectly to show that meaningful discussion of the complexity of classroom events needs to include learner-internal *and* social factors as contributors to the paradigm. This is at the heart of taking a dynamic systems perspective and acknowledges the importance of taking into consideration the 'sociocultural maze' of contextual issues (Dörnyei & Ushioda, 2011), particularly as a starting point in the DST approach. As the attractor state of silence is educationally and culturally supported in the Japanese context, learners' classroom talk systems appear to be easily drawn towards it. To not orally participate in one's foreign language class is deemed, by both students and teachers alike, to be normal behaviour. Silence therefore exists as a relatively stable state within individual, classroom, institutional and national-level systems after having emerged from a wide range of starting points. Even though this observation study has uncovered a strong trend towards silence in which its incredibly strong attractors have made student reticence a semi-permanent attractor state, we should still not consider the roots of learners' silent behaviour to be static or linear. In other words, within a single lesson there may be multiple, interrelated causes for a student's silence influenced by both dynamically changing external factors and internal learner attributes. De Bot, Lowie and Verspoor (2007) have termed this *complete interconnectedness*. For example, in the case of ST20, the somnolent student described previously, his silence may be related to any number of dynamically changing, interconnected aspects, such as psychological inhibition, lack of L2 ability, exposure to a teaching method restrictive of student talk, growing up in a culture whose discourse norms encourage reticence, dislike of his instructor, or even the ill-effects of a bad bout of insomnia. Further in-depth qualitative research would be able to effectively trace back the roots of his silent behaviour.

Even so, no matter how fossilised or static a system looks, DST says that this stability is never permanent (de Bot, Lowie & Verspoor, 2007; Larsen-Freeman & Cameron, 2008). This suggests there may come a point when some form of impetus will result in the system restructuring itself. Currently, but this goes beyond the scope of this study, the restructuring process is held back by some broader attractors operating at the wider societal level. However, the state of silence is only an attractor state and hence will eventually change and evolve into something else. Indication of the system's new self-organisation is manifested by a new breed of learners emerging partly as a result of increasing opportunities for intercultural communication encounters. An example of such learners could be the *kikokushijo* (returnee) students studying in Japan's universities, whose time abroad restricts their exposure to Japan's sociocultural environment, and who to tend to return to Japan with enhanced language skills. Certainly, this is backed up conceptually by Yashima's (2002) work which has shown that increased international posture may significantly contribute to Japanese learners' willingness to communicate in L2.

In sum, while potential attractors abound, this study provides evidence of a massive, and surprisingly generalisable attractor state of silence as a system outcome in Japanese university language classrooms. This confirms the manifold ample anecdotal evidence about Japanese language learners' reticence and highlights a potentially fruitful future research direction of tracing back the variety of reasons leading to this uniform outcome, thereby identifying the attractor basin.

5.5 Conclusion

This study employed a novel approach to gather empirical, quantitative data on the silence of Japanese university language learners through its use of a specially developed classroom observation instrument called the COPS. Focusing on the macro-level silence of non-participation, rather than on the micro-silences of pauses and hesitations more suited to conversation and discourse analysis, the COPS was employed in a multi-site study across nine Japanese universities involving over 900 learners of varying L2 proficiencies. The study took a number of measures, such as multiple observations of single classes along with various reactivity-reducing strategies, to ensure the reliability and validity of the data collected. Following 48 hours of systematic observation using a minute-by-minute, real-time coding strategy, an extremely robust trend towards silence in classrooms was uncovered. It had been expected that some silence would be discovered in the course of the research but not on the scale that materialised. The data produced by the COPS was indeed surprising, as can be seen in the following overview of the study's findings:

- There was a stunning lack of student-initiated talk in classrooms. Evident from both the whole-class oral participation and the individual student modality coding categories, less than 1 per cent of class time was taken up by talk of this type.
- Conversely, although it is not particularly surprising that teachers dominated talk within classrooms (due to their status and institutional role), the extent of their dominance was striking. Instructors in the sample spent over 45 per cent of the lesson time initiating discourse, whilst concomitantly *listening to the teacher* was the task that students engaged in the most.
- Despite a growing movement towards a communicative teaching methodology in Japan, the amount of time spent on communicative activities was significantly exceeded by the number of coded instances where there was no oral participation at all by any participants. Over a quarter of class time in the study was characterised by an absence of talk from both staff and students alike.

- Learners in the study were observed to spend up to a fifth of their time in class disengaged from the learning process and off-task. This suggests a high level of apathy towards language learning amongst many Japanese university students.

The COPS has provided a solid starting point from which to investigate learner silence. But it is only a starting point. As a rather blunt instrument of structured observation, the COPS is unable to provide a fine-grained analysis of each silent episode it records. For that, we need to start looking towards an individual-level analysis using a qualitative approach in order to gain insights into why students remain silent in certain situations and how they perceive the action of remaining silent during L2 instruction. The following chapter begins this task by reporting on the findings of a semi-structured interview investigation which focused on individual students' opinions about, and experiences of, classroom silence. Research in this vein is in line with the view that qualitative methodologies are more suited to investigating dynamic systems (Dörnyei, 2009; Larsen-Freeman & Cameron, 2008). Only once we have begun to understand the dynamics of learner silence, will we be able to discover the most effective ways to reduce the allure of the seductive state of saying nothing.

6
An interview study into learners' perspectives on L2 classroom silence

6.1 Introduction

> I was asking her a question directly "Miss Yoko, what is your answer for number one?" A:nd she just sat there! ((laughs slightly)) And- and not only did she just sit there, she did not make eye contact with me (xxx) I'm making eye contact with her and I'm asking her a direct question, it's obvious that I'm speaking to her and I call her by name but she just sits there as though nobody's speaking to her and then she just sorta puts her head dow:n, like she's just shutting everything down... It was like she could've crawled into a little hole or a burrow or something because she was not responding whatsoever.
>
> (Jill, English instructor at Takayama University)

Yoko's emphatically silent response baffled her English instructor. A caring and professionally-minded language educator with many years of experience in Japan, Jill just could not fathom Yoko's behaviour. Did a lack of L2 proficiency play a significant role in her silence? Was Jill's question too difficult or poorly delivered? Did Yoko have some underlying psychological characteristic which contributed to her reluctance to reply? Was she just feeling physically ill on that particular day? Or, as DST would suggest, is it more likely that her silent behaviour was simultaneously influenced by any number of variables to varying degrees which combined to attract her into the seductive state of saying nothing? In what follows then, I provide a voice for individual language learners like Yoko in an attempt to move away once and for all from simplistic, reductionist rationalisations of classroom silence. I do this by making use of a specially designed research instrument called the Silence and Oral Participation Interview Guide (SOPIG; Appendix 2 contains a copy of the instrument, related documents and also instructions for how to use the guide).

6.2 Data collection and analysis

Complementing the quantitative data garnered from the structured observation stage of the project, a series of semi-structured interviews were conducted in order to uncover participants' fundamental beliefs about and personal experiences of silence in language classrooms. This qualitative component was essential to the study as it allowed for a deeper analysis of silence to be carried out at the level of the individual – something that is not really possible in the quantitative paradigm. Furthermore, this qualitative element was able to broaden the investigation's scope and led to enhanced opportunities for me to interpret the silences I encountered. Eleven interviewees agreed to take part in the project, with their semi-structured interviews comprising initial and follow-up sessions each lasting approximately 45 minutes. A systematic, stratified sampling strategy based on teacher and student recommendations ensured student participants met a number of set criteria in order to provide a diverse sample. The student interviewees were made up of both language and non-language majors at various stages of their tertiary education (first year undergraduate through to second year postgraduate) and these learners inhabited a very wide L2 proficiency spectrum. This chapter draws on data from eight student interviewees whose details are set out below (all names are pseudonyms).

Asako (F): A third year English language teaching major studying at a prestigious national university. Near-fluent in English, Asako had previously studied at a British university for four months. She chose to speak mainly in English over both interview sessions.

Satoshi (M): A postgraduate psychology student at a mid-ranking private university, Satoshi has 11 years of English language learning experience. He chose for both interview sessions to be conducted in Japanese.

Takuya (M): A fourth year non-language major at a provincial private university, Takuya was described by his instructors as 'Mr Average'. At the time of his interviews

	(both conducted in Japanese), he was actively juggling academic life with the pressures of job hunting.
Aya (F):	A 21-year-old third year languages student, Aya's time at a large private university had developed her confidence and language ability to the extent that she chose for both of her interview sessions to be conducted almost entirely in English. Aya had recently achieved an institutional TOEFL score of 520 and, at the time of interview, was in preparation for a long-term study abroad programme.
Sachiko (F):	A first year, non-languages postgraduate student with eight years experience of learning English. Although described by herself and her teachers as a very quiet student, Sachiko nevertheless proved to be a perceptive interviewee. Both Sachiko's interviews were carried out entirely in Japanese.
Etsuko (F):	An English major in her second year at a languages-orientated private university. Having already spent time in Australia on a short-term study abroad scheme, Etsuko was preparing for a year-long sojourn at a United States university. One of Etsuko's interviews was carried out in Japanese, the other in English.
Mikiko (F):	A fourth year, non-language major who had been studying English for eight years. Mikiko was a refreshingly direct interviewee unafraid to speak her mind, and readily admitted to a dislike of studying English. She chose for both interviews to be in Japanese.
Shizuko (F):	A second year undergraduate studying international communication at a large, private university famous for its language graduates. Shizuka was the quietest interviewee in the study (in terms of both volume and language production). Her initial interview was conducted in English, whilst the follow-up session was in Japanese.

An interesting paradox was that even though the study's focus was on silence, a number of procedural measures had to be taken to avoid excessive reticence by interviewees. Silence within interviews does not necessarily denote a failure to elicit data as it can be used for interpretive purposes (see Poland & Pederson, 1998), but the problem of non-responsive interviewees can be a particular problem in Japan where issues connected to status inequality (see Kowner, 2002), group membership (see Gudykunst & Nishida, 1993; McDaniel, 2003; Lebra, 1976, 1993) and a widespread lack of experience in intercultural communication all play significant roles in influencing the extent to which individuals are willing to interact. I therefore took a number of steps to increase interviewer–interviewee rapport and diminish perceived power disparities. These measures included the following:

- Informal pre-interview meetings were set up in order to fully explain interview procedures and to reassure participants of the confidential nature of the research. Consent forms written in Japanese further emphasised the anonymity of participants.
- Student interviewees were able to choose the language of their interview. This resulted in four sessions being in English, nine in Japanese and three that were a mixture of both languages.
- As my presence as a non-Japanese person had the potential to have an inhibiting effect on students, a female Japanese research assistant also attended each interview session (unless requested not to do so by the interviewee). The assistant's presence significantly facilitated the building of rapport, particularly with the study's female participants.
- As the dress of the interviewer sends a semiotic message about his/her status to which Japanese interviewees may be especially susceptible (see Bond & Shiraishi, 1974), I was careful to not to wear overtly formal clothing, such as a suit and tie, during the sessions.
- In addition to ensuring a comfortable interview setting, seating arrangements took into account the hierarchical contextualisation of space in Japan (Hendry, 1989; McDaniel, 2003). This meant that interviewees were given the seating position with the highest status (in the corner of the room furthest away from and facing the entrance).

The above measures also proved effective in helping combat the phenomenon of *tatamae* answers amongst interviewees. Related to one's public presentation of self, *tatemae* refers to a person's officially stated position as opposed to his/her true, innermost beliefs (Gudykunst & Nishida, 1993; Hendry, 1989). Coupled with the Japanese tendency to avoid self-disclosure (Barnlund, 1974, 1989; Lebra, 1987), *tatemae* answers present a serious challenge for the interview researcher. This was particularly so in the present study with its focus on the potentially negative topic of classroom silence. I was careful therefore to conduct all interviews in a sensitive, non-judgmental manner and repeatedly reassured interviewees that there were no right or wrong answers prior to asking them to recount their experiences and beliefs about language classroom silence.

Much of our silent behaviour operates at a semi-conscious or unconscious level. Indeed, the reasons for a person's silence are often so nebulous that they defy easy, immediate articulation. With this in mind, a Japanese version of the study's specially designed research instrument, the Silence and Oral Participation Interview Guide (SOPIG), was given to participants in the pre-interview meetings in an effort to help them externalise their thoughts about silence and to draw out accounts of their experiences that were as rich as possible. In line with Richards' (2003) view that the analysis of interview data should be an unfolding, ongoing process and not 'a simple one-off exercise' (p. 79), adjustments were made to SOPIG's questions not only following initial piloting but throughout the study as new and relevant themes emerged. Each student was interviewed twice, with the guide being used primarily in the initial interview. The subsequent follow-up sessions were used to develop lines of investigation, corroborate responses, and so on.

All interviews were audio-recorded with the participants' consent for later coding and analysis. In order to gain a deep engagement with the oral data collected, the recordings were transcribed in full. Japanese language recordings were first transcribed directly into the L1 before being translated into English. In order to ensure translation accuracy, sections of the transcriptions were then back-translated into Japanese and compared to originals. Transcriptions may represent what Miller and Crabtree term 'frozen interpretive constructs' (cited in Dörnyei, 2007, p. 246) but to reflect better the reality of the interaction that took place within the interviews, a relatively detailed transcription convention was adopted (see page xii) which also noted elements of the interviewees' non-verbal and paralinguistic behaviour. Certainly, as the study was concerned with students' silent behaviour, the convention reflected a thorough approach towards how silence within the interviews was marked. This approach was taken even though the study primarily aimed to utilise the content of the oral data rather than examine its linguistic form in the style of conversation analysis. A final source of data complementing the study's interview methodology was a research log in which I was able to reflect in depth upon the events of each interview session and thus contribute to the ongoing, iterative interpretation of data.

6.3 Results and discussion

The true complexity of classroom silence

Learners' intolerance of silence

A number of scholars have pointed to a variation in silent pause length between specific cultural groups (Enninger, 1991; Jaworski, 1993, 2000; Scollon & Scollon, 1981, 1990; Sifianou, 1997; Tannen, 1985), with the Japanese having a supposed proclivity towards silent, implicit, non-direct forms of communication (Clancy, 1990; Ishii & Bruneau, 1994; Lebra, 1987; McDaniel, 2003; Suzuki, 1986; Yamada, 1997). From this we would expect Japanese language learners to be highly tolerant of any extended periods of silence in their language classroom and to feel perfectly at ease during such episodes. However, this did not appear to be the case for some participants in the study, particularly when the silence they encountered was characterised by non-responsiveness to an instructor's questions or prompts. Interview data pointing towards some participants' relative intolerance of silence provide a useful counter-point which runs contrary to other findings in the study – findings which generally show students wanted to be silent in their university language classrooms. Such data therefore serve perfectly to illustrate that classroom silence in Japanese universities is indeed a complex phenomenon that defies simple generalisations.

One such student who was not at ease with silence and experienced difficulties tolerating it during lessons was Etsuko, a second year student majoring in English. Outlining how she and her circle of friends felt during silent episodes in her advanced-level language class, feelings of awkwardness and irritation towards classmates who were refusing to orally participate came to the fore in Etsuko's account, with a sense that the silent students were not 'pulling their weight'. She claimed, 'We think it's uncomfortable to be in a class where nobody speaks'. Similar sentiments were expressed by Asako, a third year undergraduate studying to become an English teacher. With a raised consciousness of silence following our initial interview, at the beginning of the subsequent follow-up session Asako recounted an incident during the lesson she had only just attended. She described how, after the teacher had posed a question to the class, students responded with an extended bout of silence during which a verbal answer was not forthcoming. When I asked how she felt during the silence, I was surprised by her unequivocal response:

> It's absolutely awkward! ((slight laugh)) And teacher- my profess- my professor was completely confused. But um af- after asking

a question nobody answered it and teacher went on the class so nobody answered it. So the atmosphere is absolutely awkward.

This is not what one would expect from a learner who comes from a society that is supposedly at ease with and accepting of silence as a relatively unmarked phenomenon (c.f. Sobkowiak, 1997). Both Etsuko and Asako are reasonably proficient L2 speakers who have experience of studying abroad in English-speaking countries and have had prolonged exposure to CLT and the methodology's demands for L2 oral activity. It could be argued therefore that their untypical prior learning experiences have increased their sensitivity to classroom silence as they have developed a familiarity with the *rules of engagement* (Anstey, 2003) for effective classroom discourse within a communication-orientated L2 learning environment. Even so, such a neat explanation for the paradoxical existence of students who feel discomfort during classroom silences but who are also members of a society highly tolerant of silence does not tell the whole story. It is not only higher ability learners acculturated into modes of instruction demanding productive language skills that are ill-at-ease with silence in response to teachers' questions and prompts. Less proficient students, those with a much narrower experience of L2 learning, may also feel such situations to be problematic.

This was illustrated by Sachiko, a quiet (as described by herself and her teachers) psychology postgraduate who, despite having shown little aptitude for foreign language learning throughout her time at her university, was voluntarily attending a weekly class in order to improve her basic English skills. Like Asako, Sachiko arrived at her follow-up interview having just experienced an episode of classroom silence. She talked about how there tended to be 'an atmosphere' in the class when her instructor invited students share their ideas and opinions with the group. I asked Sachiko how she felt during the silent episodes she had just experienced:

> Ah:: it's like 'Is it okay to say something or not' sort of thing. (2) Other people who I take the class with also think 'What is this silence for?', you know, so because our turn-taking and timing were not working well, the teacher even suggested bringing a dice so that we can put our names on it, throw the dice and the name that comes up has to start speaking. So the silence is that noticeable.

In the episode Sachiko refers to, the class's silence was a highly marked phenomenon which both the teacher and the students were well aware of, but apparently equally unsure how to deal with. This is not what we would expect in a society that appears to support classroom silence from both a cultural and an educational perspective. Nakane (2007, p. 51) points out that in Japan's pre-tertiary classrooms student non-responsiveness is entirely normal and that 'There is simply no competition for the floor, as students' voluntary participation is extremely rare.' Certainly students' previous classroom experiences do exert a significant influence in amongst other multiple intervening variables which attract learner silence, and it is unsurprising that a student like Sachiko, who had lamented her lack of opinions and ability to express them in public during her interviews, failed to self-select following the instructor's open-class questions. What is surprising though is the sense of awkwardness that comes across in Sachiko's account as participants sense the pedagogical discourse of their class is not progressing smoothly because of the many noticeable, extended silences. Ideally, Sachiko would like to orally participate but the attractor state of silence is too strong and she has instead settled into the routine behaviour, not verbally responding to her teacher's questions and prompts. Even though the desire to speak is there, a requisite repeller state strong enough to push Sachiko into breaking her silence does not exist and hence the system remains in a state of silent equilibrium.

Silence and high ability learners

Sachiko and Asako's feelings of discomfort during silent episodes help to illustrate that the reality of events at the classroom level is not always as straightforward as one might at first assume. Adopting a DST perspective in the examination of classroom silence forces the researcher to acknowledge the true complexity of reality and to avoid easy generalisations and simplistic, linear cause-effect explanations for language learners' lack of L2 production. Another prime example of this concerns students' L2 ability. There exists a widespread assumption amongst laypeople that Japanese students are quiet purely because they are shy and not good at English. Certainly, the Japanese education system's consistent failure to produce competent English speakers is widely acknowledged in the literature, with numerous writers (e.g. Inoguchi, 1999; McVeigh, 2002; Pritchard & Maki, 2006) alluding to the country's dismal international TOEFL ranking which sees its students on average as some of the least proficient in Asia. It is hardly surprising therefore that a fair proportion of the silence I encountered during the classroom observation phase of the project was characterised by students' inability to articulate in the foreign language they were studying because of deficiencies in comprehension and production of English. Even so, it would be quite wrong to assume that silence within Japanese university L2 classrooms is exclusively related to problems with language proficiency. The reality is much more complex than this.

In Chapter 2, I drew attention to the fact that Kurzon (1998) rightly reminds us that when interpreting silence, an important consideration is the intentionality of the silent act. This notion is very much relevant to the silent behaviour of that minority of students in Japan's language classrooms who are relatively proficient in L2. Events in Etsuko's class illustrate well how it is not only low ability learners who may remain silent in their classrooms. Following the arrival of a new instructor in her advanced programme English class, students began refusing to orally participate in lessons that they deemed insultingly easy. While some members of her group approached the teacher outside of class hours and expressed their concern that lessons were pitched at too low a level, Etsuko explained that:

> other students were just angry and didn't say anything about it although they had the ability to talk ((in English)) because they'd actually passed the exam to study abroad. All they did was to keep silent and say we don't understand this teacher's class. It's pointless to come to school, kind of thing.

The silent learners that emerged from Etsuko's account were of a level of English aptitude high enough to gain access to mainstream undergraduate courses on study abroad programmes, but, even so, they *chose* to remain silent in order to passively protest against lesson activities they perceived to be too elementary. Silence in this context closely mirrors that observed by Gilmore (1985) in her ethnographic study of the silent stylised sulking of students within an inner-city high school in the United States . As was pointed out in Chapter 2, Gilmore notes that a learner may employ silence as an effective tool for emotional management (see also Saunders, 1985) as it allows for a passive expression of dissatisfaction but minimises the threat of face loss. A further element in the case of Etsuko's class is that within the educational context of her foreign languages-orientated university, learners closely associate English proficiency with high social status (see Ryan, 2009), and so by introducing lesson content that was not appropriate to their level, Etsuko's new instructor inadvertently challenged the students' (often hard won) identities as relatively proficient L2 speakers. Seen in this light, it is perhaps unsurprising the class reacted with dismay and, in most cases, non-cooperation and silence. Although other variables would have certainly contributed to their silent behaviour, the fact that students *chose* to remain silent does help underline that classroom talk systems are indeed complex phenomena that reject naïve oversimplification that a lack of L2 ability provides the sole basis for language learner silence.

Silence as a 'risk-free' option for learners

Dynamic systems theory suggests that rather than being an incremental phenomenon, the silence found in language classrooms is actually a construct with several parallel and converging strands. One such strand concerns how students' classroom discourse is pulled towards a pattern of non-participation because of the crucial choices made by teachers concerning the pedagogical technique, lesson materials, task activities, and so on that they employ with a class. Although there were some exceptions, many of the lessons I observed during the project were dominated throughout either by a rigid Initiation Response Feedback (IRF) pattern (Sinclair & Coulthard, 1975) that only required minimal, one-word answers from students or by methods that did not require any form of active participation at all, only that the learners be present.

Facile classroom activities inevitably fail to challenge and engage learners, and thus contribute to demotivation (see Kikuchi & Sakai, 2009) and a reluctance to invest in learning tasks that are deemed 'pointless'. Rebuck (2008) rightly points out that, as long as instructors take pertinent steps to generate interest and 'sell' activities (see also Dörnyei, 2001), excessively difficult lessons using authentic materials can actually motivate learners. Etsuko commented upon the ease with which students could pass her supposedly advanced-level language class.

> my teacher only lets us do something simple, so it's easy. I think they mainly judge by attendance. I think it's up to your attendance if you can get a credit or not. ((laughs))

Etsuko's comments highlight the fact that students are often able to pass courses in Japanese universities merely by dint of attending class, regardless of what they actually do there (see Clayton, 1993; McVeigh 2002, pp. 130–2). This means that silent language learners have little difficulty in passing courses provided they have a record of regular attendance. Their silent behaviour is supported by the pedagogical choices made by instructors in that the learners have absolutely nothing to lose by avoiding talk. We can therefore see that the didactic methods adopted by language teachers clearly act as key attractors of silence when non-responsiveness and avoidance of talk present themselves as the optimal risk-free options for students.

Interviewees frequently referred to the ease of obtaining *tani* (class credits) in their language classes. Indeed, it seems that a pernicious 'culture of class credit', whereby the sole reason for attending one's language class is to obtain the credit, rather than to actually learn anything, in effect silences not only the more proficient learners who may see little benefit in the simplistic classroom activities they are asked to perform, but also those with a much lower level of English ability. Takuya, a non-language major attending a provincial university with poor language learning provision, described the ease with which he was able to acquire the credits for his English class despite his lack of L2 ability:

> the teacher told us exactly what questions were on the test during the class so getting the credit was easy. If you had regular attendance on top of that, I think there's no doubt that you'd get the credit, so it was very easy...There are lots of students who only care about getting course <u>credits</u> and the things they learned don't <u>stay</u> in their heads. I was one of them.

With course credits being spoon-fed to students, there was no need for Takuya to participate orally in his language class in order to pass. Once he had achieved his pass early on in the course by regurgitating memorised sections of the textbook, there existed even less incentive for him to speak in the L2. Takuya's subsequent silent disengagement from the learning process appears to be a far from unique phenomenon. Recollect that the observation phase of this study discovered that learners spent over a fifth of all their class time off-task and not engaged at all with lesson content.

Takuya's experiences closely mirror Japan's pre-tertiary language education system which relies heavily on a passive, receptive mode of learning and has little provision for the productive use of English. If we take an even wider perspective, we can see the country's education system in general is characterised by a transactional, traditional mode of learning and instruction, and the influence of this system presents itself as yet another salient agent in a classroom talk system pulling discourse into the silence attractor basin. Commenting on empirical studies of educational discourse in United Kingdom and United States contexts, Larsen-Freeman and Cameron (2008) point out that classroom talk systems are influenced at the higher sociocultural level because of 'accepted ideas that learning is enhanced by active participation and that contributing to classroom talk promotes such active participation and is thus to be positively valued' (p. 181). Within the Japanese context it seems that converse beliefs still dominate: learning is enhanced by remaining quiet, listening carefully and making copious notes of the teacher's pronouncements for later memorisation. A lack of active participation is positively valued as it is respectful of the instructor's superior status and allows him/her to cover the set content of the lesson unimpeded. Those students keen to learn have nothing to lose in terms of assessment by remaining silent, and the same is even true for those who are disengaged from the learning process. Active oral participation and its inherent unpredictability is where the real risk lies.

Silence and embarrassment

The previous section emphasises the important role that situational factors play in influencing Japanese language learners' production of silence. However, if we are to take a dynamic system's perspective on this issue, we also need to acknowledge that learner-internal factors, such as perception of one's status within the classroom, confidence in using L2, level of self-esteem, degree of social inhibition, and so on, also play a simultaneous role in shaping the non-responsiveness of students. In line with this, a very strong theme to emerge from the interview data was the extent to which learners dreaded the embarrassment of having to speak English publicly in front of their peers. The data show that psychological and emotional factors act as significant system attractors which draw students into a predictable pattern of oral passivity. Although such factors are in a state of constant flux because individuals' mental processes tend to evolve over time, there does appear to be a well-established pattern of excessive self-monitoring and a culturally ingrained fear of shame amongst Japanese language learners. Even though fear of embarrassment through speaking out was *the* dominant theme to emerge from the interview phase of the research, we still need to resist thinking of this silence-inducing attractor as existing solely in isolation from other agents. DST posits that at any one time there exist multiple and interrelated factors influencing a language learner's behaviour – recall de Bot, Lowie and Verspoor's (2007) notion of *complete interconnectedness* – and the existence of these various concurrent and dynamically changing factors means that student silence cannot be accounted for simply through a single, linear cause – be it contextual in nature or an internal learner attribute.

Before I outline some individual interviewees' accounts of their feelings when under scrutiny and their embarrassment when speaking in

English, it would be a good idea first to clarify why I use the term 'embarrassment' instead of what might be considered the more academically appropriate word, 'anxiety'. Even though there is now a well-established body of research on anxiety in second language learning (e.g. Horwitz, Horwitz & Cope, 1986; MacIntyre & Gardner, 1994; Oxford, 1999; Tsui, 1996), Dörnyei (2005, p. 198) draws on Scovel to highlight that the complex construct of anxiety is difficult to define, widely misunderstood and often wrongly seen as being a purely debilitative factor. I therefore favour the term *embarrassment* and its derivatives here, rather than *anxiety*, because it is an emotion that appears to have a purely negative effect on Japanese learners' levels of oral production. Furthermore, it is the expression (*hazukashii* in Japanese) participants referred to most frequently when they were asked in interviews to describe their feelings at being required to speak in the L2 in their language classrooms. The following comments by first Satoshi and then Shizuko are typical of how many interviewees' felt whilst their language classes were in progress (note Shizuko's use of silence in the extract epitomising her oral passivity):

> I worry about what the people around me think of me. If I made a mistake with a simple task- like everybody- um e:verybody knows the answer so say there's twenty-five students and if I make a mistake when all of those twenty-five people know the answer, then they would think 'Ah::, this guy is stu:pid.' ((laughs))…I worry about my pronunciation, and the combination of words, if they're in the right order or not…I don't have confidence in my answer, then I really don't like what people around me might be thinking of me (..) and that's embarrassing. (Satoshi)
>
> I think we- I think I (2) like (…) about if I'm (4.5) different to others. (2) So (6) if I- if everyone knows the answers but I don't, it's embarrassing. (3) And then (18) I- I always think 'How do they think of me?' and (they) (53) I don't know the good answer. (Shizuko)

Student embarrassment is a dynamic phenomenon because it relates not only to the fluctuating mental characteristics of individual students, but is also influenced by various immediate situational factors. Such factors may include whether a learner is familiar with the oral task he/she is asked to perform, how many peers are exposed to the learner's L2 talk, what is the level of intimacy between the learner and peers, and so on. Silence as a defensive strategy to avoid embarrassment also appears to be supported at a higher sociocultural level within the Japanese context. The enculturated notion of an ever-present and ever-watching 'other' in Japanese society (see Greer, 2000; Lebra 1976, 1993; McVeigh, 2002) contributes to learners' hyper-sensitivity towards peer reactions. This hyper-sensitivity helps engender inhibition, an egocentric preoccupation with impression management (Tedeschi, 1981) and a reluctance to orally participate in lessons. Interviewees repeatedly raised the issue of being watched and judged in their language classes in relation to their silence, and made frequent references to the 'eyes' around them:

> I think when the teacher nominates me to answer a question, I feel I become the centre of attention and also I feel I'm being watched whether I get it right or wrong. (Mikiko)
> I personally didn't speak up when I didn't know the answer (…) yeah (21.5) mmm I think people worry about other people's eyes the most. (Shizuko)
> you're judged (..) because other people are watching you, you have to be perfect or you have to speak English well. I think to speak in front of every- everyone means you would probably become a model. So mmm I think there is a cultural trait in Japan in which people care about others' eyes. (Asako)

Of course it is not a uniquely Japanese trait to 'care about others' eyes'. Learners the world over may view their classrooms as emotional danger zones (c.f. Scheidecker & Freeman, 1999) where the act of speaking out, whether in their native tongue or in an L2, carries the risk of negative evaluation and therefore the potential to cause shame and embarrassment. However, the tendency to excessively self-monitor and a heightened empathetic awareness of others (developed from infancy – see Clancy, 1990) does seem to be a pronounced trend amongst language learners in Japan and they do appear to be very adept at employing silence as a powerful defensive strategy to avoid becoming the focus of attention. Mikiko provided a specific example of this when she spoke about teachers' attempts to solicit questions:

> you know when a teacher asks students 'any questions?' and everybody goes quiet, then I wouldn't say 'yes, I have a question' because I don't want to be the centre of the attention, you know. Yeah. (Mikiko)

Such reluctance to verbally respond to the common teacher refrain of 'any questions?' is far from uncommon. Over the course of the project's 48 hours of classroom observation, this question, or its close approximation, was posed by instructors a total of 53 times (including five times in Japanese), but was met by a silent response from students on all but three occasions. As time wore on during data collection I came to marvel at the persistence of some teachers who repeatedly posed the question even though it was so clearly redundant. Perhaps these educators were indefatigably optimistic about obtaining a verbal reply, or maybe they viewed the silent response they encountered each time as a speech act having illocutionary force (see Saville-Troike, 1985) – in which case, the silence merely meant 'no'. From a DST perspective, such interactions appear to have moved into a routinised sequence which acts to reduce the complexity of the talk system. In line with Larsen-Freeman and Cameron's (2008) assertion that such sequences tend to occur either at the start or close of interactions, this particular question-silence pattern predominantly occurs at the conclusion of an instructor's explanations or instructions.

Silence by teamwork

The dynamic formation of classroom cliques and their silencing effects

Intimately linked to the notion that inhibition and embarrassment act as powerful attractors which help move classroom talk systems towards silence is the fact that over time learners often form themselves into cliques. Having the power to stymie the establishment of good interpersonal relations within a class, dominant cliques are extremely effective at inhibiting and silencing learners. When students form themselves into exclusive, inward-looking groups it can have a devastating effect on a class's levels of oral participation and this issue is particularly significant within a Japanese context because of the great emphasis placed upon being part of a group in a country that espouses the advantages of collectivism over individualism within society (see Cathcart & Cathcart, 1994; Moeran, 1986: Peak, 1989). Of course, how these groups form and students come together is of itself a truly dynamic phenomenon because groups are themselves self-organising, dynamic systems that can be influenced in their development by any number of variables.

Student interviewees outlined a range of factors which facilitated the formation of cliques within their own language classrooms. Echoing Segal's (1974) work on propinquity, Satoshi revealed he developed a close circle of friends amongst the people who happened to sit near to him during inductions and the initial classes of his first few days at university, and it was with these people that he spent nearly all of his time for the next couple of years. He explained how he and his fellow first years tended to be assigned seats according to their student number and thus cliques of students regularly placed in adjacent seats soon developed. Of course groups do not only form because of the proximity of members – DST tells us that other concurrent factors are also likely to be an influence. For example, Takuya recounted how at his university cliques tended to be organised along gender lines, with there being little or no interaction between male and female groups.

> boys belong to boys group and girls belong to girls group and it's been like that in both junior high and high school, so maybe it has become my second nature and that's why I think boys don't mix with girls. (Takuya)

It should be noted here that during the observation phase of this study, gender did not prove to be a significant factor in students' silent behaviour. Both men and women were equally reticent and uniformly avoided initiating discourse in their language classes. This goes against the expectation created by numerous previous studies (e.g. Julé, 2005; Swann, 1992) which emphasise gender differences in language production levels, with the assumption that male students will inevitably dominate classroom talk. This unexpected finding that there was not a significant difference between male and female students in the current study yet again underlines the inherent complexity and unpredictable nature of student silence within classroom talk systems.

Certainly there were no gender differences on display in one particular language class I observed at a provincial private university which had a very distinct set of cliques within it. This was because the class in question was made up entirely of male second year sports science majors who were members of the university's various sports teams. The cliques were easy to identify because small groups of students tended to arrive together, sat together and departed together each week. As they were required to attend practice most days, groups either tended to wear the garb of their particular team or carried with them the accoutrements of their sport. In line with the similarity principle of group dynamics (Forsyth, 2009) – that there is a tendency for people to affiliate with similar others – the students in each clique were even inclined to sport similar haircuts; short and severe for the baseball squad, longer for the tennis team, and luxuriantly dyed locks amongst the footballers. What was interesting though from the point of view of classroom silence was that, in addition to a complete lack of student-initiated discourse by any individual students over the entire multiple-lesson observation period, there was also an absence of inter-group talk. As DST would suggest, there were manifold concurrent variables at the classroom level which contributed to this situation – for example, a large class size of over 50 students, inappropriate lesson materials (one session focused on useful phrases when buying women's clothing), a transactional didactic method, high degrees of student apathy and disengagement, to name but a few. But a key element reinforcing this silence-orientated classroom talk system was that students did not freely integrate with each other during any of the observed sessions and no attempt was made by the instructor to manipulate students' seating in order to facilitate cooperation and the changing of partners. This absence of integration reinforced the power of the class's cliques, and thus contributed to lessons that were characterised by learner inhibition, L2 silence and a lack of inter-group oral interaction. Cliques act as attractors which drag classroom talk systems towards silence and are supported by a Japanese cultural context which sees little verbal interaction between out-group members in public situations (see Lebra, 1976, 1993; Gudykunst & Nishida, 1993; McDaniel, 2003).

Aya and her clique
Over the course of her interview sessions, one student in particular provided an enlightening account of how the inhibitive power of cliques negatively influenced her own and other students' behaviour in an English class she had attended at her large, foreign languages-orientated private university. Aya's clique had been an eight-strong, all-female group of first year students who, she believed, had initially been attracted to each other by their shared sense of, and interest in, fashion. As with the sports science students, there also appears to have been a negligible amount of inter-group oral interaction within Aya's language class. Her clique dominated and set the tone for lessons in which mistakes in the L2 met with sniggering derision from clique members, and this contributed to what was an unsupportive learning atmosphere. The negative atmosphere was further exacerbated by the non-responsiveness of Aya's clique and she recounted how her group's members actively collaborated not to respond to their teacher's questions and prompts. Of their non-responsiveness and lack of initiated discourse, she saw this behaviour as a 'kind of like teamwork, ((laughs)) teamwork to make silence', and that during lessons 'there was an atmosphere where everyone was cooperating not to raise their hand'. Cohesive groups such as Aya's may exert significant pressure on their members to conform to certain behaviours, termed *norms* in group dynamics, and these emergent, consensual standards regulate conduct and make it predictable and meaningful for

those within the group (Forsyth, 2009, p. 145). At the time, Aya thought of the silent behaviour which had emerged within her clique as the natural and obvious way to behave. She defined her group's lack of oral participation as 'common sense: don't raise hand, don't say opinion.' From a DST perspective, the norm displayed by Aya's clique reflected silence being a preferred and relatively stable phase within the development of her group's complex classroom talk system. Group members settled into a predictable pattern of non-responsiveness, thus indicating that a strong attractor state of silence had emerged with multiple, coherent attractors. But the confident third year student sitting across from me, speaking almost entirely in English throughout her two interviews, seemed very far removed from the silent, non-responsive first year student that came across in Aya's description of her earlier self. Obviously a great change had occurred, but what had happened to bring about such a transformation?

It seems a number of factors, termed *repellers* in DST, converged simultaneously to push Aya out of her set pattern of silent behaviour. Drawing on Thelen and Bates, Dörnyei (2009, p. 107) points out that when the assorted internal and external factors which shape a system converge to produce a force strong enough to disrupt the existing elements' coherence, change will occur as the system reorganises. The more settled an attractor state, the more energy is required to force a system reorganisation. This process is well illustrated by Aya's experiences and I was able to identify some of the internal and external forces that acted simultaneously to push her away from the attractor state of silence. Firstly, after a prolonged exposure to non-traditional teaching methods emphasising student communication during her first year at the university, Aya began changing the way she thought about language learning and came to invest in the belief her L2 abilities could best be developed by active oral participation in class. Also, her university is renowned for its study abroad opportunities, and Aya soon developed a strong interest in undertaking a long-term sojourn at an institution in an English-speaking country. The shift in her outlook reflects Yashima and Zenuk-Nishide's (2008) findings on the positive attitudinal and behavioural changes found amongst Japanese learners within learning contexts focusing on study abroad preparation. Yet another concurrent factor in Aya's push away from classroom silence was that crucially, after joining an extra-curricular club, she was able to rely less and less on her clique members for friendship and support, and began to reduce the amount of time spent in their presence. At the same time it was also her good fortune to meet another student in the same language class from outside of her clique who shared both her desire to gain entry to one of the university's study abroad programmes and her increasingly positive view of being orally active in class. Finally, on top of all these factors, a change of semester brought a change of instructor, someone more experienced at teaching in the Japanese tertiary context, and this contributed to what Aya believed was a better managed, more supportive learning environment. These numerous learner-internal and situational factors at the classroom level acted as salient repellers working in tandem to exert enough pressure to push Aya out of her pattern of silent behaviour. Although it was a difficult path to take and she risked the derision of its members, Aya eventually made the difficult decision to leave her clique in order to escape its negative influence on her L2 development. Underlining that her social needs could be satisfied elsewhere, she explained:

> I decided <u>next</u> semester, like sophomore, I don't make any group and I will think about myself. And I had a friend of club so I'm not gonna make group and I'm not gonna join group. This like subject class is <u>just</u> subject class to study English.

The clique's response to Aya's defection was perhaps unsurprising. Members ignored her and studiously avoided initiating any further interaction. Thus Aya's behaviour was negatively sanctioned with the group falling back on their tried and tested strategy of employing silence to effectively communicate displeasure.

The multiple agents of Mikiko's resilient classroom silence
Experienced and skilled in avoiding talk

Up to this point, a large part of the discussion has concentrated on tracing back some typical attractors which encourage silence within the complex talk systems of Japanese university L2 classrooms. The agents and elements shaping students' silences that have been uncovered thus far through qualitative interview data are by no means a full and complete taxonomy of attractors within what is a deep and powerful silence attractor basin. Even so, they do denote salient social, cultural, pedagogical and learner-internal forces at play within Japanese language classrooms. The problem with identifying individual attractors and presenting them in relative isolation is that the multiple variable, complete interconnectedness aspect of the system's dynamics may be somewhat obscured. Therefore, by drawing on data collected from interviews with Mikiko, I will conclude this section by illustrating how there may be fluctuating, multiple, interrelated forces acting at any one time to lure individual students into the seductive state of saying nothing while learning a foreign language. I will also discuss how, even when teaching methods are modified, subsequent changes to the attractor state of silence may not necessarily follow because the state has become such an entrenched phenomenon.

Over the course of her interview sessions, Mikiko admitted to having been an extremely quiet student throughout her eight years of L2 education. More conscious of silence following our initial interview, she revealed, 'I was actually amazed to realise how kind of (1.5) natural it has become for me to be quiet.' But what lay behind so many years of oral passivity in class? The first attractor that emerged was Mikiko's lack of L2 comprehension. She repeatedly referred to the difficulties she had in understanding spoken English, for example claiming, 'I've come to the conclusion that English is an incomprehensible language.' Questions from her language teacher were something to be avoided at all costs because 'it's just impossible to answer and even if I say something as an answer, I know (..) it's going to be wrong.' This last statement reveals an important connected learner-internal attractor that also became apparent in Mikiko's testimony: her profound lack of confidence in speaking L2. This lack of self-belief where English was concerned in turn helped shape Mikiko's classroom discourse by exacerbating her fear of becoming the centre of attention and making a mistake whilst publicly speaking in class. Mikiko admitted that she even avoided greeting her teacher upon entering the classroom so as to avoid subsequently becoming the centre of the class's attention. She explained:

> As soon as I catch the teacher's eye, and say something like 'good morning' or whatever, if this impression stays with the teacher, once class starts and teacher looks for someone to answer a question, I'll definitely be the first to be nominated and will be the centre of attention only because my eyes met the teacher's just before. So, as I don't want to answer any questions, I stay silent when the teacher enters the room.

When we consider the great importance placed on *aisatsu* (ritualised greetings/leave-takings) in Japanese society (see Ide, 2009), Mikiko's conscious refusal to greet her teacher shows just how strong the allure of remaining silent and hence avoiding the potentially embarrassing behaviour of speaking out in class is. Foreign language classrooms are sites of social interaction in which a learner's sense of self is constantly challenged by having to perform in an unfamiliar language and by learning processes that expose him/her to the prospect of negative public evaluation. This threat to students' self image is underlined by Granger (2004) who claims the silence of some second language learners may represent an unhealthy combination of not being to able to verbally express themselves and a diminished self-regard which means learners are trapped in a precarious identity between their L1 and L2 selves. This analysis appears to fit Mikiko very well, whose L1 self, in direct contrast to her L2 identity, came across as confident, outgoing and perceptive.

An account of Mikiko's language learning experiences from junior high school through to university show that, in addition to inhibition and the fear of embarrassment acting as profoundly powerful forces in attracting her silent behaviour, specific contextual factors at the classroom level further supported these agents. For example, even when directly nominated, she was especially reluctant to respond to teachers' questions when in a large-class environment. This stands to reason as classes containing a greater number of unfamiliar, out-group members are much more likely to contribute to one's inhibition. Surprisingly though, Mikiko expressed a preference for increased class sizes, explaining that they provided an ideal environment in which she could minimise the likelihood of being called on to speak. Reflecting the idea of 'safety in numbers', she would endeavour to obtain seating positions well towards the back of classrooms, away from the teacher's gaze, in an attempt to maintain her silence. This is just one example of how the variable context of the learning situation provides a rich source of attractors encouraging student non-responsiveness. Linked to this dynamic environmental factor, we could even consider Mikiko's physical appearance as a surprising further element within the system facilitating her avoidance behaviour. Standing at just under five feet tall (approximately 148cm), this particular student thought of her height as a real advantage in her large language classes because it meant she could hide herself 'in the shadow of someone sitting in front'. She went on to explain:

> I focus all my efforts on hiding...I want to avoid standing out as much as possible and I want to have as little a presence as possible. (1.5) Somehow or other, I try to- to sit on the edge of my chair like this ((demonstrating)) and deliberately lower my height and hide. <u>Seriously</u> hide.

Mikiko had been especially keen to hide from her non-Japanese instructor. Gudykunst (2004) conceptualises such behaviour within an *approach-avoidance* framework in which a person's tendency to avoid interactions with people from other cultures is assessed. Raised in a largely rural area of Japan, Mikiko had little or no experience of intercultural communication and this appears to have been a contributory factor in her desire to avoid L2 communication with non-Japanese teachers. Talking about her language instructor from the United States, she explained how she had 'no idea how to deal with him' and revealed that:

> Being in front of non-Japanese makes me nervous but also, as I said before, they don't look familiar, so what I mean is er firstly, I feel awkward then (...) this awkwardness becomes embarrassment.

Even so, Mikiko made it clear she had no inherent dislike of people from other cultures and was not implacably opposed to having a foreigner as her language instructor – but this was only if she could maintain her silence and avoid having to communicate with the teacher directly. Her avoidance tendencies were further highlighted when the discussion in our follow-up interview turned towards the (humorous) comparison between non-Japanese instructors and pandas: that they are nice to look at from a distance but one would not want to deal with one close up. Mikiko explained:

> I would rather look at them like looking at something rare, um it's maybe rude though. So anyway I think it's very nice to see them and to be able to look at them ... It's like I know they are a fantastic feast for my eyes but to be in a same place is a little um (...) impossible. As soon as they talk to me, I wouldn't be able to respond, you know.

Hence we can see that Mikiko's lack of intercultural communication experience and a reluctance to interact with non-Japanese instructors are further dynamic interrelated variables in the formation of her silent behaviour.

Mikiko's persistent silence in pair and small-group work

Yet another connected agent in Mikiko's classroom silence concerns the pedagogical choices made by her instructors. As the observation phase of this research illustrates so well, student silence dwells especially in teacher-centred classrooms where discourse is tightly controlled and great emphasis is placed not only on the accuracy of the content, but also on the linguistic form of learners' utterances. Supported by Japan's language education traditions, Mikiko's most recent instructor had chosen a didactic method which treated English as an academic subject, emphasising grammar and translation (see Hino, 1988), rather than as a practical tool of communication for use in real life. She described the classes as 'mind-numbing', explaining that during lessons 'we simply translate texts and answer some questions, page after page from a textbook'. Boredom and disengagement undoubtedly played a significant role in Mikiko's classroom silences and she admitted to often not even bothering to follow her instructor's pronouncements. When I asked her to describe how she felt during these lessons, her repeated use of the phrase *mendōkusai* (meaning in this context, *I couldn't be bothered*) suggests a deep-seated apathy towards language learning contributed to by both a teacher-centred, non-oral approach and an overall lack of relevance of English in Mikiko's daily life (see Kubota & McKay, 2009).

That said, I would not want to mislead the reader into assuming the entire English education system in Japan's tertiary sector consists purely of transactional, lecture-style lessons which only target students' receptive language skills. That would certainly not be to take a complexity perspective on this issue. In reality there has been a movement towards more interactional, student-centred methods of language learning in Japan since the 1970s (Poole, 2005), but as various writers have illustrated (e.g. Hato, 2005; Nishino and Watanabe, 2008; Sakui, 2004; Yoshida, 2003), recent attempts to implement an officially sanctioned communicative approach at the local level have so far proved problematic. During the observation phase of this study, I encountered a number of instructors who were indeed innovative in their use of various small-group and pair-work tasks designed to encourage the productive use of L2 amongst their students. However, as silence dynamically emerges from so many different routes and exerts such a powerful attraction for Japanese learners, even though instructors may attempt to combat it by manipulating their methodology and the classroom environment, the attraction of saying nothing appears to persist. This shows just how resistant to change the attractor state of silence has become within Japan's language classrooms.

Mikiko's experiences in one of her earlier university language classes appear to back this up. The class was relatively small (around 20 students) and her instructor employed a student-centred, communicative approach in which learners were often required to work in pairs or groups. As such an approach offers the ideal opportunity for learners to engage with the target language in a more facilitative, less threatening context, one would expect that the provision of pair- and small-group work would naturally result in increased levels of student talk. However, a complexity perspective teaches us to be wary of what at first glance appears logical, linear, cause–effect reasoning, and by examining Mikiko's beliefs and experiences in an individual-level analysis of the issue, it appears that in actual fact her language production levels did not significantly rise. During these particular lessons, Mikiko explained that she, along with most others in the class, saw pair-work speaking tasks merely as ideal opportunities for off-task chit-chat in the L1. In reality, her English production during such exercises was limited to a few, barely audible, disconnected words produced only when the instructor happened to be monitoring nearby:

> So only when the teacher is around, I speak English by some means – using a few words and gesturing so that the teacher can only just hear us. But once the teacher's gone, we start speaking Japanese again, feeling 'What a relief!'

On one occasion Mikiko did not even bother to carry out this charade at all:

> There was a time when the teacher gave us a topic and we made a pair and talked about the topic with our partner only in English ... and I couldn't be bothered to work on it <u>right in front</u> of the teacher.

Although she admitted to chatting mostly in Japanese during oral activities and was therefore not acoustically silent, if we view her behaviour from a pragmatic perspective (Jaworski, 1993), Mikiko's avoidance of L2 talk represents a clear example of learner silence. Changes in group size, teaching methodology and activity type did not result in a shift towards greater levels of L2 production from Mikiko and such stability indicates a strong attractor state of silence in which the repellers present in the system lack sufficient energy to push it out of its equilibrium.

This otherwise conscientious student's account of her language classroom experiences and her unwillingness to attempt to speak English in situations relatively non-threatening to her sense of self reflect what I witnessed during the observation phase of the project. A common ruse was for learners to give the impression of orally participating in the L2 only while the instructor was monitoring in the immediate vicinity. Even for those learners who did manage to stay on-task during pair and small-group work, there was little evidence of a willingness to make the most of very limited opportunities to speak in the target language. Time and again when students completed activities involving an oral component ahead of peers, they were observed then to sit passively in silence waiting for further instructions from the teacher. Instead of approaching these student-centred activities as valuable chances to take control of their classroom discourse and practise the target language in a society that provides few authentic opportunities to speak English, the overriding goal of most students was simply to complete the task. Japan's pre-tertiary English education system, which seeks to prepare students for examinations (e.g., see Aspinall, 2005; Kobayashi, 2001) and is thoroughly results (i.e. scores) rather than process (i.e. skills) orientated, acts as a powerful social force, working in tandem with the array of other cultural, pedagogic and learner-internal influences described above to dynamically support such behaviour and push the classroom talk of students like Mikiko into a predictable pattern of oral passivity.

6.4 Conclusion

Through a qualitative research approach focusing on individual students' beliefs about and experiences of silence, this study has begun to shed light on the multiple forms and functions of silence within Japanese university language classrooms. Considering learners' silent behaviour from a DST perspective, we can see that silence emerges from many different routes (attractors) which combine to form a large and powerful attractor basin. The dynamic interplay between learner-internal factors and multiple external contextual issues has contributed to silence becoming a robust, semi-permanent attractor state in Japan's language classrooms. This project has only really just begun the job of tracing back the various reasons for the uniform system outcome of Japanese learner silence and therefore much further research needs to be done to fully identify the various components of the system's reticence-inducing attractor basin. Even so, the testimony of this interview study's diverse sample of participants has uncovered a number of new and surprising insights into the silent behaviour of Japan's university students, with these insights helping to underline the dynamic nature of classroom silence.

- The Japanese have a supposed proclivity towards silence and intuitive understanding, suggesting they feel at ease when there is an absence of talk. However, data from the interviews show a more complex picture at the individual level, with some interviewees describing feelings of discomfort during silent episodes in their

language classrooms. Even so, it seems that this discomfort alone is unlikely to be potent enough to repel most learners out of silence and into active oral participation.
- Contrary to widespread belief, it is not only those learners lacking foreign language proficiency that do not engage in classroom dialogue in the target language. This study has identified instances where high ability learners *chose* to remain silent, even though they were perfectly capable of expressing themselves in English. These students employed their silence as a means of passively resisting their teacher's authority and methodology.
- Unlike in educational contexts such as in the United Kingdom, traditional cultures of learning in Japan do not generally value active oral participation in the classroom. Silence therefore presents itself as the risk-free option for learners, particularly in learning environments which demand very little from students in order for them to pass.
- The study found that psychological and emotional factors present significant system attractors for students' silent behaviour, with the fear of embarrassment and loss of face which may arise as a result of publicly communicating in L2 acting as a major influence. Manifested through acute hyper-sensitivity to others and an almost neurotic dread of negative evaluation, in true DST fashion, this type of silence is supported by dynamically changing factors at learner-internal, classroom and societal levels.
- A further major silence attractor emerging from both observational and interview data concerns the presence of dominant cliques in Japanese university language classrooms. Suppressing good interpersonal relations within class groups, cliques can have a profound effect on learners' oral production levels when silence becomes a preferred and relatively predictable phase in the development of small groups' classroom talk systems.
- Even though silence has now become a semi-permanent attractor state in Japan's tertiary classrooms, DST posits that change is still possible, but only when enough variables converge to produce the energy necessary to force a shift in the system. This concept was illustrated by the experiences of the interviewee Aya, whose decision to leave her clique, in conjunction with various other concurrent learner and situational factors, eventually did result in her becoming a much more orally active language student.
- The case of Mikiko exemplifies a more typical Japanese university language learner, one whose silence has been dynamically supported by powerful attractors at the learner, classroom and societal levels

from junior high school onwards. Data from Mikiko's interviews revealed how disengagement and apathy provide especially common routes through which classroom silence emerges, and even when instructors manipulate their teaching so that learners can avoid public evaluation when speaking in L2, silence remains such a strong attractor state that it may persist even with the introduction of pair- and small-group oral tasks.

So finally, let us return to Yoko, whose intractable silence so confused and frustrated her teacher Jill at the very beginning of this chapter. The preceding discussion shows us that we can only make real sense of Yoko's non-responsiveness by adopting a complex dynamic systems perspective and tracing back the multiple intervening learner and environmental variables which combine to pull her into a state of silence. These factors may include, but are not limited to, issues related to Yoko's mental characteristics, her previous learning experiences, the task she was being asked to perform at the time, her level of intercultural experience, the nature of her relationship with Jill, Jill's nationality, social group factors within the class, the physical characteristics of the classroom environment, and so on. All these elements are in addition to higher-level social and cultural forces within the Japanese context that appear to exert pressure in support of language learner silence, thus making it more likely. Unfortunately, there is a limit to the insight we can gain on this issue from analysing student testimony collected in semi-structured interviews. Data from the project's interviews have certainly proved useful in providing individual learners with a voice to describe their experiences of, and fundamental beliefs about, classroom silence. However, in order to gain insights into *specific* incidents of learner silence like Yoko's occurring at the micro-level of classroom interaction, an introspective methodology needs to be adopted. Therefore with this in mind, the following chapter draws on data from a series of stimulated recalls (Gass & Mackay, 2000) to uncover how students felt during silent periods, why they gave a silent response, and how they perceived activities and other participants whilst silence was occurring.

7
A naturalistic stimulated recall study of specific silence events

7.1 Introduction

Stimulated recall is a form of introspective inquiry that has been employed extensively in educational research, primarily as a means of investigating individuals' concurrent thinking during specific past events (e.g. Butefish, 1990; Calderhead, 1981; Fox-Turnbull, 2009; O'Brien, 1993; Peterson & Clark, 1978). This is achieved by encouraging subjects to comment in a subsequent interview on what was happening at the time an event occurred, using prompts or stimuli connected to the incident as support. As Gass and Mackey (2000) have illustrated in their extensive overview of the approach, this method of data collection has recently been gaining increasing prominence within the field of second language education. While much of this previous research has focused on teachers' decision-making (e.g. Johnson, 1992; Nunan, 1991; Woods, 1989), stimulated recall has also been employed effectively in studies focusing on a variety of language learning topics, including for example, vocabulary acquisition (e.g. Paribakht & Wesche, 1999), written composition (e.g. Bosher, 1998), and interlanguage pragmatics (e.g. Robinson, 1992). More relevant to my own investigation into Japanese language learner silence are those studies which concentrate on oral interaction, and I shall now consider a number of these investigations in more depth.

It is no exaggeration to say that studies using stimulated recall which have silence at the heart of their focus are few and far between in the literature. One rare example is Nakane's (2007) investigation into silence in intercultural communication. Employing a mixed methods research approach that included a retrospective interview component, Nakane's conversation analysis-based study included three case studies of Japanese sojourners studying on mainstream university courses in Australia. After ethnographic observations of the three learners' classroom turn-taking performances, Nakane made use of video-supported stimulated recall interviews to explore how the learners themselves, their co-learners and lecturers perceived the Japanese students' silent behaviour. Although lacking detailed discussion on the procedural aspects of the recalls she carried out, Nakane's findings are nevertheless strongly triangulated by the multiple data sources from which she collected her evidence. One key finding, in what was a wide-ranging study, was that silence poses significant problems for Japanese students studying abroad in English-speaking countries, particularly as there appears to be a mismatch in how silence is used and perceived by participants within intercultural classroom contexts.

Another quite different study investigating Japanese learners' L2 oral interactions can be seen in Sato (2007). He employed a stimulated recall methodology to examine how eight first year university students modified their oral output differently depending on whether they were interacting with a peer or one of four native speakers (NS) of English. This quasi-experimental study found that self-initiated modified output was greater in learner-learner dyads when compared to learner-NS dyads. In addition, learner participants tended to feign understanding (see also Ellis, Tanaka & Yamazaki, 1994) and engaged in less negotiation of meaning when speaking to non-Japanese partners. Sato also explored the connection between social relationships and interactional moves by examining learners' perceptions of their interlocutors and the effect this had on the number of repetitions they produced. Interestingly, some of Sato's retrospective data suggest that repetitions were significantly higher amongst learner-NS dyads partly because learners wanted to show verbally that they were listening to their partner's talk and thought that to have remained silent might have appeared excessively rude.

Mackey has been involved in a number of retrospective studies focusing on language learners' oral interactions (e.g. Mackey, Gass & McDonough, 2000; Mackey, 2006). Building upon the notion that interaction facilitates second language acquisition, Mackey's (2002) study used a stimulated recall methodology to examine 46 language learners' perceptions of conversational interactions taking place in classroom and dyadic settings. Supported by a detailed description of research procedures, the investigation discovered a significant overlap between learners' insights and researchers' previous claims (e.g. Gass, 1997) about the benefits of L2 conversational interaction. For example, a common pattern in the data was that learners perceived interaction as providing an opportunity to negotiate meaning with interlocutors and make input more comprehensible at the point when there is a communicative need for that input (Mackey, 2002, p. 387). While underlining the benefits of oral interaction for L2 learners, studies in the vein of Mackey's serve to emphasise how excessive silence and non-participation in spoken tasks may have a negative influence on a language learner's L2 development.

Using a psycholinguistic conceptual framework based on Levelt's (1989, 1993, 1995) model of speech production, Dörnyei and Kormos's (1998) study employed a stimulated recall approach to investigate how speakers manage problems in L2 communication. Forty-four Hungarian learners of English were audio-recorded performing three communicative tasks. The recordings were played back to each participant and, after listening to their own elicited speech, they were asked to comment on the communication difficulties they had encountered. The four main sources of communication problems were: resource deficits, processing time pressure, perceived deficiencies in output, and perceived deficiencies in the interlocutor's performance. Dörnyei and Kormos identify the use of micro-level silences in the form of nonlexicalised, unfilled pauses as one of a range of communication strategies which help manage processing time pressure. Even so, they point out that L2 speakers are aware of 'the need to avoid lengthy silences, which can terminate the conversation or deter the interlocutor' (Dörnyei & Kormos, 1998, p. 368) and present various other stalling mechanisms (e.g. the use of fillers or repetition) that allow for extended cognitive processing time.

In the current study I use dynamic systems theory (DST) as a primary analytical framework because this conceptual approach recognises the true complexity of events which occur in language classrooms and acknowledges that learner behaviour may be influenced by multiple, concurrent variables (termed *attractors* in DST) whose influence may shift over time (see de Bot & Larsen-Freeman, 2011; Dörnyei, 2009; N. C. Ellis, 2007; Larsen-Freeman & Cameron, 2008; van Geert 2008). MacIntyre and Legatto (2011) also utilised a DST approach in their idiodynamic-based stimulated recall study of 'willingness to communicate' (WTC). Six female Canadian learners of French were asked to perform eight L2 communicative tasks adapted from MacIntyre, Babin and Clément's (1999) work on L1 WTC. The participants used special software to continuously rate their WTC while watching video recordings of their performance during the tasks. They were then shown the video again and, with the aid of a graph detailing their self-ratings, asked to describe why changes in WTC occurred at particular points. MacIntyre and Legatto found that in their sample, WTC was an interconnected dynamic phenomenon affected by a range of factors, including the process of retrieving vocabulary from memory and the presence of language anxiety. The researchers posit that WTC is produced by interconnected linguistic, social, cognitive and emotional systems:

> When the systems function together to facilitate communication, we see WTC as an attractor state. When the systems interfere with each other, such as when vocabulary items are absent or a threat to self-esteem is detected, we see a repeller state where communication is abandoned (MacIntyre & Legatto, 2011, p. 169).

While MacIntyre and Legatto's innovative research provides a useful conceptual background for my own investigation into language learner silence, the two studies do differ significantly in character. As is now clear, the stimulated recall phase of my project makes up just one source of data within a much wider, mixed-methods investigation. In addition to establishing the actual existence of classroom silence in Japan's universities, the observation phase of the research has also proved crucial in providing key qualitative data to complement learners' retrospective accounts of their silences, thereby providing insights that would not be possible by examining spoken retrospective interview data alone. Furthermore, the stimulated recall data presented in this chapter are based on interactions within naturalistic classroom settings (see Lyle, 2003), and is therefore quite different to MacIntyre and Legatto's more controlled, laboratory-based approach which they liken to 'an oral exam's question-and-answer format' (2011, p. 168).

The above select overview of retrospective studies only hints at the great variety of ways in which research employing this methodological paradigm may be carried out. A stimulated recall approach is a far from unproblematic method of data collection (for a comprehensive overview of the method's limitations and pitfalls, see Gass & Mackey, 2000) and researchers who utilise it are faced with a number of procedural decisions likely to prove crucial if they are to gain reliable and valid data for their projects. Consequently, a detailed description of research procedures is vital in order to ensure confidence in the quality of any data yielded. The following section therefore provides a purposely detailed account of the stimulated recall research procedures I employed, in an attempt to make sense of individual learners' silent behaviour in Japanese university language classrooms.

7.2 Data collection

A series of seven stimulated recalls were undertaken in order to explore learners' perceptions of specific silence events which they either produced or directly experienced during lessons forming part of the observation phase of this study. This introspective method of data collection proved to be a fruitful way of uncovering students' thoughts and feelings about silence at the micro-level of classroom interaction, particularly as silence is a phenomenon which is heavily context-dependent and often requires a high degree of inference to gauge its meaning (Jaworski, 1993). In order to better reflect the variety of tertiary institutions which exist in Japan, data were collected at three sites: a small municipal university specialising in fine arts, a medium-sized, middle-ranking provincial university known for its economics and pharmacy courses, and a large, urban university specialising in foreign languages.

Participants

Unlike the semi-structured interview phase of the research, it was not possible to choose participants for stimulated recalls based on prior staff/student recommendations. Instead, I approached learners whose individual modality had been tracked over the course of three classroom observations. All of these students had been observed to remain silent in specific situations when talk was expected of them during their language classes; for example, during whole-class drilling exercises, small-group speaking activities, in response to teachers' questions, and so on. Although this approach guaranteed recalls could be conducted with learners who had actually been silent, it did also run the risk of singling out reticent, inarticulate participants who may have been lacking in perception. Of course, this is one of the major challenges facing silence researchers: how do you get people to talk about not talking, especially when silence tends to operate at a semi-conscious or unconscious level? A range of measures were therefore put in place to diminish the possibility of participant non-responsiveness during retrospective interviews. The measures were effective and in the end I was able to gain usable data from five of the study's participants, whose details are set out in the table below (all names are pseudonyms).

Table 3 Participant details for stimulated recall study

	Gender	Year	Uni	Major	Class name/type	No. of students in class
Nao	F	1	X	Pharmacy	English Conversation (c)	16
Yuri	F	1	Y	English	Intensive Academic English	24
Jiro	M	2	X	Sports Science	General English (c)	52
Miho	F	1	Z	Art	General English (c)	26
Tamaki	F	1	Y	English	Intensive Academic English	20

Uni – university; c – class is compulsory component of student's course

These participants, who were all in their late teens or early twenties, nicely reflect the broad range of student experience on offer within the language classrooms of Japanese universities. At one end of the spectrum are reasonably proficient language majors like Yuri and Tamaki who benefit from at least 24 hours of contact time per week in classes limited to a maximum of 25 students, while at the other end of the scale, non-language majors, such as Jiro, can expect only 90 minutes of foreign language education in a week, often provided in lecture-style sessions containing over 50 learners. All the students in the study had received the six years of pre-tertiary English language education that is compulsory upon entering Japan's junior high schools from the age of 11.

Classroom observations

Each participant's class was observed on three separate occasions, with silent episodes occurring during the final observation forming the main basis of subsequent recalls. This multiple-observation approach had the twin benefits of enhancing the reliability of any observational data collected, whilst at the same time reducing reactivity amongst students (see Allwright & Bailey, 1991) as my presence became a familiar aspect of the language lessons. Using the COPS scheme, I was able to successfully code classroom events on a minute-by-minute basis to form a chronological representation of the oral participation which occurred in each lesson. The simplicity of the COPS design allowed me to use completed coded sheets as an effective stimulus for the subsequent recall sessions. This was in addition to the use of recorded audio sequences of classroom events as a further prompt. As silence and reticence tend to be deemed negative phenomena in classrooms (c.f. Li, 2001; Reda, 2009), students were informed I was conducting research into language learner interaction rather than focusing specifically on silence. The above measures, coupled with my non-intrusive seating position and careful avoidance of any interaction with the learners I was observing, meant that participants were able to arrive at their stimulated recall sessions in a position to provide unbiased accounts of natural classroom behaviour involving targeted silent episodes.

Developing rapport with informants

In any research interview situation, it is vital that subjects are put at ease and some sort of rapport is established so that a non-threatening atmosphere is created in which the interviewees feel comfortable enough to express themselves freely. Unlike the semi-structured interview phase of the project, it was not possible to facilitate this by conducting informal pre-interview meetings with participants because of the need to undertake stimulated recalls relatively quickly after classroom events had occurred. I therefore had to be careful to ensure rapport was built and students were put at their ease within the short space of time between the end of their observed lesson and the commencement of recall activities. This was not a wholly straightforward task when one considers that many Japanese people, especially outside of the large urban centres, lack intercultural communication experience and, in the words of Kowner (2002, p. 339), 'perceive communication with non-Japanese as an embarrassing and unpleasant, if not frightening experience'. With this is mind, the presence of a female Japanese research assistant proved vital in helping me to facilitate a friendly and non-threatening atmosphere in which recalls could be carried out successfully.

The timing of the retrospective interviews

The timing of stimulated recalls is crucial to maintaining the validity of retrospective data. A long delay between the task and the recall session makes interference more likely, as participants are forced to retrieve from long-term memory, thus increasing the possibility of them saying merely what they think the researcher wants to hear (Gass & Mackey, 2000; Mackey & Gass, 2005). In order to avoid memory decay and to maintain the validity of the retrospective data collected, all stimulated recall sessions in the study were conducted in line with Dörnyei's (2007) recommendation that a time lapse of less than 24 hours between event and recall is preferable (for a further enlightening discussion on how timing affects the veridicality of verbal protocols, see Ericsson & Simon, 1993).

The language of the retrospective interviews

In addition to consent forms and procedural explanations being provided in Japanese, the recall sessions themselves were also conducted primarily in the participants' first language. As Gass and Mackey (2000) rightly point out, learners of limited L2 proficiency may not only misunderstand the instructions and questions of the researcher; there also exists the possibility that these learners will only verbalise what they *can* during recalls, instead of providing a full account of their cognitive processes. The problem of limited verbalisation is exacerbated when the focus of the research is on something as intangible as the participant's silence; an aspect of classroom behaviour he/she is likely to have never even considered before. Although conducting recalls in the L1 should not be considered a panacea to the limitations of this type of research – some students did still experience difficulties in producing a verbal account of their silent behaviour – the use of L1 certainly helped subjects to make incursions into their implicit knowledge more easily, and enabled them to externalise any thoughts and feelings discovered there much better. With the participants' consent, each recall session was audio-recorded and subsequently transcribed directly into the L1 before being translated into English. Sections of the data were then back-translated (see Brislin, 1970) into the source language so as to ensure the reliability of the original translation.

Silence as a sensitive topic

A language student's silent classroom behaviour, particularly when it is characterised by non-responsiveness and the intentional avoidance of talk, can be a potentially sensitive topic. Unless attention is paid to setting the scene of the interview (see Cohen, Manion & Morrison, 2007) – during which, for example, participants are reassured the procedure is not some kind of test and there are no correct or incorrect responses – it may be difficult to gain the full cooperation of recall interviewees as they may be reluctant to discuss their silences in an honest and open manner. Great care was taken in the initial stages of recall sessions to also reassure participants of their anonymity and the confidentiality of their answers. In each encounter it was made clear that the researchers held no official affiliation with the institution where the research was being conducted and, in an effort to address status and power dynamics, that they should not be considered to be figures of authority in any way. In a further attempt to encourage honest, accurate accounts of silence incidents from the students' own perspectives, participants were asked to avoid *tatamae* answers during recall sessions. Relating to one's socially tuned, publicly stated opinion rather than one's true, innermost feelings, *tatamae* (see Barnlund, 1974; Gudykunst & Nishida, 1993; Hendry, 1989; Lebra, 1976) was specifically referred to in the research protocol because it is a Japanese cultural concept which participants could readily understand and relate to.

Procedures within the retrospective interviews

During the retrospective interviews learners were shown completed observation coding sheets and were played audio recordings of specific classroom episodes involving silences in order to access their concurrent interpretations of events. The recordings helped to provide context around which silence incidents occurred, for example, by allowing a learner to listen again to the teacher's question which he/she did not respond to, or to be reminded of a whole-class choral drill in which he/she failed to participate. Even so, the immediacy of the stimulated recall after the task, coupled to the use of a chronologically ordered observation coding sheet acting as a strong stimulus, meant that a number of participants were able to clearly remember targeted incidents even before an audio recording was played to them. Following Gass and Mackey (2000), learners were asked to remember what they were thinking and feeling *at the time* the silence occurred, rather than provide comments on their thoughts about the episode now (i.e. in the recall session) with the benefit of hindsight. Even so, the focus of the interviews was not exclusively cognitive in orientation and learners were able to provide other interesting insights about, for example, their impressions of the teaching methodology employed in their language classrooms. We, as researchers, were careful to adopt the role of relatively passive listeners during participants' responses and were mindful of asking leading or biased questions. Instead of peppering interviewees with a string of questions, we employed extensive use of silence and echo probing in order to provide enough space for learners to retrieve and verbalise valid, if not always particularly eloquent, retrospective accounts of their silent classroom behaviour.

7.3 Results and discussion

Nao: 'I'm not interested. I'm not listening to the class'

Nao, a first year non-language major studying pharmacy at a large provincial university in the west of Japan, was consistently silent and unresponsive throughout the small-sized (comprising less than 20 students) English conversation classes I observed her attend. Over the course of three structured observations, Nao never once initiated discourse within the class, nor did she verbally respond to any of her teacher's questions or prompts. Her silent behaviour was profound and in the third and final observed lesson, which acted as the arena for the subsequent stimulated recall session, Nao was observed to avoid speech even during the relative anonymity of whole-class choral drills, when learners' L2 oral production moves out of the public and into the private sphere. These drills formed the tasks which were subsequently recalled during a retrospective interview conducted immediately after the lesson had ended.

The first point to make about Nao's recall session is that it provided me with the somewhat ironic task of having to encourage an inarticulate, reticent learner to provide a verbal account of her silent classroom behaviour. Even so, as Nao spoke entirely in Japanese throughout the recall session, the procedure did allow me to observe at first hand her lack of verbal expressiveness when communicating in her own language. After being asked to describe what she had been thinking whilst she remained silent during a whole-class speaking drill in which learners were required to repeat phrases from a shopping dialogue modelled by their instructor, Nao indicated she was able to recall the episode and made the following response:

> Eh (4.5) we:ll (7) mm (hhh) (3.5) ((sniffs)) (14.5) (hh) (6) er::m (10) (hhh) °I don't know° (30) no, say something- (7.5) say- (13) ((laughs slightly)) (6) I didn't consider replying (3) something. (3) Well (1.5) er:m (2) Perhaps, I always don't say anything. Come to think of it, I remember. (1.5) About- (9.5) hm (8) eh? I don't- I don't know.

Although from a cognitive perspective, this extract provides us with little useful data about Nao's concurrent thought processes during the episode of classroom silence in question, the 130.5 seconds of silence contained within this short passage do provide an indicative example of Nao extensively using silence in a communicative situation and, related to this, her lack of ability in expressing herself verbally in her own language. There is a strong argument to be made that Nao's inarticulateness in the L1 transfers directly to her L2 performance, thereby contributing to her limited oral production in language classes. Interestingly, throughout the above exchange, the participant was observed to remain perfectly at ease and displayed no outward signs of embarrassment or discomfort during her silences, apart from a single brief laugh after the 13 second pause. This behaviour points towards a learner who is both accepting of silence and one who treats the absence of talk as a relatively unmarked phenomenon (see Sobkowiak, 1997).

Further data from Nao's recall session revealed that deep feelings of apathy and a lack of engagement with the subject were major additional factors contributing to her avoidance of talk during the lesson. Speaking about her thoughts during one of the lesson's choral drills, she revealed:

I didn't feel anything special about everybody else speaking. (3) I didn't think anything. (5.5) I don't think but (22) I wasn't like- I couldn't be bothered to do it sort of thing. ((laughs slightly))

Nao's failure to orally participate in the lesson's choral drill appears, then, to emerge partly from her disengagement from a language learning process in which she is not prepared to invest much effort. Her silence was, to a degree, born from her inattention and she freely admitted that, 'I'm not interested. I'm not listening to the class.' Nao may have been physically present in the lesson, but cognitively speaking, she was somewhere else. Rather than performing some form of cognitive or interactive function (for more on the relationship between silence and communication, see e.g. Bruneau, 1973; Jaworski, 1993), her silence during the choral drill was inactive and without communicative meaning. Indeed, when asked to describe what she was thinking during a subsequent activity in which she also failed to participate, Nao freely acknowledged her thoughts were:

'Now is the chance to sleep', °kind of thing° (hhh) ((very slightly laughs)) while the teacher was talking, we:ll (7) it'll probably be alright.

Such an attitude is supported by Japan's education system which, while placing great emphasis on attendance, appears less concerned with what learners actually do whilst the lesson is in progress and, consequently, is highly tolerant towards sleeping in class (see Steger, 2006). Indeed, I recorded in my research notes one conversation with a senior Japanese professor who informed me (not entirely in jest) that he was quite content for students to sleep while he taught them because slumbering learners tended to cause him fewer classroom management problems than the conscious ones! The issue of sleeping aside, although various concurrent factors would have acted to contribute to Nao's silent disengagement, her instructor's use of a highly structured teaching methodology would certainly not have helped to stimulate her interest. With a rigid emphasis on lexical and grammatical accuracy, all L2 discourse within Nao's class was tightly controlled by the instructor, with students allowed very little freedom of expression. It is perhaps therefore unsurprising that, in addition to Nao, significant number of learners were observed to be off-task and not orally participating over the course of the observation period.

Looking at Nao's silence during the targeted choral drill from a DST perspective, as the above discussion shows, it was certainly not the result of just one factor. Rather, it emerged because of multiple, interrelated silence attractors present both within Nao herself, and also within the immediate classroom environment around her. Her silent behaviour was shaped not only by learner-internal aspects such as her lack of oral expressiveness, apathy towards the task, and general lack of interest in learning a foreign language. It was also influenced concurrently by external agents, such as her instructor's approach to teaching and his strict control over classroom discourse. All of these elements worked together within an interconnected dynamic system to produce a relatively stable attractor state of silence within Nao's classroom discourse system, meaning she rarely spoke whilst lessons were in progress.

Yuri: 'I thought I'd better behave myself'

An English-major in her first year of study at a large, foreign languages-orientated university, at the time of data collection Yuri was a member of the university's intensive English programme. This two-year module consists of a minimum of 24 classroom contact hours per week, ostensibly in an English-only environment, and aims to help prepare students for potential study abroad placements. The programme is streamed and even though the class I observed Yuri participate in was one of the lower-ranked groups (sixth out of eight), its learners could still be considered to have above-average foreign language skills when compared to Japan's general undergraduate population. Entry onto the programme had ensured that Yuri and her peers were regularly exposed to a wide range of communicative language learning activities, and that discussion and other oral activities played a key role in their L2 development.

The silence which formed the basis for Yuri's stimulated recall occurred during one such speaking activity. The 24 students in her class were invited by their non-Japanese instructor to form small groups of four members in order to discuss a text they had read earlier focusing on physical appearance, a topic easily accessible to them. To help direct the exchange, the teacher provided three discussion questions on the board and afterwards slowly moved around the room monitoring each group of learners, occasionally joining in with discussions but not taking a dominant role in groups' exchanges. Two minutes into the activity, I observed that when the teacher approached Yuri's group (made up of two male and two female students), they immediately ceased talking and remained silent until the instructor moved away again a short time later.

Later in her stimulated recall session, Yuri provided an ingenuous account of her classroom behaviour during the class. When questioned about what she had been thinking at the time the silent episode described above occurred, she recalled:

> I thought 'Oops!' Because we were talking about something else ((spoken while slightly laughing)) if he'd heard what we were talking about, we would've been in trouble, (·hhh) yeah. It doesn't mean I behaved badly in the class but we drifted onto a different topic so ((sniffs)) we went quiet because we all realised that we were talking about something else. ((sniffs))

Although Yuri and her group had been conducting their discussion primarily in English, she was concerned that their off-topic talk would displease the teacher and stated that when he arrived, 'I thought I'd better behave myself'. This is interesting as her instructor, who has many years of experience teaching in Japan's tertiary sector, was the antithesis of what could be called a disciplinarian and conducted his lessons in an approachable, easy-going manner throughout the three sessions I observed. It was therefore highly unlikely the group would have been reproached for straying off-topic during their L2 discussion. This begs the question, what lay behind Yuri's avoidance of relevant talk during this particular classroom event?

We can better understand how her silence emerged if we remember there exists a significant relationship between power disparities and a person's silent behaviour (see Braithwaite, 1990; Saville-Troike, 1985), and correspondingly, as Carlsen (1991) rightly notes, classroom interaction tends to reflect status inequalities and the differences in authority which exist between teachers and their students. The silence that emerged in this particular incident presents a prime example of this phenomenon, with Yuri and her peers employing silence in an attempt to negotiate what they perceived to be a potentially face-threatening encounter with a person deemed to have superior status. Yuri's behaviour was supported at a societal level by Japan's particularistic orientation towards social relationships which reinforces power disparities and results in a well-defined superior–subordinate environment (see Nakane, 1988) in which juniors tend to assume a silent, passive role in the presence of seniors (McDaniel, 2003; c.f. Kurzon, 1992). We may therefore consider Yuri's silence, manifested in the form of her intentional avoidance of talk, to have been an effective defensive strategy that ultimately saw the instructor retreat from the group and for their L2 talk to resume once more.

Viewed from a complexity perspective, this silence incident during small-group work provides us with a clear example of the dynamic nature of one language learner's silent behaviour. DST posits that systems are self-organising and even seemingly fossilised systems are capable of change (de Bot, Lowie & Verspoor, 2007; Larsen-Freeman & Cameron, 2008). In the case of Yuri, her classroom talk system, supported by social and cultural elements encouraging silent behaviour, entered into a silence attractor state when the instructor approached to monitor the group during their L2 discussion. The fact that her silence did not persist once the instructor had walked away, illustrates that Yuri's silent behaviour was not a static phenomenon and that fluctuating variables encouraged on-the-fly change within her classroom talk system.

Jiro: 'I was thinking something else'

At the time of his retrospective interview, Jiro was a second year sports science student studying English once a week at a medium-sized, provincial university in the west of Japan. This language class formed a compulsory component of Jiro's course and the lessons he attended contained over 50 students, all of whom were male. A member of his university's baseball team, Jiro came across as an intelligent and confident young man whose interests clearly did not lie in the field of foreign language education. Despite this, his record of attendance at the English class was generally good and he did display reasonably proficient receptive L2 skills in comparison to some of his classmates.

During the final session that I observed of his class, Jiro remained silent throughout a choral exercise in which the instructor read aloud a dialogue in English and invited the whole class to repeat after him the various phrases contained within. The dialogue focused on the functional language of how to first reserve and then check into a hotel room. Jiro failed to orally participate for the entire duration of the task, which lasted around nine minutes. He was not alone in his avoidance of talk; the majority of learners in the class remained silent during the exercise and those that did participate did so with such a lack of enthusiasm and expression that I recorded in my research notes their efforts produced what could best be described as 'a terrible murmur of voices'.

In the stimulated recall session, after being shown the relevant section of the observation coding sheet and having listened to a recording of the task, Jiro was quickly able to remember that he had indeed not orally participated in the choral drill task. When I asked him what he had been thinking and feeling during this specific episode of classroom silence, he replied:

> (·hhh) You know, it's like ((clears throat)) er:m always the same lesson so ((spoken while slightly laughing)) all I need to do really is study before the exam and er (...) mmm well I couldn't be bothered. ((spoken while slightly laughing)) That was one thing and (..) (·hhh) er I was thinking something else like it'll soon be break time so I'll be able to take it easy – totally different stuff to the class. ((spoken while slightly laughing))

Jiro's reference to only needing to study for the exam is unsurprising, coming as it does from a learner who is a product of an education system which McVeigh (2006) terms Japan's 'examocracy'. The important thing for Jiro is merely to pass the end-of-term exam and gain a credit for the course. He therefore had very little to lose by not participating in the drill as he was indifferent to improving his L2 speaking ability. He knew his oral performance was not being assessed during the activity, and that neither would it be subsequently in any examination.

This learner's silent behaviour appears, then, to be very similar to that of Nao, whose disengagement and apathy were strong factors in the emergence of her classroom silence. Jiro used the same phrase as Nao, *mendōkusai* – meaning 'I couldn't be bothered', when he described how he felt during the targeted exercise, and his admission that he was thinking about something completely disconnected to the L2 task in hand illustrates a fairly typical silence attractor which emerges in large-sized Japanese university language classes whose learners have not chosen to be there. However, it is the context of Jiro's silence that differs from Nao's which I would now like to examine in more depth.

Always surrounded by teammates from his sports club, Jiro was part of a clearly defined sub-group within the classroom. Whilst lessons were in progress I observed there to be little integration and no interaction between members of this sports science class's various sporting cliques, and in his retrospective interview Jiro underlined this lack of assimilation when he explained, 'Football club members, they sit at the back and baseball club members, we sit in the front.' Following Sifianou's (1997) work on silence and politeness, we could interpret Jiro's silent behaviour during the targeted choral drill as representing a positive politeness strategy in which his avoidance of talk contributed towards a feeling of solidarity with similarly silent in-group members. Certainly, Jiro considered his actions in the class to be within the public domain and therefore open to the scrutiny of fellow group members whose close physical proximity to each other meant that any L2 oral contributions could be easily heard. Jiro himself made a distinction between his lack of volubility in public situations such as in a classroom, compared to his private talk:

> But in my case ((clears throat)) in the class, I don't usually- I mean I talk a lot in private life but when it comes to the class, I tend to fall into a long silence or think about something else...

Such comments again support the concept that we should not consider a person's silent behaviour to be a static phenomenon, but rather it is dynamic and highly dependent upon the here-and-now of contextual factors. From a DST perspective, we could say that Jiro's silence had been *softly assembled* (Thelan & Smith, 1994), in that it was a non-permanent, adaptive action produced in response to the task in hand and the various contextual influences that were concurrently in play at the time.

When I asked what those in his group would have thought of him if he had actively participated in the choral drill, Jiro's response was, 'maybe my friends would probably think I'm odd- odd.' Indeed, over the course of my three observations of his class, on the rare occasions that members of Jiro's clique did participate in choral drilling, they did so only very briefly and in a theatrical, almost mocking manner – much to the amusement of those around them. Along with Jiro's comments, such performances suggests that active oral participation had come to represent out-of-the-ordinary behaviour for these learners and that their classroom silence had emerged as a predictable, consensual norm within the development of the group's classroom L2 talk.

Miho: 'I understood only the name "Shakespeare"'

At the time of her stimulated recall session, Miho, a first year fine arts student at a small municipal university located in a rural area of Japan's main island of Honshu, was studying English for 90 minutes a week in a compulsory class comprising over 25 learners. The non-Japanese instructor of the class rated Miho's cohort as having an L2 proficiency level slightly above average in comparison to undergraduates he had taught at other universities in the area. He ascribed this to the fact that places at Miho's university were highly sought after amongst local high school students attracted by the reduced tuition fees charged by a public institution. Despite this assessment of his learners' L2 abilities, I observed Miho to communicate only once in the target language over the course of the three observation sessions I conducted with her class, and in the final session she remained persistently silent throughout.

It was Miho's silent responses to her instructor's various questions and prompts that I wished to explore in more depth during the stimulated recall interview which followed immediately after the concluding observation session. On a number of occasions during the lesson, the teacher, speaking in the target language, either attempted to elicit verbal answers to short written exercises the students had performed, or tried to interact with the group by posing open-class questions related to various topics which arose as the lesson content progressed. In one particular incident, the class was asked what William Shakespeare was famous for. Miho, who up until this point had had her eyes lowered, staring at the textbook open on the desk in front of her, suddenly looked up at the teacher as he spoke but did not attempt to make a verbal response. In her retrospective interview, after being shown the relevant observation coding sheet and listening to an audio recording of the incident, Miho quickly recalled what had happened, explaining:

> At that point, I understood only the name 'Shakespeare' and er a little- I also knew only some titles of his works.

Clearly then, rather than having understood the teacher's L2 utterance in its entirety, Miho had only been able to recognise and process just one word: 'Shakespeare'. Although her recognition of the bard's name momentarily ignited an interest in the teacher's discourse, which was displayed physically by a change in gaze direction and body posture, her inability to comprehend the instructor's whole message proved to be a major contributory factor in her silent non-responsiveness. But attributing Miho's silence to a deficiency in her L2 aural skills does not tell the whole story. As DST emphasises that multiple concurrent variables may influence one's classroom behaviour at any one time, rather than focusing on the learner in isolation, it would be germane to also consider how the actions of those others present during the interaction contributed to the production of Miho's silence. With this in mind, let us now examine how Miho's instructor played a key role in attracting her silent behaviour.

The first point to make is that discourse in Miho's class was almost completely dominated by her teacher. That he was responsible for the majority of classroom talk is not particularly remarkable, given the instructor's institutional status and his power in determining topics and accessibility to the floor. But the extent to which he monopolised talk was surprising. During the lesson which provided the focus for Miho's stimulated recall session, data from the COPS reveals that the teacher was responsible for an incredible 96 per cent of all talk, with there being no recorded instances at all of students initiating discourse in the target language. Other studies focusing on interaction in foreign language classrooms (e.g. Tsui, 1985) have also pointed to an acute imbalance in the distribution of classroom talk between educators and learners, but not to the extent found in the current study. This excessive teacher talking time (TTT) appears to have led to the divergent process of what Tannen (1981), drawing on Bateson, calls 'complementary schismogenesis', whereby the more the teacher talks, the more silent students become, and the more silent students become, the more the teacher talks.

Furthermore, it appears Miho's instructor may have over-estimated the students' abilities to comprehend his English. This contributed to a failure in sufficiently modifying his language, for example, by slowing the pace of delivery or by producing less grammatically/syntactically complex sentences (see Walsh, 2002), with the result being a wall of incomprehensible input for Miho. As Allwright and Bailey (1991) rightly note, it is notoriously difficult to assess learners' levels of cognitive involvement during tasks and this is particularly true when the activity involves listening. Even so, in her stimulated recall interview, Miho estimated she had been able to understand only about 30 to 40 per cent of the teacher's talk, before quickly adding she thought this estimation was perhaps a little high. The instructor's incomprehensible L2 input was further exacerbated by his tendency either to pause only very briefly or not to pause at all after posing a question or inviting a comment, with the effect that general solicits to the class were liable to blend in to a kind of 'white noise' of teacher talk. Various researchers (e.g. Rowe, 1986; Shrum, 1984; Tobin, 1987) have highlighted the benefits of educators extending their silent wait-time after solicits as a way of combating student nonresponsiveness. Extended pauses allow students space for cognitive processing during which they can deal with input and formulate appropriate responses in the target language. From a DST perspective, a change in her teacher's wait-time behaviour could help shift Miho's classroom discourse system out of its silence attractor state and towards a different trajectory.

Tamaki: 'It's kind of my role to be the listener'

Tamaki was the most highly proficient learner to take part in the study. A first year undergraduate studying at the same foreign languages-orientated university as Yuri (discussed above), Tamaki had gained entry into her year's most advanced English class after scoring very highly on the university's institutional TOEFL test. Her class included some learners who possessed near native-like L2 skills, with a number being *kikokushijo* (returnees) (see Kanno, 2003) who had completed the majority of their secondary education abroad. While perhaps not quite up to this level of proficiency, Tamaki nevertheless possessed language skills of a standard high enough to make it unlikely that any episodes of classroom silence on her part would be down to a lack of L2 ability. There is an understandable tendency for language learner silence to be viewed purely as an issue related to deficiencies in ability in the target language, but Tamaki's case helps illustrate that the reality of events at the classroom level is not always as straightforward as this and that language learner silence is indeed a complex phenomenon.

The specific incident discussed here which saw Tamaki refrain from talk at a time when talk was reasonably expected of her occurred during an English language content lesson focusing on the topic of art. Following an engaging slide presentation entitled 'What is art?' by Tamaki's instructor, the class divided into groups of four in order to discuss a questionnaire related to this subject which they had completed earlier. This small-group oral exercise lasted for approximately five minutes and saw Tamaki remain silent for the majority of the discussion. When I later questioned her about the incident in the subsequent stimulated recall session, Tamaki explained she had had little to contribute to the discussion because her opinions had not differed greatly from those of the other group members. She went on to reveal that she had been more interested in hearing what the other members had to say, with the implication being that her own similar-sounding answers might have been of little consequence to the rest of the group. This suggests a lack confidence more in the content rather than in the L2 form of any potential utterance and is perhaps a little surprising, coming as it did from a student raised in a society which places such a high value on the building of consensus. Indeed, citing a sociocultural background which stresses the importance of group-mindedness and harmony, Anderson (1993) goes as far to say that Japanese learners who express original ideas and initiate discussion tend to be viewed as social misfits by their peers and, consequently, this type of behaviour is not usually expected in language classrooms. Even so, the L2 ability of Tamaki's class, combined with their past educational and international experiences, meant that they were much more adaptable to the cut and thrust of debate and discussion in English than the average Japanese undergraduates to which Anderson refers. Despite this, Tamaki still remained orally passive during the targeted discussion task and so it is to yet another concurrent variable that emerged during her stimulated recall session that we will now turn our attention in order to better understand the roots of her silent behaviour.

Tamaki described how, even though she did have a desire to talk, she always seemed to end up as the listener during classroom tasks. When asked why this was, she replied:

> Well it's been like that since the beginning- from the off. By the time I realised, I'd already become like a listener. When I want to speak, I do but mmm it's kind of my role to be the listener. I could be wrong but I'm maybe under the impression that it's my role so I've become someone who doesn't initiate speaking much.

From this extract we can see that Tamaki's self-concept in relation to her co-participants appears to act as an important agent influencing her interactional behaviour during oral tasks. She sees herself more as an orally passive listener rather than as an initiator of interaction in classroom situations. This insight reflects the fact that identity construction (see Benwell & Stokoe, 2006; Edwards, 2009; Morita, 2012) can be a useful avenue of inquiry for the DST silence researcher wishing to trace back the multiple routes of individual learners' classroom silences. Recently, applied linguists such as Richards (2006) in relation to classroom talk and Ushioda (2009) writing about language learner motivation, have found Zimmerman's (1998) model of social and discoursal identity to be a helpful analytical framework for exploring interaction-relevant identity. Explained briefly, this framework includes three aspects of identity: 'discourse identity' which dynamically shifts on a moment-by-moment basis so that within the course of an interaction a person may take on the role of questioner, listener, initiator, and so on; 'situated identity' relating to the specific context of an interaction and which would include participants orientating themselves towards the roles of, for example, teacher or student within a classroom situation; and finally, latent 'transportable identity' based on physical or cultural insignia that ' "tag along" with individuals as they move through their daily routines' (Zimmerman, 1998, p. 90). The interesting point about Tamaki's performance during the discussion task in question relates to Zimmerman's idea of a dynamic discourse identity. Throughout the activity, although Tamaki remained engaged and displayed supportive non-verbal responses to her co-participants' talk, her discourse identity patently did not shift as the interaction progressed and remained steadfastly fixed in the role of listener. This empirical observation of Tamaki's performance during the 'What is art?' discussion, in tandem with her spoken data gained from the subsequent retrospective interview, seems to suggest that Tamaki's L2 classroom talk system has settled into a stable attractor state of silence, and that a repeated orientation towards a listener discourse identity during L2 tasks seems to be a major factor amongst the multiple, concurrent agents supporting her silent behaviour.

7.4 Conclusion

By employing a stimulated recall methodology, backed up by empirical qualitative data garnered from relevant classroom observations, this phase of the research has been able to explore event-specific examples of Japanese university language learner silence. Such an approach has allowed for a fine-grained analysis of individual episodes of classroom silence, thereby providing insights into why students refrained from talk in certain situations and what they were thinking or feeling whilst these silent episodes were in progress. The study's series of retrospective interviews resulted not only in cognitive-related data concerning learners' concurrent interpretations of silence events at the micro-level of classroom interaction, but also provided a useful forum in which interviewees were able to voice their perceptions about co-participants, the L2 tasks they encountered, and to express fundamental beliefs about their silent behaviour.

The results of the study point towards the underlying complex nature of language learner silence, highlighting it as a phenomenon which may emerge during any number of L2 oral task activities. The current study focused on five event-specific instances of silence which arose in the following scenarios: during whole-class choral drills; in the course of small-group discussions; and following a teacher's general solicits to the class. Viewed through the prism of dynamic systems theory we can see that single cause–effect explanations for why participants in the study failed to talk in classroom situations where talk was expected of them are not valid, and that in reality multiple, interconnected concurrent variables were at play influencing learners' silent behaviour on a moment-by-moment basis. The diverse set of silence attractors uncovered in the study include learner-internal factors (relating to areas such as L2 processing, identity construction, and affect), in addition to a myriad of external environmental factors (with elements and agents at classroom, institutional and societal levels). Because silence emerges from such a wide range of starting points, and because it is both educationally and culturally supported in Japan, learners in the study appeared to be easily drawn towards what is the seemingly normal behaviour of not speaking in their language classes.

8
Summary and conclusions

This final chapter of the book is divided into three main sections. It begins with a summary of the principal research findings for each phase of the project. As the mixed-methods investigation into Japanese university students' silent behaviour presented here is novel (both in topic and research design terms), I accompany the discussion of the investigation's major findings with a brief recap of some of the methodological challenges I faced when investigating the intangible phenomenon of silence. The subsequent section of the chapter outlines the study's limitations and provides numerous suggestions for future research. Where appropriate, the ideas that I provide for further silence-focused investigations take into account the current project's drawbacks. This part of the chapter also includes discussion centring on potentially fruitful strategies for future DST-orientated research into language learner silence. To end the chapter, I address the study's practical implications and tentatively discuss practical pedagogical strategies which could prove effective in combating learner silence and oral unresponsiveness in the language classroom.

8.1 Summary of research findings

'Training in silence'

Amongst the most notable themes examined in the study's literature review was the idea put forward by researchers such as Clancy (1990), Lebra (1993) and Yamada (1997) that from an early age Japanese children are socialised into patterns of communication which rely heavily on non-vocal, implicit understanding and which eschew direct verbalisation. This 'training in silence', it is suggested, requires a developed sense of empathetic understanding in order to anticipate and gauge meaning from unspoken messages, and hence children are encouraged to perform the silent listener role well within interactions. (It should be noted though that I also discussed in Chapter 3 how the ability to infer meaning is a pragmatic skill not unique to Japanese people and silence during Japanese L1 interactions does still have the potential to be misinterpreted by interlocutors.) Related to the concept that there is a link between silence and empathy is the idea that one's sensitivity to others may become over-developed and thus contribute to inhibition and the avoidance of talk. With this in mind, I examined silence from a socio-psychological perspective, and discussed how a hyper-sensitivity to others and a fear of negative evaluation by peers appear to contribute to Japanese students avoiding talk and using silence as a means of maintaining some form of control when confronted by situations which appear to threaten the self. To better understand such behaviour, we need to remember that silence, under-elaboration and the avoidance of direct speech are themes strongly supported at a sociocultural level in Japan. As the literature review illustrates clearly, a positive valuation of such behaviour is immediately apparent within Japan's proverbs, poetry and literature.

The structured observation study results

The structured observation phase of the study provides a number of intriguing findings concerning oral participation patterns within Japanese university L2 classrooms and hence tells us much about the prevalence of silence within this particular educational context. In order to obtain reliable quantitative data on participants' silent classroom behaviour, I developed a novel low-inference observation scheme called the COPS which used a minute-by-minute, real-time coding strategy. Focusing on the macro-level silences of non-participation and unresponsiveness, the scheme was employed in a multi-site study that included a broad, heterogeneous class sample aptly reflecting the variety of English language education on offer within Japan's tertiary sector. In all, this unique large-scale observation study collected data from 30 different classes situated across nine universities and comprised a student population of 924.

The findings of this phase of the inquiry provide clear evidence of a robust and generalisable national trend towards learner silence within Japan's university L2 classrooms. The reticence and oral passivity of learners within this setting become immediately apparent when we examine data which focused on the incidence of student-initiated talk during lessons. Results from the COPS's whole-class oral participation section reveal what can only be described as a dramatic lack of discourse initiation from students. Indeed, less than a quarter of 1 per cent of lesson time was found to be taken up by learners producing self-selected turns at talk. Over the course of the study's 48 hours of minute-by-minute observation there were a mere seven coded instances of this form of oral production by students. This is in startling comparison to the 1,297 coded instances of teacher-initiated talk recorded over the same period, a figure which saw instructors in the study occupy slightly more than 45 per cent of total lesson time initiating discourse. Data from the COPS' individual student modality section fully supports these whole-class oral participation results. There were just three coded incidences of initiated talk produced amongst the 90 learners whose behaviour was individually monitored over the course of their language lessons.

Further evidence of the extent of silence within Japan's tertiary sector language classrooms is apparent in the coded instances of no oral participation by any participants (i.e. neither staff nor students spoke during the coding interval), accounting for more than a quarter of the total observed lesson time throughout the study. I should note that while silence within this coding category is not solely an indication of non-participation or unresponsiveness, as it includes periods when audio/audio-visual equipment was playing and episodes when learners were engaged in task activities not requiring verbalisation (e.g. silently reading), the suffusion of coded instances occurring within this category clearly indicates what amounts to a thoroughly reduced opportunity for learners to be orally active in the target language whilst lessons were in progress. This narrow opportunity to speak appears even further restricted when we consider that individually monitored learners were observed to spend over 37 per cent of lesson time engaged in the task of listening to the teacher's talk – an activity that accounted for most of the students' time. A final notable finding worth mentioning here is that individually monitored students were found to be off-task and disengaged from the language learning process for more than a fifth of the total lesson time. This suggests widespread apathy towards foreign language learning amongst Japan's university population – of course, learners who are not engaged in the learning process cannot orally participate in task activities in any meaningful way.

If we view the empirical evidence of language classroom silence produced by the COPS from a theoretical perspective, strong resonances and similarities with some of the major tenets of DST begin to become apparent. The robust nation-wide trend towards silence, which displayed minimal variation across diverse learning contexts, suggests that silence has now formed a semi-permanent attractor state within Japan's university language classrooms. If we define the system in terms of a classroom discourse system composed of multiple, individual learners' classroom talk sub-systems, we can see that the system outcome of silence has settled into a seemingly fossilised and relatively predictable state at both local and national levels. This indicates that a single-cause, linear explanation for Japanese language learner silence is unlikely, and suggests that silence in fact emerges through a number of different routes. These routes, which correspond to DST's notion of attractors, are so numerous and powerful that learners appear to be easily drawn towards them and hence reticence is considered to be a normal part of learner behaviour within Japanese L2 educational contexts.

The semi-structured interview study results

While the structured observation study described in Chapter 6 provided an appropriate research methodology for proving the actual existence of silence within Japan's tertiary L2 classrooms, data produced by the COPS are essentially quantitative in nature and, as such, do not allow for a detailed, individual-level analysis of learners' silent classroom behaviour to be gained. The research design therefore included a parallel phase in the project, entailing a series of semi-structured interviews which aimed to uncover L2 learners' personal experiences of silence and their fundamental beliefs about not speaking in language classrooms. As interview studies focusing on language learner reticence are relatively uncommon, before I outline some important findings it is worth reiterating here some strategies I employed to discourage informants from lapsing into silence when faced with questions about that very topic.

To combat the fact that a great deal of one's silent behaviour tends to operate at an unconscious or semi-conscious level, participants were provided with a copy of the SOPIG interview guide (written in Japanese) prior to their interview sessions. This assisted the informants in collecting their thoughts about silence and facilitated them in providing much richer accounts of the silence-related classroom experiences they had been involved in than would otherwise have been the case had they had entered the interview 'cold'. In addition to these measures, I also had to pay careful attention to numerous other procedural aspects of the interviews in order to increase interviewer–interviewee rapport and thus minimise participants' tendency towards reticence. To give just one example of the initiatives I implemented, informal pre-interview meetings were conducted which enabled me to reassure participants about their anonymity and the confidentiality of their answers. The meetings were also an opportunity to explain about the format of the interview sessions that the informant would later encounter. Naturally, the study's consent forms did provide this information but, as Mackey and Gass (2005, p. 35) rightly point out, within some cultures signed consent is looked upon with suspicion as it does not form part of the normal research process and hence could be an indication that something unpleasant may occur. Pre-interview meetings helped mitigate any such qualms and provided an effective forum for building interviewer–interviewee trust.

A diverse sample of student interviewees, comprising both undergraduates and postgraduates who possessed varying levels of L2 proficiency, produced data which served to underline the dynamic and complex nature of Japanese language learner silence. Interestingly, a number of interviewees recounted having experienced feelings of discomfort whilst episodes of classroom silence were taking place in lessons they were attending. This unease is surprising when we consider that these learners were brought up in a society which has a supposed inclination towards silent intuitive understanding and a distrust of overt verbalisation, and is one which emphasises the value of prudence in speech. The evidence pointing to some informants' feelings of intolerance of classroom silence was in stark contrast to the study's wider findings which suggest that Japanese language learners prefer to remain silent and non-responsive in their language classes. This was not the only finding suggesting that silence within L2 learning contexts is a complex phenomenon and is not something to which we should apply simplistic generalisations. There is a commonly held view that Japanese learners tend not to speak in their language classes simply because they lack L2 ability. While it is true that deficiencies in students' comprehension and language production skills did contribute to a fair proportion of the reticence I observed over the course of the project, classroom silence may also occur when students have consciously chosen to refrain from speech. This point was well illustrated by one particular interviewee, Etsuko, who revealed how students in her advanced-level English class chose not to orally participate in classroom activities, even though they were perfectly capable of doing so, as a means of passively resisting their teacher's authority and protesting about his pedagogical methods. Rather than denoting blank incomprehension, the silence that emerged from Etsuko's account is full of meaning and can be construed as being a group-determined tactical construct expressing non-cooperation and disapproval not likely to entail a significant threat to the perpetrators' face. This second example of the complexity of classroom silence emerging from the interview study provides further confirmation that simplistic generalisations are best avoided if we are to gain a true understanding of learner behaviour at the level of classroom events.

As has been stated previously, DST posits that language learner silence develops through a multiplicity of routes. The semi-structured interview phase of the research project proved crucial in tracing back and identifying some key attractors which act together to pull learners' classroom talk systems into a pattern of silence and non-participation. One such set of factors concerned the choices made by instructors about the methods of teaching and assessment, the lesson materials and the task activities they employ with their classes. For example, one informant, Takuya, a non-language major who possessed a low level of L2 proficiency, spoke about how easy it was for him to pass his English language class. All that Takuya's instructor required of the students was to obtain a reasonable level of attendance and memorise certain sections of the textbook for later paper testing. Silence therefore presented itself as a 'risk-free' option for this learner and his peers. Indeed, why engage in the uncertain business of speaking out in the target language when one can be just as successful in assessment terms by avoiding L2 discourse altogether? Takuya's experiences reflect the fact that traditional cultures of learning in Japan do not place great value on active oral participation and instead emphasise a much more passive, receptive mode of education.

Other silence attractors to emerge from the interview data concerned how, in addition to external situational influences, learner-internal factors also play a major role in shaping the non-vocal behaviour of students. This is in accordance with the DST concept that systems depend on both external and internal resources, and that these resources interact with each other (de Bot & Larsen-Freeman, 2011). A strong theme to emerge in Chapter 6 was that psychological and emotional factors act as highly influential attractors drawing learners' classroom talk systems into a predictable pattern of non-participation and silence. Interviewees made frequent references to the embarrassment and potential loss of face that publicly communicating in the target language might bring to them and described a near-neurotic dread of being negatively evaluated by their classmates. Echoing in particular the work of Greer (2000), interviewees alluded to inhibitory feelings of being watched and having 'eyes' around them whilst they engaged in tasks in their language classrooms.

A final intriguing finding from this phase of the study concerned the possibility of change within a learner's classroom talk system. Aya, a third year foreign languages undergraduate, recounted how a powerful all-female classroom clique of which she had been a member, exerted significant pressure on her to conform to a group norm of non-cooperative silence during lessons. The clique's classroom discourse system displayed a predictable, stable pattern of oral unresponsiveness. Even so, DST posits that change within a system is possible even when fossilisation appears to have occurred, but it may only take place when sufficient factors converge, producing enough energy to compel the system to reorganise. Aya's experiences illustrated this concept perfectly. Her bold decision to risk social ostracism and leave her clique worked in conjunction with developments in various other learner-internal (particularly attitudinal) and situational factors, to eventually repel Aya out of an established pattern of oral non-participation. I should note, however, that the shift in Aya's classroom talk system in effect amounts to a negative case example, and that as Japanese language learner silence is dynamically supported by such a powerful host of attractors at learner, classroom and societal levels, the disengaged and apathetic silence of students like Mikiko, whose beliefs and experiences were also discussed in Chapter 6, unfortunately appears to be much more typical.

The stimulated recall study results

The third and final concurrent phase of the research project involved the collection of retrospective data with the aim of investigating specific silence incidents within naturalistic L2 learning contexts. To this end, Chapter 7 reported on a novel stimulated recall study which analysed students' perceptions of classroom silence that they had either produced or had directly experienced during intact lessons forming part of the observation phase of the project. Using completed COPS coding sheets and audio recordings as effective stimuli to aid participants' recall of events, this phase of the research successfully uncovered data on individual learners' thoughts and feelings about silence at the micro-level of classroom interaction, in addition to gaining useful insights into how students perceived both the language learning tasks they were confronted with and their co-participants at the time of targeted silence events.

The practical research dilemma of how best to encourage reticent students to talk about language learner silence was even more pronounced in the stimulated recall study than it had been for the semi-structured interview sessions. When obtaining a student sample for the semi-structured interviews, I had been able to rely on staff/student recommendations as a means of identifying potential informants who possessed a requisite level of perceptiveness. I had also been able to encourage participants to start thinking about the esoteric topic of silence in pre-interview meetings so that later when interviewed they would be better able to externalise their implicit beliefs about not speaking in L2 educational contexts. Neither of these approaches was possible for the retrospective interviews as the sample had to be made up solely of learners who I had observed to remain silent during classroom events in which there had been a reasonable expectation of talk. Furthermore, it was vital for these participants to arrive at recall sessions unaware of the specific topic of my investigation. Prior knowledge that the research was focused on learners' oral unresponsiveness may have resulted in biased behaviour during observed lessons and unreliable subsequent accounts of the silence incidents occurring therein. A compromise solution was to inform learners prior to observations that my research was focused on the oral communication that takes place in foreign language classes in Japan. Ultimately, the timing and the language of the recall sessions proved crucial elements in mitigating the reticence of interviewees. All sessions were conducted as soon as was possible after the targeted incidents had transpired, and all informants were able to use their L1 during recalls. These measures had the additional benefit of helping to ensure the veridicality of the retrospective data that I collected.

Nao, a first year non-languages major of average L2 ability, was observed to be consistently silent and unresponsive throughout the three English conversation classes I watched her attend. The targeted silence incident which formed the basis for Nao's subsequent recall session occurred when she failed to participate in a whole-class choral drill task during the final observed lesson. What came across strongly in this participant's recall data was the overwhelming sense of listlessness she felt whilst the targeted drill was in progress and the chronic ennui that studying a foreign language instilled in her. Although various concurrent factors, including the restrictive, teacher-centred methodology employed by her instructor, appear to have contributed to Nao's silent disengagement, it was her inattentive apathy towards the task which stood out in the data as the most salient attractor sustaining her individual classroom talk system in its settled state of silence. There is also a very strong case to be made that the marked L1 inarticulateness displayed by this learner transfers directly to her L2 performance and hence further contributes to any lack of oral production in the target language.

The comparison with Jiro, a second year sports science major, is interesting. Like Nao, he was observed to refrain from speech for the duration of a whole-class speaking drill. He too attended a compulsory English class whose discourse was rigidly controlled by the instructor (not a single instance of student-initiated talk was coded for either student's class over the course of six observations). Jiro's recall data revealed that he also experienced feelings of apathy and disengagement during the targeted exercise. As had been the case with Nao, cognitively-speaking Jiro was somewhere else entirely during the drill and was not thinking about anything connected to the language learning task occurring around him. In their retrospective interviews, both informants used the phrase *mendōkusai* – meaning 'I couldn't be bothered/it was too much trouble' – to describe how they felt in their respective classes. However, unlike Nao, Jiro was not a reticent, inarticulate L1 user and he came across as self-confident and perfectly capable of expressing himself in Japanese. He even admitted to being rather garrulous once outside of a classroom setting. Firstly, Jiro's case is important because, along with Nao's, it illustrates a fairly typical attractor state of silence experienced by the thousands of non-language majors in Japan who, even though they are thoroughly disengaged from the L2 learning process, are compelled to attend mandatory English classes in order to progress with their studies. Secondly, Jiro's testimony provides insights into how, rather than being something static, a learner's silent behaviour is actually a dynamic phenomenon heavily influenced by here-and-now contextual factors. Jiro's vocality outside of a classroom setting points towards his silence as having been a *softly assembled* (Thelan & Smith, 1994) non-permanent, adaptive action. As anyone who has ever been in a clamorous university corridor in Japan between class periods will attest, the stereotype of the silent Japanese learner needs to be approached with caution because one's performances of silence tend to be highly context-dependent and may not hold true across settings.

Two other stimulated recall participants provided interesting contrasts in their retrospective data. Miho, a first year fine arts student, had been silent and non-communicative in response to various questions and solicits posed by her instructor. In the subsequent retrospective interview, she admitted to having experienced severe difficulties comprehending the teacher's relatively unmodified, extensive L2 input. This suggested that Miho's classroom talk system was drawn towards a pattern of silence primarily because of learner-internal factors related to a lack of L2 ability. These factors are, of course, interrelated to the behaviour of the instructor whose excessive (accounting for 96 per cent of all coded talk in the lesson) and overly-complex target language talk appears to have exacerbated Miho's unresponsiveness. These findings are in contrast to those of another informant, Tamaki, who was observed to remain silent throughout a small-group discussion task in her advanced-level English class. A first year undergraduate studying at a foreign languages-orientated university, unlike Miho, Tamaki was in possession of highly proficient L2 skills, making it unlikely in her case that L2 processing difficulties contributed to the reticence I observed during the targeted episode. From the retrospective account of the incident that Tamaki provided, it seems that her silent behaviour was in part influenced by her self-concept in relation to the co-participants in the task. She believed her role within the class had developed into that of an orally passive listener during learning activities rather than as an initiator of discourse. This is an interesting finding because it suggests that identity construction, particularly in relation to Zimmerman's (1998) model of social and discoursal identity, may well prove a fruitful avenue of inquiry for silence researchers hoping to trace back the various concurrent causes of a language learner's silence.

8.2   Limitations, and suggestions for future research

There are a number of limitations to the research presented in this book and I will now discuss these in more detail. Where appropriate I will provide suggestions for future research which takes into account the limitations described.

Regarding the classroom observation phase of the research, one of the drawbacks of the COPS was that it only allowed for the identification of macro-level, non-participatory silences and was not ideally suited to measuring the micro-silences of learners' pauses and hesitations. It is apparent that structured observation of intact classes is not an appropriate methodology for quantitatively measuring the frequency of these types of silences. An acoustical-orientated method (e.g. Mattys, Pleydell-Pearce, Melhorn & Whitecross, 2005) is one potential, though rather technical, approach to analysing language learners' most minute unfilled pauses, although the sensitivity of the equipment needed to accurately record hesitation phenomena in milliseconds would probably preclude its use in a naturalistic classroom setting, making a laboratory study more feasible. Even so, a conversation analysis approach measuring Japanese university language learners' classroom micro-silences in tenths rather than thousandths of seconds would be achievable. Following Sacks, Schegloff and Jefferson's (1974) notion that these tiny gaps in discourse have interactional significance (see also Wilson & Zimmerman, 1986), Nakane (2007) has demonstrated how conversation analysis can successfully provide insights into the silent behaviour of Japanese students in study-abroad contexts. There is no reason why a similar approach would not also provide further useful non-elicited data on Japanese learners' micro-silences within the context of university L2 classrooms in their own country.

Limited resources meant that the observation phase of the research was conducted by a single researcher – myself. During the process of piloting the COPS, I found that it was only possible for one observer to reliably monitor the modality of a maximum of three individual learners during each coding interval. This restricted the number of individually monitored students for the whole study to 90. Although this is a respectable enough number, future research involving more than one observer in each classroom would make an increased sample size of individually observed students for each class. An alternative strategy might be to use multiple observers to reduce the COPS' one-minute coding interval, rather than as a way of increasing student sample sizes within individual classes. Having, for example, four researchers on hand could make it possible for one to record the whole-class oral participation aspects of the lesson, while the other three observers coded individual learners' behaviour. In this way, the coding interval could be significantly reduced, leading to an even more detailed chronological representation of classroom events than the COPS currently allows for. A word of caution though – increasing the number of observers present during classroom events may also have significant drawbacks. Firstly, special attention has to be paid to ensuring inter-observer reliability as the presence of more than one researcher in the classroom can lead to inconsistent results (Allwright & Bailey, 1991; Cohen, Manion & Morrison, 2007; Mackey & Gass, 2005). This problem can be counteracted though through a process of careful observer training which focuses on coding consistency and by performing statistical procedures designed to check inter-rater reliability (see Mackey & Gass, 2005, pp. 242–6). A second, more difficult problem to overcome is that the presence of multiple observers within a single classroom would likely prove intrusive, and could lead to increased levels of reactivity amongst participants, thereby invalidating any data collected. Covert observation is one solution to the dilemma, but this approach raises some serious ethical and logistical concerns. A more realistic solution would be a process of habituation whereby students gradually become accustomed to the presence of multiple observers in their classroom over a period of time, eventually reverting back to their natural classroom behaviour.

The COPS' uncomplicated design and low-inference content categories make it an ideal observation scheme for use in classroom contexts other than those presented in Chapter 5. With this in mind, it is worth noting that the current study would benefit from being extended to include observational data on oral participation within non-foreign language classes at Japanese universities. In this way, it would be possible to find out whether the attractor state of silence so prevalent within the country's tertiary language classrooms also exists within mainstream learning contexts operating wholly in an L1 medium. If this were to be the case, and significant levels of silence were uncovered, it would be further evidence that Japanese language learners' silences cannot exclusively be attributable to L2 linguistic difficulties. Continuing with this theme of the need for future silence-orientated research to address a wider range of contexts, if we are to move away from the spurious *nihonjinron* notion that the Japanese are in some way unique in their tendency towards silent behaviour in certain situations (see discussion in Chapter 3; Dale, 1986), further research using the COPS in L2 learning contexts outside of Japan and involving students of other nationalities is essential. As someone who has taught in a number of different countries around the world, I can testify that the Japanese certainly do not have a monopoly on reticent students, and that silent learners can of course be found within other national contexts. However, the intriguing questions are: how does the extent of other cultural groups' silent behaviour compare to that of Japanese L2 learners, and does their silence emerge through similar routes?

The semi-structured interview phase of the project elicited data from a diverse sample of Japanese university students and provided valuable insights into these learners' personal beliefs about not speaking during the process of studying a foreign language. However, in order to gain an even deeper understanding of L2 classroom silence, there is a need to examine the phenomenon from the instructor's point of view as well. Although broadening the interviewee sample further to include a comprehensive staff sample was beyond the scope of the current study, it would be useful to discover whether L2 teachers in Japan perceive classroom unresponsiveness differently to their students, and how their ideas about students' oral participation patterns relate to their conception of effective L2 instruction. Such research would build upon not only my own work within a Japanese tertiary context, but it would also complement Tsui's (1996) study which used language learning anxiety as its conceptual background to examine how Hong Kong secondary school English teachers perceived the problem of their students' reticence.

As I have discussed previously, one of the major limitations of a stimulated recall approach is that it is highly dependent upon the verbal skills and perceptiveness of participants for its success. In Chapter 7, I outlined in detail the various ways in which the current study's research design attempted to meet these challenges. It should be acknowledged though that even if such measures are instigated, they do not guarantee access to participants' event-specific mental processes in their entirety, as so much of our silent behaviour operates at a deep unconscious level and is therefore inaccessible. What is more, as Dörnyei (2007) draws on Cohen to point out, a further drawback in this method of investigation is that even some conscious processes may be too complex for participants to accurately recall. Even so, it should be noted that whilst the current stimulated recall study's informants may have sometimes struggled to retrospectively access their prior thought and reasoning processes, they appear to have experienced far less difficulty in describing both their feelings during targeted events and how they perceived specific learning tasks.

Although I agree with Richards' (2003, p. 299) assertion that it is the appropriateness of an inquiry which is important and we should not confuse size with quality, I think it is fair to say that the retrospective phase of the investigation might have benefitted from a slightly larger sample. I had been rather restricted in my choice of participants in this phase of the inquiry because the use of completed coding sheets as recall stimuli meant I was only able to select those learners whose individual modality had been monitored during the third and final observation of their class and who had produced an episode of silence within this ultimate lesson. On several occasions during the first and second observation classes, I witnessed individually tracked students produce a marked silent answer in response to a directly nominated question posed by the instructor. Unfortunately, I was precluded from focusing on these silences in an immediate recall interview, as to have done so prior the final observation would have risked subsequent biased classroom behaviour from the participant. To have asked about these early silence events in recall interviews following final observations was also not viable because this strategy would have forced the participant to access his/her long-term memory, thus threatening the quality of the recall data provided. While the stimulated recall stage of my project did not produce what might be described as an over-abundance of eloquent data, its findings are reliable, valid and certainly of enough interest to warrant further larger-scale retrospective-orientated studies focusing on language learner silence within naturalistic classroom settings.

In this project I have adopted an over-arching DST conceptual framework through which to interpret the study's results. This complexity approach has allowed me a certain theoretical flexibility in interpreting the diverse silent episodes I have encountered and has acted as a fitting complement to the interdisciplinary nature of the study. As the project's findings developed, it became apparent that strong resonances exist between some of the major tenets of DST and the phenomenon of silence within Japanese university L2 classes. This was particularly so in relation to firstly, the notion of a stable attractor state of silence existing across diverse L2 tertiary contexts; secondly, the idea that students' silent behaviour is influenced by multiple, concurrent attractors; and thirdly, the concept that these attractors are likely to be related to both learner-internal factors and external environmental agents acting in concert. However, one drawback of the research design is that it is essentially cross-sectional in nature and therefore does not allow one to track developments within systems displaying silence outcomes from a longitudinal perspective (although I should note here that the semi-structured interview investigation did uncover data on long-term change within one particular informant's classroom talk system, detailing the multiple agents in her transformation from being a silent language learner into a much more orally productive student). Dörnyei (2009, 2010) has identified the adoption of longitudinal designs as one out of a number of key strategies in the new area of DST-based applied linguistic research, and in light of this, it is apparent there is a need for empirical qualitative research which examines developments in individual learners' silent behaviour over a prolonged period of time. A case study approach (see Gomm, Hammersley & Foster, 2000; Stake, 1995; van Lier, 2005) would appear to be an obvious, potentially fruitful avenue for further investigations in this vein.

Of course, longitudinal research is not the only option open to researchers keen to conduct future studies on Japanese language learner silence from a DST perspective. In the current project, one of the goals of the qualitative component was to trace back some of the principal and also less anticipated attractors which seduce students into a pattern of non-vocalisation and oral passivity. Although I was able to successfully uncover a wide assortment of learner and environmental variables which contribute to L2 classroom silence, I can by no means claim to have identified a full taxonomy of silence attractors. There is still work to be done in this area. One potentially rewarding approach to such a task could involve the use of a novel DST-orientated qualitative method called 'retrodictive qualitative system modelling'. Dörnyei (in press) has illustrated how this approach seeks to understand why a system has arrived at a settled state by producing a retrospective qualitative model of the system's development based on data elicited from a systematic series of interviews with students who embody prototypical system outcomes. By conducting interviews with several members of the same class, it would likely be possible to gain enough oral data for a comprehensive overview of how their class functions (Dörnyei, in press, p. 7). If it could be adapted to investigate silence as a salient system outcome, this approach could undoubtedly provide useful insights into why some learners display such a stable and predictable pattern of non-vocalisation in their language classrooms.

8.3 Practical implications of the study

Pedagogical suggestions

This project suggests a number of practical implications relating not only to micro-level issues connected to pedagogical technique, but also to the macro-level issue of language education planning in Japan. Regarding the former, as the current research did not focus specifically on measuring the effectiveness of specific strategies to combat L2 classroom silence and reduce learner unresponsiveness, the pedagogical suggestions I present here are offered only in a very tentative manner.

The current project found convincing evidence that there is a strong and generalisable trend towards silence within the L2 classrooms of Japan's universities. In line with this, the book has discussed how, rather than there being one single, linear cause–effect explanation for why learners' classroom talk systems are drawn towards a predictable system outcome of silence, students' von-vocal behaviour is in reality governed by a powerful conglomeration of concurrent, interconnected variables. Having a powerful set of attractors governing a stable system outcome means that a requisite number of variables need to converge in order to produce the energy necessary for a shift in the system to take place. Translated into practical terms, this means that if we attempt to alter just one variable relating to a learner's silent behaviour, there is a distinct possibility that a meaningful and prolonged modification towards increased oral production may not occur. This in turn implies that teachers aiming to encourage increased levels of active oral participation in their classrooms would be better off adopting a multi-strategy approach which manipulates a range of learner and environmental factors *simultaneously*. A multi-strategy approach based on data from a retrodictive qualitative system modelling inquiry carried out within a single class would likely provide for a particularly well-focused intervention. Although it could be argued that it is the learner's responsibility to deal with his/her own nonresponsive behaviour, Larsen-Freeman and Cameron (2008) are quite right when they point out that the agent in the system most likely to be able to instigate a system reorganisation is the teacher. Based on these and other concepts discussed throughout this volume, I would like to draw attention to a number of practical pedagogical suggestions which might contribute to such a multi-strategy intervention:

- A movement away from traditional, teacher-centred didactic methods towards a more communicative approach forms a challenging key strategy for reducing learner silence. Lecture-style language classes are ideal for imparting large amounts of sequential information detailing discrete lexico-grammatical points, but they do not serve learners' practical language development and communicative competence needs well. Furthermore, this type of teaching reinforces a hierarchical relationship between the teacher and the taught. As was seen in the case of Yuri in Chapter 7, the presence of status inequalities amongst co-participants within an interaction do tend to contribute to silent behaviour on the part of subordinates.
- Linked to the above, it is essential that educators plan sufficient time within lessons for students to actually speak in the target language. This would begin to redress the massive imbalance in the distribution of classroom talk between teachers and their learners that currently exists. As we have seen in the present research, excessive TTT, a rigid IRF exchange structure, plus the veritable plethora of non-oral learning activities available to educators mean that many Japanese learners only receive a very condensed opportunity for L2 production within their language lessons. This narrow opportunity for talk assumes even more importance when we consider that there are few chances for meaningful L2 interaction outside of classroom contexts in Japan.
- Regarding the quality rather than the quantity of teachers' talk, close attention should be paid to systematically modifying one's speech in order to align its lexical and grammatical complexity to the needs of the class. In this way, learners will not be faced with a barrage of attention-draining incomprehensible input. Instructors need to be highly aware of what is appropriate language for their teaching aim (see Walsh, 2002).

- Also with reference to the quality of teachers' talk, instructors may be able to use their own silence as a useful strategy for counteracting learner unresponsiveness. Research into wait-time has shown that if teachers extend the time they wait after posing a question, it increases the likelihood of a response from learners and may also improve the quality of the response (see Rowe, 1974, 1986; Shrum, 1984; Tobin, 1987). By extending their silent pause after solicits, teachers allow learners increased space for cognitive processing. A caveat accompanying this strategy is provided by Tobin (1987) who warns that maintaining the unnatural behaviour of extending silent wait-time in the long term after initial training may prove problematic for teachers.
- Choosing appropriate learning materials from which students can develop their L2 skills is essential. Outdated, irrelevant texts will do little to stimulate interaction between students. Gilmore's (2011) innovative quasi-experimental study on the use of authentic materials with Japanese university L2 learners suggests that such materials significantly aid the development of a range of communicative competencies, particularly with regard to fluency in the target language, when materials focus on conversational strategies.
- Taking into account the feelings of inhibition and fear of embarrassment informants in the current research described in relation to publicly speaking in the target language, efforts should be made to ensure that learners have opportunities for meaningful L2 interaction which are non-public (i.e. not open to whole-class scrutiny) and therefore not excessively face-threatening. Task-based learning (Ellis, 2003) using small groups presents itself as an ideal approach for encouraging more active learner involvement – providing teachers are able to adapt the method to meet the demands of their own particular teaching contexts (see Littlewood, 2007).
- Teachers should aim to create a supportive and collaborative learning atmosphere in which students are encouraged to take risks in their target language use. Reduced levels of error correction and an emphasis on spoken fluency rather than accuracy could prove conducive to creating such a facilitative environment. Adopting an approachable manner both inside and outside of the classroom can also work well in this respect and should help to promote increased communication with students.
- Finally, one of the potentially most effective ways we can contribute to the diminishing of language learner silence is by paying very close attention to the systematic manipulation of group dynamics

within a classroom (see Dörnyei & Murphey, 2003). For example, to avoid the negative silencing effects of in-group/out-group distinctions and the formation of cliques, group membership should be changed regularly and, ideally, in a random way. As the spatial organisation of the classroom influences the participation patterns of students, the class environment (e.g. seating arrangements) should be manipulated in such a way that communication between students is encouraged.

While the pedagogical suggestions presented above may by no means be considered an exhaustive taxonomy of practical strategies addressing language learner silence, they do provide a number of salient ideas for educators wishing to instigate a multi-strategy intervention within a Japanese context. Even though each of the strategies relates to themes which have been previously discussed in this book, I should reiterate once more that they are provided only in a tentative manner, as the project was not concerned with examining the efficacy of such interventions.

Implications for L2 education planning in Japan

The project's findings make it apparent that Japan's current system of L2 education continues on its relentless course of failing to produce learners capable of displaying either communicative or sociolinguistic competence. The high levels of student silence observed in this study provide a damning indictment of an examination-orientated system which is characterised by top-down curriculum planning at the pre-tertiary level. Language educators within Japan's tertiary sector tend to enjoy some autonomy in choosing what they teach and how they teach it. Unfortunately for many learners, by the time they reach this late stage of their L2 education, it may be too late. I would therefore like to briefly present three implications that the study suggests for language education planning in Japan.

- Firstly, it seems clear to me that we cannot expect learners to actively speak in the target language if their instructors are not prepared to do so either. I acknowledge the concept that L1 may play a role in L2 instruction (e.g., see Auerbach, 1993; Ford, 2009), but currently too many JTEs lack the proficiency and confidence to use English as an instructional medium (see the discussion in Chapter 4). More attention needs to be paid to enhancing JTEs' practical L2 skills and pedagogical repertoires, and thus empower them to at least be in a

position to choose whether or not they engage in the target language whilst teaching.
- While MEXT's rhetoric regarding language education reform is increasingly moving towards advocating a more communicative-orientated approach (see MEXT, 2003, 2011), its policy documents fail to acknowledge constraints at the local level, such as a lack of effective teacher training and negligible time for language instruction within schools (see Chapter 4). It is questionable whether any meaningful reforms can be enacted whilst the system remains so preoccupied with preparing learners for entrance exams.
- The epidemic levels of learner disengagement uncovered in this study raise some serious concerns which education policy planners at Japanese universities need to address. While English as a compulsory subject for all undergraduates is wonderful news for foreign language practitioners who have a vested interest in maintaining as broad a student base as possible, one has to question whether students' interests might not be better served by making the subject an elective. As the system stands at present, it would appear that too many L2 classes for non-language majors are at best an irrelevance and at worst an elaborate institutional exercise in killing time.

8.4 Final thoughts

This book has taken an unapologetically negative view of macro-level silence in the L2 classroom when it is characterised by learner unresponsiveness, a lack of oral participation and the avoidance of talk in the target language. Even so, I trust the mixed-methods research presented here has illustrated that one can never make easy assumptions about the silent episodes one may encounter when teaching or learning a second language. As we have seen, silence has a multiplicity of both forms and functions and these make it an inherently complex and ambiguous phenomenon to deal with. I hope the empirical evidence uncovered by this study, along with the accompanying conceptual discussion, can perhaps go some way in helping applied linguistics practitioners gain an increased awareness and deeper understanding of the much neglected issue of silence.

References

Agyekum, K. (2002). The communicative role of silence in Akan. *Pragmatics*, *12*(1): 31–52.

Akasu, K., & Asao, K. (1993). Sociolinguistic factors influencing communication in Japan and the United States. In W. B. Gudykunst (ed.), *Communication in Japan and the United States* (pp. 88–121). New York: SUNY Press.

Alderson, J. C., & Hamp-Lyons, L. (1996). TOEFL preparation courses: A study of washback. *Language Testing*, *13*(3): 280–97.

Allwright, D., & Bailey, K. M. (1991). *Focus on the Language Classroom: An introduction to classroom research for language teachers*. Cambridge: Cambridge University Press.

Anderson, F. E. (1993). The enigma of the college classroom: Nails that don't stick up. In P. Wadden (ed.), *A Handbook for Teaching English at Japanese Colleges and Universities* (pp. 101–10). Oxford: Oxford University Press.

Anstey, M. E. (2003). Examining classrooms as sites of literate practice and literacy learning. In G. Bull & M. E. Anstey (eds.), *The Literacy Lexicon* (pp. 103–21). Frenchs Forest, NSW: Pearson Education.

Aspinall, R. W. (2005). University entrance in Japan. In J. S. Eades, R. Goodman & Y. Hada (eds.), *The 'Big Bang' in Japanese Higher Education: The 2004 reforms and the dynamics of change* (pp. 199–218). Rosanna, VIC: Trans Pacific Press.

Aspinall, R. W. (2008). An overview of outsourcing. *The Language Teacher*, *32*(1): 39–40.

Aspinall, R. W. (2003). Japanese nationalism and the reform of English language teaching. In R. Goodman & D. Phillips (eds.), *Can the Japanese Change their Education System?* (pp. 103–17). Oxford: Symposium.

Auerbach, E. R. (1993). Reexamining English only in the ESL classroom. *TESOL Quarterly*, *28*: 693–97.

Barnlund, D. C. (1974). The public and the private self in Japan and the United States. In J. C. Condon & M. Saito (eds.), *Intercultural Encounters with Japan: Communication - contact and conflict* (pp. 27–96). Tokyo: Simul Press.

Barnlund, D. C. (1989). *Communicative Styles of Japanese and Americans*. Belmont, CA: Wadsworth.

Basso, K. (1990). 'To give up on words': Silence in Western Apache culture. In D. Carbaugh (ed.), *Cultural Communication and Intercultural Contact* (pp. 303–20). Hillsdale, NJ: Lawrence Erlbaum Associates.

Befu, H. (1986). An ethnography of dinner entertainment in Japan. In T. S. Lebra & W. P. Lebra (eds.), *Japanese Culture and Behavior: Selected readings* (Revised edn, pp. 108–20). Honolulu: University of Hawaii Press.

Befu, H. (2001). *Hegemony of Homogeneity: An anthropological analysis of Nihonjinron*. Melbourne: Trans Pacific Press.

Benwell, B., & Stokoe, E. H. (2006). *Discourse and Identity*. Edinburgh: Edinburgh University Press.

Bernstein, B. (1971). *Class, Codes and Control: Theoretical studies toward a sociology of language*. London: Routledge & Kegan Paul.

Blimes, J. (1994). Constituting silence: Life in the world of total meaning. *Semiotica*, *98*(1/2): 73–87.

Bond, M. H. (2002). Reclaiming the individual from Hofstede's ecological analysis – a 20-year odyssey: Comment on Oyserman *et al.* (2002). *Psychological Bulletin*, *128*(1): 73–7.

Bond, M. H., & Shiraishi, D. (1974). The effect of body lean and status of an interviewer on the non-verbal behavior of Japanese interviewees. *International Journal of Psychology*, *9*(2): 117–28.

Bosher, S. (1998). The composing processes of three Southeast Asian writers at post-secondary level: An exploratory study. *Journal of Second Language Writing*, *7*(2): 205–41.

Braithwaite, C. A. (1990). Communicative silence: A cross-cultural study of Basso's hypothesis. In D. Carbaugh (ed.), *Cultural Communication and Intercultural Contact* (pp. 321–7). Hillsdale, NJ: Lawrence Erlbaum Associates.

Brislin, R. W. (1970). Back-translation for cross-cultural research. *Journal of Cross-Cultural Psychology*, *1*(3): 185–216.

Britzman, D. P. (1998). *Lost Subjects, Contested Objects: Toward a psychoanalytic inquiry of learning*. Albany: SUNY Press.

Brown, J. D. (2000). University entrance examinations: Strategies for creating positive washback on English language teaching in Japan. *Shiken: JALT Testing & Evaluation SIG Newsletter*, *3*(2): 2–7.

Brown, J. D. (2002). English language entrance examinations: A progress report. In *Curriculum Innovation, Testing and Evaluation: Proceedings of the 1st Annual JALT Pan-SIG Conference* (pp. 95–105). Kyoto Institute of Technology, Japan: JALT.

Brown, J. D., & Yamashita, S. O. (1995). English language tests at Japanese universities: What do we know about them? *JALT Journal*, *17*(1): 7–30.

Brown, P., & Levinson, S. (1987). *Politeness: Some universals in language usage*. Cambridge: Cambridge University Press.

Browne, C., & Wada, M. (1998). Current issues in high school English teaching in Japan: An exploratory survey. *Language, Culture and Curriculum*, *11*(1): 96–111.

Bruneau, T. J. (1973). Communicative silences: Forms and functions. *The Journal of Communication*, *23*(1): 17–46.

Butefish, W. L. (1990). Science teachers' perceptions of their interactive decisions. *Journal of Educational Research*, *84*(2): 107–14.

Butler, Y. G., & Iino, M. (2005). Current Japanese reforms in English language education: The 2003 'Action Plan'. *Language Policy*, *4*(1): 25–45.

CLAIR (The Council of Local Authorities for International Relations). (2003). *The JET Programme Pamphlet 2003–2004*. Tokyo: CLAIR.

CLAIR (2010). *The JET Programme 2010–2011*. Tokyo: CLAIR.

Calderhead, J. (1981). Stimulated recall: A method for research on teaching. *British Journal of Educational Psychology*, *51*(2): 211–17.

Camras, L. A., Campos, J., Campos, R., Miyake, K., Oster, H., Ujiie, T., *et al.* (1998). Production of emotional facial expressions in European American, Japanese, and Chinese infants. *Developmental Psychology*, *34*(4): 616–28.

Canale, M. (1983). From communicative competence to language pedagogy. In J. Richards & J. Schmidt (eds.), *Language and Communication* (pp. 2–27). London: Longman.

Canale, M., & Swain, M. (1980). Theoretical bases of communicative approaches to second language teaching and testing. *Applied Linguistics*, 1(1): 1–47.

Carlsen, W. S. (1991). Questioning in classrooms: A sociolinguistic perspective. *Review of Educational Research*, 61(2): 157–78.

Cathcart, D., & Cathcart, R. (1994). The group. A Japanese context. In L. A. Samovar & R. E. Porter (eds.), *Intercultural Communication: A reader* (7th edn, pp. 293–304). Belmont, CA: Thomson Wadsworth.

Caudill, W., & Weinstein, H. (1969). Maternal care and infant behavior in Japan and America. *Psychiatry*, 32(1): 12–43.

Cave, P. (2003). Japanese educational reform: Developments and prospects at primary and secondary level. In R. Goodman (ed.), *Can the Japanese Save their Education System?* (pp. 87–102). Oxford: Symposium.

Cave, P. (2004). 'Bukatsudō': The educational role of Japanese school clubs. *Journal of Japanese Studies*, 30(2): 383–415.

Chafe, W. L. (1985). Some reasons for hesitating. In D. Tannen & M. Saville-Troike (eds.), *Perspectives on Silence* (pp. 77–89). Norwood, NJ: Ablex.

Cheng, X. (2000). Asian students' reticence revisited. *System*, 28(3): 435–46.

Clancy, P. M. (1990). Acquiring communicative style in Japanese. In R. C. Scarcella, E. S. Anderson & S. D. Krashen (eds.), *Developing Communicative Competence in a Second Language* (pp. 27–35). New York: Newbury House.

Clayton, T. (1993). ABC's of evaluating your students: Options to consider. In P. Wadden (ed.), *A Handbook for Teaching English at Japanese Colleges and Universities* (pp. 126–34). Oxford: Oxford University Press.

Cohen, L., Manion, L., & Morrison, K. (2007). *Research Methods in Education* (6th edn). Abingdon: Routledge.

Crown, C. L., & Feldstein, S. (1985). Psychological correlates of silence and sound in conversational interaction. In D. Tannen & M. Saville-Troike (eds.), *Perspectives on Silence* (pp. 31–54). Norwood, NJ: Ablex.

Dale, P. N. (1986). *The Myth of Japanese Uniqueness*. London: Routledge.

Dauenhauer, B. P. (1980). *Silence, the Phenomenon and its Ontological Significance*. Bloomington, IN: Indiana University Press.

Daulton, F. E. (2002). Biracials and bullying: Preparing kids for school. *The Language Teacher*, 26(5): 7–10.

Daulton, F. E., & Seki, A. (2000). Bullying and biracial children in Japan. *The Language Teacher*, 24(11): 31–4.

de Bot, K. (1996). The psycholinguistics of the Output Hypothesis. *Language Learning*, 46(3): 529–55.

de Bot, K., & Larsen-Freeman, D. (2011). Researching second language development from a dynamic systems theory perspective. In M. Verspoor, K. de Bot & W. Lowie (eds.), *A Dynamic Approach to Second Language Development* (pp. 5–23). Amsterdam: John Benjamins.

de Bot, K., Lowie, W., & Verspoor, M. (2005). *An Introduction to Second Language Acquisition: Dynamic aspects*. London: Routledge.

de Bot, K., Lowie, W., & Verspoor, M. (2007). A dynamic systems theory approach to second language acquisition. *Bilingualism: Language and Cognition*, 10(1): 7–21.

De Mente, B. L. (2004). *Japan's Cultural Code Words*. Clarendon, VT: Tuttle.

Doi, T. (1973). *The Anatomy of Dependence*. Tokyo: Kodansha.

Doi, T. (1974). Some psychological themes in Japanese human relationships. In J. C. Condon & M. Saito (eds.), *Intercultural Encounters with Japan: Communication - contact and conflict* (pp. 17–26). Tokyo: Simul Press.

Doi, T. (1988). Dependency in human relationships. In D. I. Okimoto & T. P. Rohlen (eds.), *Inside the Japanese System: Readings on contemporary society and political economy* (pp. 20–5). Stanford, CA: Stanford University Press.

Dollinger, M. J. (1988). Confucian ethics and Japanese management practices. *Journal of Business Ethics*, 7(8): 575–84.

Doyon, P. (2000). Shyness in the Japanese EFL class: Why it is a problem, what it is, what causes it, and what to do about it. *The Language Teacher*, 24(1): 11–16, 37.

Doyon, P. (2001). A review of higher education reform in Japan. *Higher Education*, 41(4): 443–70.

Dörnyei, Z. (1997). Psychological processes in cooperative language learning: Group dynamics and motivation. *The Modern Language Journal*, 81(4): 482–93.

Dörnyei, Z. (2001). *Motivational Strategies in the Language Classroom*. Cambridge: Cambridge University Press.

Dörnyei, Z. (2005). *The Psychology of the Language Learner: Individual differences in second language acquisition*. Mahwah, NJ: Lawrence Erlbaum.

Dörnyei, Z. (2007). *Research Methods in Applied Linguistics: Quantitative, qualitative, and mixed methodologies*. Oxford: Oxford University Press.

Dörnyei, Z. (2009). *The Psychology of Second Language Acquisition*. Oxford: Oxford University Press.

Dörnyei, Z. (2010). Researching complex dynamic systems: Focus on L2 motivation. Paper presented at the American Association for Applied Linguistics Annual Conference, 8 March 2010, Atlanta, GA.

Dörnyei, Z. (in press). Researching complex dynamic systems: 'Retrodictive qualitative modelling' in the language classroom. *Language Teaching*.

Dörnyei, Z., & Kormos, J. (1998). Problem-solving mechanisms in L2 communication: A psycholinguistic perspective. *Studies in Second Language Acquisition*, 20(3): 349–85.

Dörnyei, Z., & Murphey, T. (2003). *Group Dynamics in the Language Classroom*. Cambridge: Cambridge University Press.

Dörnyei, Z., & Ushioda, E. (2011). *Teaching and Researching Motivation* (2nd edn). Harlow: Pearson Education.

Edwards, J. (2009). *Language and Identity*. Cambridge: Cambridge University Press.

Ehrman, M. E., & Dörnyei, Z. (1998). *Interpersonal Dynamics in Second Language Learning: The visible and invisible classroom*. Thousand Oaks, CA: Sage.

Ellis, N. C. (2007). Dynamic systems and SLA: The wood and the trees. *Bilingualism: Language and Cognition*, 10(1): 23–5.

Ellis, R. (1999). *Learning a Second Language through Interaction*. Amsterdam: John Benjamins.

Ellis, R. (2003). *Task-based Language Learning and Teaching*. Oxford: Oxford University Press.

Ellis, R., Tanaka, Y., & Yamazaki, A. (1994). Classroom interaction, comprehension, and the acquisition of L2 word meanings *Language Learning*, 44(3): 449–91.

Enninger, W. (1991). Focus on silence across cultures. *Intercultural Communication Studies*, 1(1): 1–37.

Ephratt, M. (2008). The functions of silence. *Journal of Pragmatics*, 40(11): 1909–38.
Ericsson, K. A., & Simon, H. A. (1993). *Protocol Analysis: Verbal reports as data* (2nd edn). Cambridge, MA: MIT Press.
Essau, C. A., Sasagawa, S., Chen, J., & Sakano, Y. (2012). Taijin kyofusho and social phobia symptoms in young adults in England and in Japan. *Journal of Cross-Cultural Psychology*, 43(2): 219–32.
Falout, J., & Maruyama, M. (2004). A comparative study of proficiency and learner demotivation. *The Language Teacher*, 28(8): 3–9.
Feldstein, S., & Sloan, B. (1984). Actual and stereotyped speech tempos of extraverts and introverts. *Journal of Personality*, 52(2): 188–204.
Feldstein, S., Alberti, L., & BenDebba, M. (1979). Self-attributed personality characteristics and the pacing of conversational interaction. In A. W. Siegman & S. Feldstein (eds.), *Of Speech and Time: Temporal speech patterns in interpersonal contexts* (pp. 73–87). Hillsdale, NJ: Lawrence Erlbaum.
Fennelly, M., & Luxton, R. (2011). Are they ready? On the verge of compulsory English, elementary school teachers lack confidence. *The Language Teacher*, 35(2): 19–24.
Fischer, J. L., & Yoshida, T. (1968). The nature of speech according to Japanese proverbs. *The Journal of American Folklore*, 81(319): 34–43.
Flynn, C. (2009). ALT furniture: A look at dispatch ALT contracts. *The Language Teacher*, 33(5): 39–40.
Fogel, A., Toda, S., & Kawai, M. (1988). Mother–infant face-to-face interaction in Japan and the United States: A laboratory comparison using 3-month-old infants. *Developmental Psychology*, 24(3): 398–406.
Ford, K. (2009). Principles and practices of L1/L2 use in the Japanese university classroom. *JALT Journal*, 31(1): 63–80.
Forsyth, D. R. (2009). *Group Dynamics* (5th edn). Belmont, CA: Wadsworth, Cengage Learning.
Fotos, S. (2005). Traditional and grammar translation methods for second language teaching. In E. Hinkel (ed.), *Handbook of Research in Second Language Teaching and Learning* (pp. 653–70). Mahwah, NJ: Lawrence Erlbaum.
Fox-Turnbull, W. (2009). Stimulated recall using autophotography - A method for investigating technology education. Paper presented at the PATT-22 Conference, August 24–28, Delft, Netherlands.
Franks, P. H. (2000). Silence/listening and intercultural differences. Paper presented at the 21st Annual Meeting of the International Listening Association, March 7–12, Virginia Beach, Virginia.
Gass, S. M. (1997). *Input, Interaction, and the Second Language Learner*. Mahwah, NJ: Lawrence Erlbaum Associates.
Gass, S. M., & Mackey, A. (2000). *Stimulated Recall Methodology in Second Language Research*. Mahwah, NJ: Lawrence Erlbaum.
Gilbert, R., & Yoneoka, J. (2000). From 5-7-5 to 8-8-8: An investigation of Japanese haiku metrics and implications for English haiku. *Language Issues: Journal of the Foreign Language Education Center, Prefectural University of Kumamoto*, 6(1): 1–35.
Gilmore, A. (2011). 'I prefer not text': Developing Japanese learners' communicative competence with authentic materials. *Language Learning*, 61(3): 768–819.
Gilmore, P. (1985). Silence and sulking: Emotional displays in the classroom. In D. Tannen & M. Saville-Troike (eds.), *Perspectives on Silence* (pp. 139–62). Norwood, NJ: Ablex.

Goffman, E. (1967). *Interaction Ritual*. Garden City, NY: Doubleday.
Goffman, E. (2006). On face-work: Analysis of ritual elements in social interaction. In A. Jaworski & N. Coupland (eds.), *The Discourse Reader* (2nd edn, pp. 299–310). Abingdon: Routledge.
Gomm, R., Hammersley, M., & Foster, P. (eds.) (2000). *Case Study Method*. London: Sage.
Goodman, R. (2005). W(h)ither the Japanese university? An introduction to the 2004 Higher Education Reforms in Japan. In J. S. Eades, R. Goodman & Y. Hada (eds.), *The 'Big Bang' in Japanese Higher Education: The 2004 reforms and the dynamics of change* (pp. 1–31). Rosanna, VIC: Trans Pacific Press.
Gorsuch, G. J. (1998). Yakudoku EFL instruction in two Japanese high schools: An exploratory study. *JALT Journal*, 20(1): 6–32.
Gorsuch, G. J. (2000). EFL educational policies and educational cultures: Influences on teachers' approval of communicative activities. *TESOL Quarterly*, 34(4): 675–710.
Gorsuch, G. J. (2002). Assistant foreign language teachers in Japanese high schools: Focus on the hosting of Japanese teachers. *JALT Journal*, 24(1): 5–32.
Granger, C. A. (2004). *Silence in Second Language Learning: A psychoanalytic reading*. Clevedon: Multilingual Matters.
Greer, D. L. (2000). 'The eyes of *hito*': A Japanese cultural monitor of behavior in the communicative language classroom. *JALT Journal*, 22(1): 183–95.
Gudykunst, W. B. (2004). *Bridging Differences: Effective intergroup communication* (4th edn). Thousand Oaks, CA: Sage.
Gudykunst, W. B., & Nishida, T. (1993). Interpersonal and intergroup communication in Japan and the United States. In W. B. Gudykunst (ed.), *Communication in Japan and the United States* (pp. 149–214). New York: SUNY Press.
Gudykunst, W. B., & San Antonio, P. (1993). Approaches to the study of communication in Japan and the United States. In W. B. Gudykunst (ed.), *Communication in Japan and the United States* (pp. 18–48). New York: SUNY Press.
Guest, M. (2000). What's wrong with Japanese English teachers? *The Language Teacher*, 24(1): 30–1.
Guest, M. (2002). A critical 'checkbook' for culture learning and teaching. *ELT Journal*, 56(2): 154–61.
Guest, M. (2008). Japanese university entrance exams: What teachers should know. *The Language Teacher*, 32(2): 15–19.
Hall, E. T. (1981). *Beyond Culture*. New York: Anchor Books.
Hane, M. (2000). *Japan: A Short History*. Oxford: Oneworld.
Harumi, S. (2006). Japanese learners of English and their use of silence. Retrieved November 3, 2008, from The East Asian Learner website: http://owww.brookes.ac.uk/schools/education/eal/jl-archive/jl-bestof/23.pdf
Hato, Y. (2005). Problems in top-down goal setting in second language education: A case study of the 'Action Plan to Cultivate "Japanese with English Abilities"'. *JALT Journal*, 27(1): 33–52.
Helgesen, M. (1993). Dismantling a wall of silence: The 'English conversation' class. In P. Wadden (ed.), *A Handbook for Teaching English at Japanese Colleges and Universities* (pp. 37–49). Oxford: Oxford University Press.
Hendry, J. (1986). *Becoming Japanese: The world of the pre-school child*. Manchester: Manchester University Press.
Hendry, J. (1989). *Understanding Japanese Society*. London: Routledge.

Henrichsen, L. E. (1989). *Diffusion of Innovations in English Language Teaching: The ELEC effort in Japan.* New York: Greenwood Press.

Hino, N. (1988). Yakudoku: Japan's dominant tradition in foreign language learning. *JALT Journal,* 10(1/2): 45–55.

Hofstede, G. (1980). *Culture's Consequences.* Beverly Hills, CA: Sage.

Holliday, A. (1994). *Appropriate Methodology and Social Context.* Cambridge: Cambridge University Press.

Horwitz, E. K., Horwitz, M. B., & Cope, J. (1986). Foreign language classroom anxiety. *Modern Language Journal,* 70(2): 125–32.

Hudson, R. A. (1980). *Sociolinguistics.* Cambridge: Cambridge University Press.

Hymes, D. (1964). Introduction: Toward ethnographies of communication. In J. J. Gumperz & D. Hymes (eds.), *The Ethnography of Communication* (pp. 1–34). Washington, DC: American Anthropologist Association.

Hymes, D. (1974). *Foundations in Sociolinguistics: An ethnographic approach.* Philadelphia, PA: University of Pennsylvania Press.

Ide, R. (2009). Aisatsu. In G. Senft, J-O. Östman & J. Verschueren (eds.), *Culture and Language Use* (pp. 18–28). Amsterdam: John Benjamins.

Inoguchi, T. (1999). Japan's failing grade in English. *Japan Echo,* 26(5): 8–11.

Ishii, S., & Bruneau, T. J. (1994). Silence and silences in cross-cultural perspective: Japan and the United States. In L. A. Samovar & R. E. Porter (eds.), *Intercultural Communication: A reader* (7th edn, pp. 246–51). Belmont, CA: Thomson Wadsworth.

Iwashita, N. (2003). Negative feedback and positive evidence in task-based interaction. *Studies in Second Language Acquisition,* 25(1): 1–36.

Izumi, S. (2003). Comprehension and production processes in second language learning: In search of the psycholinguistic rationale of the Output Hypothesis. *Applied Linguistics,* 24(2): 168–96.

Jandt, F. E. (2007). *An Introduction to Intercultural Communication: Identities in a global community* (5th edn). Thousand Oaks, CA: Sage.

Jaworski, A. (1993). *The Power of Silence: Social and pragmatic perspectives.* London: Sage.

Jaworski, A. (2000). Silence and small talk. In J. Coupland (ed.), *Small Talk* (pp. 110–32). Harlow: Pearson Education.

Jaworski, A. (ed.) (1997). *Silence: Interdisciplinary perspectives.* Berlin: Mouton de Gruyter.

Jaworski, A., & Sachdev, I. (1998). Beliefs about silence in the classroom. *Language and Education,* 12(4): 273–92.

Jaworski, A., & Sachdev, I. (2004). Teachers' beliefs about students' talk and silence: Constructing academic success and failure through metapragmatic comments. In A. Jaworski, N. Coupland & D. Galasinski (eds.), *Metalanguage: Social and Ideological Perspectives* (pp. 227–44). Berlin: Mouton de Gruyter.

Johnson, K. E. (1992). The instructional decisions of pre-service ESL teachers: New directions for teacher preparation programs. In J. Flowerdew, M. Brock & S. Hsia (eds.), *Perspectives on Second Language Teacher Education* (pp. 115–34). Hong Kong: City Polytechnic of Hong Kong.

Jones, J. F. (1999). From silence to talk: Cross-cultural ideas on students' participation in academic group discussion. *English for Specific Purposes,* 18(3): 243–59.

Julé, A. (2005). *Gender, Participation and Silence in the Language Classroom: Sh-shushing the girls*. Basingstoke and New York: Palgrave Macmillan.

Kamada, L. D. (2010). *Hybrid Identities and Adolescent Girls: Being 'half' in Japan*. Bristol: Multilingual Matters.

Kamiya, S. (2009, January 20). 'Exam hell' now not so hot. *The Japan Times*. Retrieved January 21, 2009, from http://search.japantimes.co.jp/cgi-bin/nn20090120i1.html

Kanno, Y. (2003). *Negotiating Bilingual and Bicultural Identities: Japanese returnees betwixt two worlds*. Mahwah, NJ: Lawrence Erlbaum.

Kasahara, Y. (1986). Fear of eye-to-eye confrontation among neurotic patients in Japan. In T. S. Lebra & W. P. Lebra (eds.), *Japanese Culture and Behavior: Selected readings* (Revised edn, pp. 379–87). Honolulu: University of Hawaii Press.

Kember, D., & Gow, L. (1991). A challenge to the anecdotal stereotype of the Asian student. *Studies in Higher Education*, 16(2): 117–28.

Kerr, A. (2001). *Dogs and Demons: Tales from the dark side of Japan*. New York: Hill & Wang.

Kikuchi, K. (2006). Revisiting English entrance examinations at Japanese universities after a decade. *JALT Journal*, 28(1): 77–96.

Kikuchi, K., & Sakai, H. (2009). Japanese learners' demotivation to study English: A survey study. *JALT Journal*, 31(2): 183–204.

King, J. (2005). Supervision and appraisal through classroom observation: Time for a change of approach. *Explorations in Teacher Education*, 13(3): 9–15.

King, J. (2013). Silence in the second language classrooms of Japanese universities. *Applied Linguistics*, 34(3), 325–43.

King, J., & Lind, S. L. (2007). Cultural factors behind the in-class somnolent behaviour of university second-language learners. Paper presented at The 5th ASIA TEFL International Conference, June 8-10, Kuala Lumpur, Malaysia.

Kinmonth, E. H. (2005). From selection to seduction: The impact of demographic change on private higher education in Japan. In J. S. Eades, R. Goodman & Y. Hada (eds.), *The 'Big Bang' in Japanese Higher Education: The 2004 reforms and the dynamics of change* (pp. 106–35). Rosanna, VIC: Trans Pacific Press.

Kleinknecht, R. A., Dinnel, D. L., & Kleinknecht, E. E. (1997). Cultural factors in social anxiety: A comparison of social phobia symptons and *taijin kyofusho*. *Journal of Anxiety Disorders*, 11(2): 157–77.

Knapp. K. (2000). Metaphorical and interactional uses of silence. *EESE: Erfurt Electronic Studies in English*, 7. Retrieved June 16, 2009, from http://webdoc.sub.gwdg.de/edoc/ia/eese/artic20/knapp/7_2000.html

Kobayashi, Y. (2001). The learning of English at academic high schools in Japan: Students caught between exams and internationalisation. *Language Learning Journal*, 23(1): 67–72.

Korst, T. J. (1997). Answer, please answer! A perspective on Japanese university students' silent response to questions. *JALT Journal*, 19(2): 279–91.

Kotloff, L. J. (1996). '...And Tomoko wrote this song for us'. In T. P. Rohlen & G. K. LeTendre (eds.), *Teaching and Learning in Japan* (pp. 98–118). Cambridge: Cambridge University Press.

Kowner, R. (2002). Japanese communication in intercultural encounters: The barrier of status-related behavior. *International Journal of Intercultural Relations*, 26(4): 339–61.

Kowner, R. (2003). Japanese miscommunication with foreigners: In search for valid accounts and effective remedies. *Japanstudien*, 15: 117–51.

Kramsch, C. (1998). *Language and Culture*. Oxford: Oxford University Press.

Kubota, R. (1999). Japanese culture constructed by discourses: Implications for applied linguistics research and ELT. *TESOL Quarterly*, 33(1): 9–35.

Kubota, R., & McKay, S. (2009). Globalization and language learning in rural Japan: The role of English in the local linguistic ecology. *TESOL Quarterly*, 43(4): 593–619.

Kurzon, D. (1992). When silence may mean power. *Journal of Pragmatics*, 18(1): 92–5.

Kurzon, D. (1995). The right of silence: A socio-pragmatic model of interpretation. *Journal of Pragmatics*, 23(1): 55–69.

Kurzon, D. (1998). *Discourse of Silence*. Amsterdam: John Benjamins.

Labov, W. (1972). *Sociolinguistic Patterns*. Philadelphia, PA: University of Pennsylvania Press.

Lane, R. C., Koetting, M. G., & Bishop, J. (2002). Silence as communication in psychodynamic psychotherapy. *Clinical Psychology Review*, 22(7): 1091–104.

Larsen-Freeman, D. (1997). Chaos/complexity science and second language acquisition. *Applied Linguistics*, 18(2): 141–65.

Larsen-Freeman, D., & Cameron, L. (2008). *Complex Systems and Applied Linguistics*. Oxford: Oxford University Press.

Law, G. (1995). Ideologies of English language teaching in Japan. *JALT Journal*, 17(2): 213–24.

Lawrie, A. (2006). Don't interrupt, I'm thinking! Paper presented at the BALEAP Conference on The East Asian Learner, February 25, University of Winchester, Winchester.

Lebra, T. S. (1976). *Japanese Patterns of Behavior*. Honolulu: University Press of Hawaii.

Lebra, T. S. (1987). The cultural significance of silence in Japanese communication. *Multilingua*, 6(4): 343–57.

Lebra, T. S. (1993). Culture, self, and communication in Japan and the United States. In W. B. Gudykunst (ed.), *Communication in Japan and the United States* (pp. 51–87). New York: SUNY Press.

Lee-Cunin, M. (2005). The Japanese student perspective on universities. In J. S. Eades, R. Goodman & Y. Hada (eds.), *The 'Big Bang' in Japanese Higher Education: The 2004 reforms and the dynamics of change* (pp. 136–64). Rosanna, VIC: Trans Pacific Press.

Levelt, W. J. M. (1989). *Speaking: From intention to articulation*. Cambridge, MA: MIT Press.

Levelt, W. J. M. (1993). Language use in normal speakers and its disorders. In G. Blanken, J. Dittman, H. Grimm, J. C. Marshall & C-W. Wallesch (eds.), *Linguistic Disorders and Pathologies*. Berlin: Mouton de Gruyter.

Levelt, W. J. M. (1995). The ability to speak: From intentions to spoken words. *European Review*, 3(1): 13–23.

Lewis, C. C. (1984). Cooperation and control in Japanese nursery schools. *Comparative Education Review*, 28(1): 69–84.

Li, H. (2001). Silences and silencing silences. In *Philosophy of Education Studies Yearbook* (pp. 157–65). Champaign, IL: University of Illinois Press.

Lincicome, M. (1993). Nationalism, internationalization and the dilemma of educational reform in Japan. *Comparative Education Review*, 37(2): 123–51.

Littlejohn, S. W., & Foss, K. A. (2005). *Theories of Human Communication* (8th edn). Belmont, CA: Thomson Wadsworth.

Littlewood, W. (2000). Do Asian students really want to listen and obey? *ELT Journal*, 54(1): 31–6.

Littlewood, W. (2007). Communicative and task-based language teaching in East Asian classrooms. *Language Teaching*, 40(3): 243–49.

Long, M. H. (1996). The role of the linguistic environment in second language acquisition. In W. C. Ritchie & T. K. Bhatia (eds.), *Handbook of Language Acquisition (Vol. 2: Second language acquisition)* (pp. 413–68). New York: Academic Press.

Loveday, L. (1982). *The Sociolinguistics of Learning and Using a Non-native Language*. Oxford: Pergamon Press.

Lyle, J. (2003). Stimulated recall: A report on its use in naturalistic research. *British Educational Research Journal*, 29(6): 861–78.

MEXT (The Ministry of Education, Culture, Sport, Science and Technology). (2003). *Regarding the establishment of an action plan to cultivate 'Japanese with English abilities'*. Retrieved April 12, 2010, from http://mext.go.jp/english/topics/03072801.htm

MEXT. (2010). *Monbu kagaku tōkei yōran (heisei 22 nenban) [Statistical abstract: Education, culture, sports, science, and technology (2009)]*. Tokyo: Nikkei Insatsu Kabushikigaisha.

MEXT. (2011). *Official curriculum guidelines for elementary schools: Chapter 4 Foreign language activities*. Retrieved May 18, 2011, from http://www.mext.go.jp/component/english/_icsFiles/afieldfile/2011/03/17/1303755_011.pdf

MacIntyre, P. D., & Gardner, R. C. (1994). The subtle effects of language learner anxiety on cognitive processing in the second language. *Language Learning*, 44(2): 283–305.

MacIntyre, P. D., & Legatto, J. J. (2011). A dynamic system approach to willingness to communicate: Developing an idiodynamic method to capture readily changing affect. *Applied Linguistics*, 32(2): 149–71.

MacIntyre, P. D., Babin, P. A., & Clément, R. (1999). Willingness to communicate: Antecedents and consequences. *Communication Quarterly*, 47(2): 215–29.

Mackey, A. (2002). Beyond production: Learners' perceptions about interactional processes. *International Journal of Educational Research*, 37(3/4): 379–94.

Mackey, A. (2006). Feedback, noticing and instructed second language learning. *Applied Linguistics*, 27(3): 405–30.

Mackey, A., & Gass, S. M. (2005). *Second Language Research: Methodology and design*. Mahwah, NJ: Laurence Erlbaum.

Mackey, A., Gass, S. M., & McDonough, K. (2000). How do learners perceive interactional feedback? *Studies in Second Language Acquisition*, 22(4): 471–97.

Maeda, R. (1999). 'Ijime': An exploratory study of a collective form of bullying among Japanese students. Paper presented at the *Biennial Meeting of the Society for Research in Child Development*, April 15–18, Albuquerque, New Mexico.

Mahoney, S. (2004). Role controversy among team teachers in the JET Programme. *JALT Journal*, 26(2): 223–44.

Mattys, S. L., Pleydell-Pearce, C. W., Melhorn, J. F., & Whitecross, S. E. (2005). Detecting silent pauses in speech: A new tool for measuring on-line lexical and semantic processing. *Psychological Science*, 16(12): 958–64.

McCafferty, S. G., Jacobs, G. M., & DaSilva Iddings, C. (eds.) (2006). *Cooperative Learning and Second Language Teaching*. New York: Cambridge University Press.

McCarthy, M. (2000). Mutually captive audiences: Small talk and the genre of close-contact service encounters. In J. Coupland (ed.), *Small Talk* (pp. 84–109). Harlow: Pearson Education.

McConnell, D. L. (1996). Education for global integration in Japan: A case study of the JET Program. *Human Organisation*, 55(4), 446-457.

McConnell, D. L. (2000). *Importing Diversity: Inside Japan's JET program*. Berkeley: University of California Press.

McDaniel, E. R. (2003). Japanese nonverbal communication: A reflection of cultural themes. In L. A. Samovar & R. E. Porter (eds.), *Intercultural Communication: A reader* (10th edn, pp. 253–61). Belmont, CA: Wadsworth.

McPake, J., & Powney, J. (1998). A mirror to ourselves? The educational experiences of Japanese children at school in the UK. *Educational Research*, 40(2): 169–79.

McVeigh, B. J. (1997). *Life in a Japanese Women's College: Learning to be ladylike*. London: Routledge.

McVeigh, B. J. (2002). *Japanese Higher Education as Myth*. New York: M. E. Sharpe.

McVeigh, B. J. (2006). *The State Bearing Gifts: Deception and disaffection in Japanese higher education*. Lanham, MD: Lexington.

Mitchell, R. G. (1993). *Secrecy in Fieldwork*. London: Sage.

Miyazato, K. (2009). Power-sharing between NS and NNS teachers: Linguistically powerful AETs vs. culturally powerful JTEs. *JALT Journal*, 31(1): 35–62.

Moeran, B. (1986). Individual, group and *seishin*: Japan's internal cultural debate. In T. S. Lebra & W. P. Lebra (eds.), *Japanese Culture and Behavior: Selected readings* (Revised edn, pp. 62–79). Honolulu: University of Hawaii Press.

Morita, N. (2012). Identity: The situated construction of identity and positionality in multilingual classrooms. In S. Mercer, S. Ryan & M. Williams (eds.), *Psychology for Language Learning: Insights from research, theory and practice* (pp. 26–41). Basingstoke and New York: Palgrave Macmillan.

Moskowitz, G. (1971). Interaction analysis: A new modern language for supervisors. *Foreign Language Annals*, 5(2): 211–21.

Mulligan, C. (2005). No English educational reforms will be effective unless Japanese English teachers can and will speak English in the classroom. *The Language Teacher*, 29(5): 33–5.

Mulvey, B. (1999). The myth of influence: Japanese university entrance exams and their effect on junior and senior high school reading pedagogy. *JALT Journal*, 21(1): 125–42.

Mulvey, B. (2001). The role and influence of Japan's university entrance exams: A reassessment. *The Language Teacher*, 27(7): 11–17.

Murphey, T. (2001). Nonmeritorious features of the entrance exam system in Japan. *The Language Teacher*, 25(10): 37–9.

Murphey, T. (2004). Participation, (dis-) identification, and Japanese university entrance exams. *TESOL Quarterly*, 38(4): 700–10.

Murphy, J. M. (1992). An etiquette for the nonsupervisory observation of L2 classrooms. *Foreign Language Annals*, 25(3): 215–25.

Naito, T., & Gielen, U. P. (2005). Bullying and *ijime* in Japanese schools: A sociocultural perspective. In F. Denmark, H. H. Krauss, R. W. Wesner, E. Midlarsky & U. P. Gielen (eds.), *Violence in Schools: Cross-national and cross-cultural perspectives* (pp. 169–90). New York: Springer Science.

Nakane, C. (1988). Hierarchy in Japanese society. In D. I. Okimoto & T. P. Rohlen (eds.), *Inside the Japanese System: Readings on contemporary society and political economy* (pp. 8–14). Stanford, CA: Stanford University Press.

Nakane, I. (2006). Silence and politeness in intercultural communication in university seminars. *Journal of Pragmatics*, 38(11): 1811–35.

Nakane, I. (2007). *Silence in Intercultural Communication*. Amsterdam: John Benjamins.

Nakatani, A. (2006). The emergence of 'nurturing fathers': Discourses and practices of fatherhood in contemporary Japan. In M. Rebick & A. Takenaka (eds.), *The Changing Japanese Family* (pp. 94–108). London: Routledge.

National Center for University Entrance Exams. (2010, 5 February). *Heisei 22 nendo sentā shiken jishi kekka no gaiyou [Summary of the 2010 sentā shiken results]*. Retrieved April 12, 2010, from http://www.dnc.ac.jp/modules/news/content0337.html

Nikolov, M., & Djigunovič, M. J. (2006). Recent research on age, second language acquisition, and early foreign language learning. *Annual Review of Applied Linguistics*, 26: 234–60.

Nishino, T. (2008). Japanese secondary school teachers' beliefs and practices regarding communicative language teaching: An exploratory study. *JALT Journal*, 30(1): 27–50.

Nishino, T., & Watanabe, M. (2008). Communication-orientated policies versus classroom realities in Japan. *TESOL Quarterly*, 42(1): 133–8.

Nunan, D. (1991). *Classroom Interaction*. Sydney: National Centre for English Language Teaching and Research.

Nwoye, G. (1985). Eloquent silence among the Igbo of Nigeria. In D. Tannen & M. Saville-Troike (eds.), *Perspectives on Silence* (pp. 185–91). Norwood, NJ: Ablex.

O'Brien, J. (1993). Action research through stimulated recall. *Research in Science Education*, 23(1): 214–21.

O'Donnell, K. (2005). Japanese secondary English teachers: Negotiation of educational roles in the face of curricular reform. *Language, Culture and Curriculum*, 18(3): 300–15.

Oxford, R. L. (1997). Cooperative learning, collaborative learning, and interaction: Three communicative strands in the language classroom. *Modern Language Journal*, 81(4): 443–56.

Oxford, R. L. (1999). Anxiety and the language learner: New insights. In J. Arnold (ed.), *Affect in Language Learning* (pp. 58–67). Cambridge: Cambridge University Press.

Oyserman, D., Coon, H. M., & Kemmelmeier, M. (2002). Rethinking individualism and collectivism: Evaluation of theoretical assumptions and meta-analyses. *Psychological Bulletin*, 128(1): 3–72.

Paribakht, T. S., & Wesche, M. (1999). Reading and 'incidental' L2 vocabulary acquisition: An introspective study on lexical inferencing. *Studies in Second Language Acquisition*, 21(2): 195–224.

Peak, L. (1989). Learning to become part of the group. The Japanese child's transition to preschool life. *Journal of Japanese Studies*, 15(1): 93–123.

Peterson, P. L., & Clark, C. M. (1978). Teachers' reports of their cognitive processes. *American Educational Research Journal*, 15(4): 555–65.

Philips, S. U. (1976). Some sources of cultural variability in the regulation of talk. *Language in Society*, 5(1): 81–95.

Poland, B., & Pederson, A. (1998). Reading between the lines: Interpreting silences in qualitative research. *Qualitative Inquiry*, 4(2): 293–312.

Poole, G. S. (2005). Reform of the university English language teaching curriculum in Japan: A case study. In J. S. Eades, R. Goodman & Y. Hada (eds.), *The 'Big Bang' in Japanese Higher Education: The 2004 reforms and the dynamics of change* (pp. 242–73). Rosanna, VIC: Trans Pacific Press.

Pritchard, R. M. O. (1995). Amae and the Japanese learner of English: An action research study. *Language, Culture and Curriculum*, 8(3): 249–64.

Pritchard, R. M. O., & Maki, H. (2006). The changing self-perceptions of Japanese university students of English. *Journal of Studies in International Education*, 10(2): 141–56.

Rebuck, M. (2008). The effect of excessively difficult listening lessons on motivation and the influence of authentic listening as a 'lesson-selling' tag. *JALT Journal*, 30(2): 197–222.

Reda, M. M. (2009). *Between Speaking and Silence: A study of quiet students*. Albany, NY: SUNY Press.

Richards, K. (2003). *Qualitative Inquiry in TESOL*. Basingstoke and New York: Palgrave Macmillan.

Richards, K. (2006). 'Being the teacher': Identity and classroom conversation. *Applied Linguistics*, 27(1): 51–77.

Robinson, M. A. (1992). Introspective methodology in interlanguage pragmatics research. In G. Kasper (ed.), *Pragmatics of Japanese as Native and Target Language* (pp. 27–82). Honolulu: University of Hawai'i Press.

Rose, K. (1996). American English, Japanese and directness: More than stereotypes. *JALT Journal*, 18(1): 67–80.

Rovine, H. (1987). *Silence in Shakespeare: Drama, power, and gender*. Ann Arbor, MI: UMI Research Press.

Rowe, M. B. (1974). Pausing phenomena: Influence on the quality of instruction. *Journal of Psycholinguistic Research*, 3(3): 203–24.

Rowe, M. B. (1986). Wait time: Slowing down may be a way of speeding up. *Journal of Teacher Education*, 37(1): 43–50.

Ryan, S. (2009). Ambivalence and commitment, liberation and challenge: Investigating the attitudes of young Japanese people towards learning English. *Journal of Multilingual and Multicultural Development*, 30(5): 405–20.

Sacks, H., Schegloff, E., & Jefferson, G. (1974). A simplest systematics for the organization of turn-taking in conversation. *Language*, 50(4): 696–35.

Sakui, K. (2004). Wearing two pairs of shoes: Language teaching in Japan. *ELT Journal*, 58(2): 155–63.

Sakuragi, T. (2004). Association of culture with shyness among Japanese and American university students. *Perceptual and Motor Skills*, 98: 803–13.

Samimy, K. K., & Kobayashi, C. (2004). Toward the development of intercultural communicative competence: Theoretical and pedagogical implications for Japanese English teachers. *JALT Journal*, 26(2): 245–61.

Samovar, L. A., & Porter, R. E. (2003). Understanding intercultural communication: An introduction and overview. In L. A. Samovar & R. E. Porter (eds.), *Intercultural Communication: A reader* (10th edn, pp. 6–17). Belmont, CA: Thomson Wadsworth.

Sato, C. J. (1982). Ethnic styles in classroom discourse. In M. Hines & W. Rutherford (eds.), *On TESOL '81* (pp. 11–24). Washington, DC: TESOL.

Sato, M. (2007). Social relationships in conversational interaction: Comparison of learner-learner and learner-NS dyads. *JALT Journal, 29*(2): 183–208.

Saunders, G. R. (1985). Silence and noise as emotion management styles: An Italian case. In D. Tannen & M. Saville-Troike (eds.), *Perspectives on Silence* (pp. 165–83). Norwood, NJ: Ablex.

Saville-Troike, M. (1985). The place of silence in an integrated theory of communication. In D. Tannen & M. Saville-Troike (eds.), *Perspectives on Silence* (pp. 3–18). Norwood, NJ: Ablex.

Saville-Troike, M. (1989). *The Ethnography of Communication: An introduction*. Oxford: Basil Blackwell.

Scheidecker, D., & Freeman, W. (1999). *Bringing Out the Best in Students: How legendary teachers motivate kids*. Thousand Oaks, CA: Corwin Press.

Scollon, R. (1985). The machine stops: Silence in the metaphor of malfunction. In D. Tannen & M. Saville-Troike (eds.), *Perspectives on Silence* (pp. 21–30). Norwood, NJ: Ablex.

Scollon, R., & Scollon, S. W. (1981). *Narrative, Literacy, and Face in Interethnic Communication*. Norwood, NJ: Ablex.

Scollon, R., & Scollon, S. W. (1990). Athabaskan-English Interethnic communication. In D. Carbaugh (ed.), *Cultural Communication and Intercultural Contact* (pp. 259–86). Hillsdale, NJ: Lawrence Erlbaum Associates.

Seargeant, P. (2008). Ideologies of English in Japan: The perspective of policy and pedagogy. *Language Policy, 7*(2): 121–42.

Segal, M. W. (1974). Alphabet and attraction: An unobtrusive measure of the effect of propinquity in a field setting. *Journal of Personality and Social Psychology, 30*(5): 654–57.

Sekeres, A. (2010). Dispatching a lower quality of education. *The Language Teacher, 34*(2): 74–5.

Shrum, J. L. (1984). Wait-time and student performance level in second language classrooms. *Journal of Classroom Interaction, 20*(1): 29–35.

Shrum, J. L. (1985). Wait-time and the use of target or native languages. *Foreign Language Annals, 18*(4): 305–13.

Sifianou, M. (1997). Silence and politeness. In A. Jaworski (ed.), *Silence: Interdisciplinary perspectives* (pp. 63–84). Berlin: Mouton de Gruyter.

Sinclair, J., & Coulthard, M. (1975). *Towards an Analysis of Discourse*. Oxford: Oxford University Press.

Sobkowiak, W. (1997). Silence and markedness theory. In A. Jaworski (ed.), *Silence: Interdisciplinary perspectives* (pp. 39–61). Berlin: Mouton de Gruyter.

Spada, N., & Fröhlich, M. (1995). *COLT Communicative Orientation of Language Teaching Observation Scheme: Coding conventions and applications*. Sydney: Macquarie University, National Centre for English Language Teaching and Research.

Spratt, M. (2005). Washback and the classroom: The implications for teaching and learning of studies of washback from exams. *Language Teaching Research, 9*(1): 5–29.

Stake, R. (1995). *The Art of Case Study Research*. Thousand Oaks, CA: Sage.

Stapleton, P. (1995). The role of Confucianism in Japanese education. *The Language Teacher*, 19(4): 13–16.
Steger, B. (2006). Sleeping through class to success: Japanese notions of time and diligence. *Time & Society*, 15(2/3): 197–214.
Susser, B. (1998). EFL's othering of Japan: Orientalism in English language teaching. *JALT Journal*, 20(1): 49–82.
Suzuki, T. (1986). Language and behavior in Japan: The conceptualization of personal relations. In T. S. Lebra & W. P. Lebra (eds.), *Japanese Culture and Behavior: Selected readings* (Revised edn, pp. 142–57). Honolulu: University of Hawaii Press.
Swain, M. (1995). Three functions of output in second language learning. In G. Cook & B. Seidlhofer (eds.), *Principles and Practice in Applied Linguistics: Studies in honour of H. G. Widdowson* (pp. 125–44). Oxford: Oxford University Press.
Swain, M. (2005). The output hypothesis: Theory and research. In E. Hinkel (ed.), *Handbook of Research in Second Language Teaching and Learning* (pp. 471–83). Mahwah, NJ: Lawrence Erlbaum.
Swain, M., & Lapkin, S. (1998). Interaction and second language learning: Two adolescent French students working together *Modern Language Journal*, 82(3): 320–37.
Swann, J. (1992). *Girls, Boys and Language*. Oxford: Blackwell.
Taguchi, N. (2005). The communicative approach in Japanese secondary schools: Teachers' perceptions and practice. *The Language Teacher*, 29(3): 3–11.
Tanabe, Y. (2004). What the 2003 MEXT Action Plan proposes to teachers of English. *The Language Teacher*, 28(3): 3–8.
Tannen, D. (1981). The machine-gun question: An example of conversational style. *Journal of Pragmatics*, 5(5): 383–97.
Tannen, D. (1984). *Conversational Style: Analysing talk among friends*. Norwood, NJ: Ablex.
Tannen, D. (1985). Silence: Anything but. In D. Tannen & M. Saville-Troike (eds.), *Perspectives on Silence* (pp. 93–111). Norwood, NJ: Ablex.
Tannen, D. (1990). Silence as conflict management in fiction and drama: Pinter's *Betrayal* and a short story, 'Great Wits'. In A. Grimshaw (ed.), *Conflict Talk* (pp. 260–79). Cambridge: Cambridge University Press.
Tedeschi, J. T. (ed.). (1981). *Impression Management Theory and Social Psychological Research*. New York: Academic Press.
Terao, Y., Suzuki, M., Nasukawa, T., & Takahashi, M. (2010). Yōchien de no eigokatsudō no kokoromi ni yoru enji no manabi to kyōin no manabi: Hyōgo to kyōin e no chōsa ni motozuite [What children and teachers learned through English activity lessons in a kindergarten class: Based on the questionnaire survey toward parents and interview to teachers]. *The Journal of the School of Education, Hyogo University of Teacher Education*, 22: 1–12.
Thelan, E., & Smith, L. (1994). *A Dynamic Systems Approach to the Development of Cognition and Action*. Cambridge, MA: MIT Press.
Thorp. D. (1991). Confused encounters: Differing expectations in the EAP classroom. *ELT Journal*, 45(2): 108–18.
Tobin, K. G. (1987). The role of wait-time in higher cognitive learning. *Review of Educational Research*, 57(1): 69–95.

Trompenaars, F. (1993). *Riding the Waves of Culture: Understanding cultural diversity in business*. London: The Economist.
Tsuda, Y. (2000). *Eigo beta no susume: Eigo shinkō wa mō suteyō [A recommendation for bad English: Let's get rid of English worship]*. Tokyo: Wani no NEW Shinsho.
Tsui, A. B. M. (1985). Analyzing input and interaction in second language classrooms. *RELC Journal*, 16(1): 8–32.
Tsui, A. B. M. (1996). Reticence and anxiety in second language learning. In K. M. Bailey & D. Nunan (eds.), *Voices from the Language Classroom: Qualitative research in second language education* (pp. 145–67). Cambridge: Cambridge University Press.
Tsunoda, T. (1985). *The Japanese Brain: Uniqueness and universality*. Tokyo: Taishukan.
Ushioda, E. (2009). A person-in-context relational view of emergent motivation, self and identity. In Z. Dornyei & E. Ushioda (eds.), *Motivation, Language Identity and the L2 Self* (pp. 215–28). Bristol: Multilingual Matters.
van Geert, P. (2008). The dynamic systems approach in the study of L1 and L2 acquisition: An introduction. *The Modern Language Journal*, 92(2): 179–99.
van Lier, L. (2005). Case study. In E. Hinkel (ed.), *Handbook of Research in Second Language Learning and Teaching* (pp. 195–208). Mahwah, NJ: Lawrence Erlbaum.
Vogel, E. (1963). *Japan's New Middle Class: The salary man and his family in a Tokyo suburb*. Berkeley, CA: University of California Press.
Wada, M., & Cominos, A. (1994). *Studies in Team Teaching*. Tokyo: Kenkyusha.
Walsh, S. (2002). Construction or obstruction: Teacher talk and learner involvement in the EFL classroom. *Language Teaching Research*, 6(1): 3–23.
Watanabe, Y. (1996). Does grammar translation come from the entrance examination? Preliminary findings from classroom-based research. *Language Testing*, 13(3): 318–33.
Watts, R. J. (1997). Silence and the acquisition of status in verbal interaction. In A. Jaworski (ed.), *Silence: Interdisciplinary perspectives* (pp. 87–115). Berlin: Mouton de Gruyter.
Weiner, M. (ed.) (1997). *Japan's Minorities: The illusion of homogeneity*. New York: Routledge.
Wilson, T. P., & Zimmerman, D. H. (1986). The structure of silence between turns in two-party conversation. *Discourse Processes*, 9(4): 375–90.
Woods, D. (1989). Studying ESL teachers' decision-making: Rationale, methodological issues and initial results. *Carleton Papers in Applied Linguistics*, 6: 107–23.
Yamada, H. (1997). *Different Games, Different Rules: Why Americans and Japanese misunderstand each other*. New York: Oxford University Press.
Yashima, T. (2002). Willingness to communicate in a second language: The Japanese EFL context. *The Modern Language Journal*, 86(1): 54–66.
Yashima, T. (2010). The effects of international volunteer work experiences on intercultural competence of Japanese youth. *International Journal of Intercultural Relations*, 34(3): 268–82.
Yashima, T., & Zenuk-Nishide, L. (2008). The impact of learning contexts on proficiency, attitudes, and L2 communication: Creating an imagined international community. *System*, 36(4): 566–85.
Yohena, S. O. (2003). Conversational styles and ellipsis in Japanese couples' conversations. In L. J. Thiesmeyer (ed.), *Discourse and Silencing* (pp. 79–110). Philadelphia, PA: John Benjamins.

Yokoyama, A. (1999). Yochien ni okeru eigokyoiku no kōka ni tsuite no kenkyu [A study on the effects of teaching English to kindergarten children]. *Bulletin of Kyushu Women's University*, 35(3): 1–18.

Yoneyama, S. (1999). *The Japanese High School: Silence and resistance*. New York: Routledge.

Yoshida, K. (2003). Language education policy in Japan: The problem of espoused objectives versus practice. *The Modern Language Journal*, 87(2): 290–2.

Yule, G. (1996). *Pragmatics*. Oxford: Oxford University Press.

Yule, G. (2006). *The Study of Language* (3rd edn). Cambridge: Cambridge University Press

Yum, J. O. (1994). The impact of Confucianism on interpersonal relationships and communication patterns in East Asia. In L. A. Samovar & R. E. Porter (eds.), *Intercultural Communication: A reader* (7th edn, pp. 75–86). Belmont, CA: Wadsworth Thomson.

Zimmerman, D. H. (1998). Discoursal identities and social identities. In C. Antaki & S. Widdicombe (eds.), *Identities in Talk* (pp. 87–106). London: Sage.

Zimmerman, M. A. (1985). *Dealing with the Japanese*. London: Unwin.

Zuengler, J., Ford, C., & Fassnacht, C. (1998). *Analyst Eyes and Camera Eyes: Theoretical and technical considerations in 'seeing' the details of classroom interaction*. Albany, NY: School of Education, University of Albany.

Glossary of selected Japanese terms

The following Japanese terms have been included in the text either because they are commonly referred to in English-language academic works focusing on education in Japan; a direct English translation does not exist; or their English translation produces a slightly different connotation to the original.

aisatsu	ritualised greetings/leave-takings involving highly predictable set phrases
amae	emotional dependence; sometimes translated as 'sweet dependence'
a-un no kokyuu	lit., ah-hm breathing; used to signify two people are on the same wavelength
daigaku nyūshi sentā shiken	National Center Test for University Admissions (Center Test)
eigo shinkō	lit., English worship; refers to the exalted status afforded to study of the English language in Japan
gaijin mitai	like a foreigner
gaijin	lit., outside person – a foreigner; shortened and less polite form of *gaikokujin*, hence widely considered a derogatory term
hāfu	lit., half; used to denote a person (child) of mixed Japanese-foreign ethnicity; widely considered to be pejorative
haiku	traditional three-line Japanese poetry using a set number of syllables
haragei	lit., belly art; following the traditional Japanese belief that one's true emotions are located in the stomach, *haragei* refers to unspoken, implicit communication; used extensively in *nihonjinron* literature
hazukashii	embarrassed/embarrassing
hensachi	deviation score used to indicate one's academic ranking
hito	person or people at large; may be used to refer to a ubiquitous, watching 'other'
ijime	bullying; has the connotation of collective bullying of an individual
juken eigo	examination English; used to refer to a form of English studied in schools which stresses detailed linguistic knowledge over communicative competence
juku	private cram school where students study out of regular school hours
kikokushijo	returnee; students who have returned from living abroad
kōhai	a junior; someone younger/subordinate within a group (cf. *senpai*)
kotowaza	proverbs; common sayings

Glossary of selected Japanese terms

mawari	the periphery, surroundings; may be used to describe the people around one
mendōkusai	'I can't be bothered' or 'It's too much trouble'
nihonjinron	theories of the Japanese; a body of pseudo-sociological and pseudo-psychological literature aimed at illustrating the uniqueness of the Japanese race
niji shiken	lit., Second Tests; university entrance examinations set and administered by individual faculties
omoiyari	empathy; the ability to show consideration for and understand the feelings of others
rōnin	lit., a masterless samurai; used to denote a failed university entrance exam candidate no longer of high school age preparing to retake the exam/exams
sasshi	guess or conjecture; used to denote the skill of being able to surmise a person's under-elaborated meaning; linked to the concept of empathy
seken	society; the people around one
senpai	a senior; someone older/of higher status within a group (cf. *kōhai*)
shūi	the periphery, surroundings; see *seken*, *mawari* (appears as *shui* (sic) in text)
shutaisei	individual autonomy
soto	outside; often used to refer to individuals not members of one's own group (cf. *uchi*)
tani	credits needed for passing a class
tatemae	one's socially acceptable and officially stated position as opposed to one's true, innermost beliefs
uchi	inside; often used to refer to individuals who are members of one's own group (cf. *soto*)
yakudoku	a traditional grammar-translation language learning method
yōchien	a nursery school for children up to the age of five years

Appendix 1: The Classroom Oral Participation Scheme (COPS)

190 *Appendix 1: The Classroom Oral Participation Scheme (COPS)*

A step-by-step guide to using the COPS

The Classroom Oral Participation Scheme (COPS) has been designed to be a relatively easy-to-use, uncomplicated research instrument which can provide clear quantitative data about oral participation and student modality over the course of a language lesson. You do not need to be an experienced researcher to use the COPS and below I provide a simple step-by-step guide to using the scheme effectively.

1. After choosing the class you intend to observe, ensure appropriate ethical protocols are followed by gaining consent from relevant parties. Note that it would be impossible for a teacher both to use the COPS and to teach a class at the same time. In order to collect reliable data, it is necessary to devote all one's attention solely to observing events.

2. A pre-observation meeting with the participant instructor is a good opportunity to establish trust and emphasise the need to avoid putting on a 'show lesson' for your benefit. It is important that the instructor deems your observation to be non-threatening, otherwise you will encounter out-of-the-ordinary behaviour. Reassure him/her that you will be non-judgmental and stress the confidentiality of any data collected.

3. Decide how many times you will observe the class. The more, the better is the general rule of thumb here. One idea is to discard data from a couple of early sessions and instead use these observations as a means of familiarising yourself with the instrument and reducing *observer effect* by helping participants get used to your presence.

4. Take up a good vantage point from which to observe events, making sure your position is non-intrusive. I recommend being seated (thus creating a smaller presence) and avoiding movement around the room (this distracts students and will consequently distort your data). Avoid sitting at the back of the room as you will be unable to observe students' faces.

5. Initially some learners may be curious about who you are and what you are doing so it is a good idea to introduce yourself right at the start of the first observation session. Keep this introduction as brief and as general as possible. In-depth explanations about your silence-orientated research are to be avoided as they will likely inhibit learners' oral participation even more.

6. Decide upon the three individual students who you will track for the session. Your sampling strategy here will depend upon the focus of your research. It is a good idea to ask instructors for recommendations about whom to watch but do bear in mind that they might well be keen for you to follow their most active students. It is particularly important that you have a clear line of sight to each of the three individually observed students.

7. I do not recommend making a video recording of the class, because the presence of a camera can be rather off-putting and does tend to cause atypical behaviour amongst students (and teachers too!). Much better to make a high quality sound recording to go along with the information you collect on the COPS. Having a sound recording as a back-up source of data can prove useful if you need to check something later on. Make sure to test your equipment thoroughly prior to data collection in order to ensure the

Appendix 1: The Classroom Oral Participation Scheme (COPS)

recording is of an acceptable quality. Always carry spare batteries for the recording device and check there is sufficient space left on its file/tape.

8. Wait until everyone is settled in their seats, the register has been called and the lesson proper has actually begun before commencing with data collection. Use the time at the beginning of the class to get your bearings and locate the three individual students you have decided to track.
9. Try to avoid eye contact with class members and try not to initiate any interaction. Your aim from now on is to be as invisible as possible.
10. The COPS has two sections. The first, on the left of the scheme, focuses on the overall participant organisation of oral interaction (i.e. who in the class is speaking and how this talk is organised). The second section looks at the modality of the three individual students (i.e. whether the student is speaking, writing, listening, and so on). Using the timer on your digital recorder (or a stopwatch if your recording device does not have a timer), spend one minute observing the class as a whole and the three individual students.
11. When the minute is up, simply place a tick in the appropriate boxes on the COPS to indicate the events you have observed. There should be one tick for the whole-class section and one for each of the three students. The coding categories are explained in detail on pages 87 to 89.
12. In the event of students performing a combination of skills during the minute of observation, follow a primary focus coding convention. This means it is the most significant activity and the one which takes up the most time during the segment that is recorded on the scheme.
13. The intensity of your observation will make it difficult, but, if you are able, make any brief notes in the column on the left of the COPS.
14. To build up a chronological picture of events within the classroom, after the class has ended, simply add up the ticks for each column. These totals represent the number of minutes a behaviour or activity was observed to have occurred.

Appendix 2: The Silence and Oral Participation Interview Guide (SOPIG)

English version

Sociolinguistic competence

- There is a saying in Japanese: *iwanu ga hana* (to say nothing is a flower). We don't have this saying in English. Can you explain what it means? Would it be relevant in a classroom?
- In classroom situations in my country, there are times to speak and times to be quiet. There are also times when one is invited to speak but it's difficult. Do you have these in your classroom?
- We know that some Japanese students remain silent in class because they lack foreign language ability. However, I find it interesting that students with a relatively high level of ability sometimes also stay silent in the classroom. Can you explain why this is?

Silence as a politeness strategy

- Studies have shown that some East Asian students tend to avoid asking their teacher questions in public through fear of the teacher losing face if s/he doesn't know the answer. Do students in Japan show a similar concern for protecting the teacher's face?
- We know that some students avoid speaking out in front of the rest of the class because they feel it takes valuable time away from their classmates? Can you explain this behaviour? Are students who often take the floor selfish and inconsiderate towards their classmates?
- Is it easier to speak to the teacher in private? Is there usually a chance to do this?

Group dynamics

- Research has shown that some students stay silent in class when they feel intimidated by the other students watching and judging them. Why does this happen?
- When is it easy to speak English in front of others? When is it particularly difficult?

Practical strategies

- If you don't understand something in your English class, what do you do? Honestly!
- Have you ever wanted to ask the teacher a question but didn't? What happened? Be honest!
- We know that some students miss opportunities to speak in the classroom because they are slowed down by meticulously translating everything in their heads before speaking. Do you feel you get enough thinking time in class? Do you ever feel rushed in your English class? When?

Valuations

- Are good students in Japan quiet or talkative?
- In sum: is silence good or bad?

Closing

- Is there anything that you would like to add before we finish?
- Can you think of a good question I should ask in my next interview?
- Follow-up interview? Details?

Japanese version

インタビューガイド

社会言語学
- 日本には『言わぬが花』ということわざがありますが、英語にはありません。このことわざ、どういう時に使われますか？教室内において『言わぬが花』の状況がありますか？
- 私の国の場合、授業中には、話している時間と静かにしている時間があります。また、発言を求められることもありますが難しいです。あなたの外国語の授業ではどうですか？授業の様子を教えてください。
- 語学力が不十分のため授業中に発言しない日本人学生は分かりますが、十分な語学力があっても発言しない生徒がいます。どうして発言しないのだと思いますか？

丁寧行動の方略としての沈黙
- 調査によると、東アジア諸国の学生の中には、先生が自分の質問に答えられず面目を失ってしまうことを気遣い、公の場での先生への質問は避ける傾向にあるようです。日本でも、生徒は先生の面目を守るために何か気を遣いますか？
- 生徒の中には、クラスメートの貴重な時間を自分の発言によって奪いたくないという理由から、みんなの前での発言は避けている生徒もいるようです。この行動の、真の理由は何なのでしょうか？発言する生徒は自己中心的で、思いやりがないのでしょうか？
- 先生とはみんなの前よりプライベートでの方が話しやすいですか？通常、先生とプライベートで話す機会はありますか？

グループ内での他者への感受性
- 研究では、生徒が授業中、発言せず黙ったままでいるのは、他の生徒に見られていることや、自分の発言に対する評価を恐れているためであることを明らかにしています。どうしてこのような状況が起こるのでしょうか？
- 他の生徒の前でも英語で気楽に話せるのはどういうときですか？どういうときに特に話しづらいですか？

教室内での実際的戦略
- 英語の授業中、分からないことがあったら、あなたはどうしますか？正直に教えてください。
- 先生に聞きたいことがあったけど、実際には聞かなかった、という経験がありますか？どうしてですか？正直に話してください。
- 生徒の中には、頭の中で単語を1つずつ訳している間に時がたち、発言の機会を無くしてしまった生徒もいるようです。授業では、考える時間が十分にありますか？英語の授業で急かされていると感じたことがありますか？どんな時ですか？

全般評価
- 日本では、良い生徒とは、静かな生徒とよく話す生徒のどちらですか？
- つまり、沈黙は良いことですか、悪いことですか？

終わりに
- インタビューを終了する前に何か言い加えたいことがありますか？
- 他の人のインタビューで聞いた方がいいような、いい質問がありますか？
- 次のインタビューはいつにしますか？時期、詳細。

A step-by-step guide to using the SOPIG

Interviewing learners about classroom silence is no easy task. This brief, step-by-step guide to using the Silence and Oral Participation Interview Guide (SOPIG) outlines a sequence of strategies for effectively investigating participants' beliefs and experiences about not speaking in class. The SOPIG has been designed to be used in semi-structured interviews, meaning it is not essential to work your way religiously through all of its questions. Indeed, it is important to be flexible during the interview by pursuing interesting lines of enquiry as and when they emerge, drawing on the SOPIG only when you think it necessary to keep the encounter moving along productively. The steps below focus on preparing for and conducting data collection. For a detailed overview of interview data analysis, I recommend Richards (2003).

1. Sampling is of course a crucial factor in the success of any interview research. Although my own project included a number of student interviewees who regarded themselves and were regarded by others as extremely taciturn, I think perceptiveness is a much more important quality for an interviewee to have. Use student and teacher recommendations as a means to identify learners who will be able to provide you with a certain level of insight.
2. It is important to have a pre-interview meeting with your participant. This is an opportunity for you to explain the research procedures and make reassurances about subject anonymity and the confidentiality of the data. Go through the consent form (see below) and answer any questions the participant may have.
3. The pre-interview meeting is a time for creating rapport and trust with the participant. Be ready to engage in small talk, emphasise that the interview is not some kind of test and make it clear there are no right or wrong answers to your questions. It is better to come across as competent but slightly clueless about the topic under investigation. If you come across as some kind of important, expert professor, the interviewee may become inhibited and clam up.
4. Give the interviewee a copy of the SOPIG (preferably written in his/her L1). You do not want pre-prepared, memorised answers but you do want the participant to start thinking about some of the areas that the SOPIG covers. This stage is important because classroom silence is an issue that the interviewee may not have considered before.
5. If possible, provide the participant with a choice of language for the interview. In the research presented in this book, some students chose L1, some L2 and others a mixture of both Japanese and English. A choice of language should encourage your participants to produce richer data.
6. Choose your interview room with care. Somewhere that you will not be disturbed (a sign on the door is a good idea) and which will be comfortable for the interviewee is ideal. Arrange the room's furniture in such a way that hierarchies are reduced. For example, if one chair is slightly higher than others, offer it to your participant.
7. Check, double check and triple check that your recording device has sufficient power for the interview's duration and that it has enough file/tape

Appendix 2: The Silence and Oral Participation Interview Guide (SOPIG)

space left for the data. Ensure you have a foolproof system for naming all of the files/tapes that you produce.

8. Before the interview proper begins, a little small talk usually should help the participant to relax. After the consent form has been signed and the recorder switched on, start with some basic bio-data questions that the interviewee can answer easily. It is better not to take notes as this may be too distracting both for you and the interviewee.

9. The SOPIG is divided into seven sections covering six areas connected to learner silence and oral participation (sociolinguistic competence, silence as a politeness strategy, group dynamics, practical strategies, valuations and closings). It is not strictly necessary to cover the sections in the order they appear on the guide (though 'closings' should of course come last!) but the questions have been designed to logically progress with a certain amount of coherence.

10. Remember that it is the interviewee's job to talk, and ideally, the interviewer should say as little as possible, only breaking in to ensure the participant's testimony remains relevant. There are a number of ways to prompt participants but I find one of the most effective is merely to repeat in a questioning tone a key word that has been used by the interviewee.

11. As the interview progresses, it is important not respond critically to what your participant says. Be aware of your body language. Try to remain supportive and non-judgmental in order to encourage an open and honest account about, what is for many learners, quite a sensitive topic.

12. Aim for the interview to last around 45 minutes, although feel free to extend this if things are going particularly well and insightful, interesting data is flowing freely from your interviewee!

13. The final section of the SOPIG helps to close the encounter, providing the respondent with an opportunity to raise any points that were not covered during the interview. This section also asks for details of a follow-up interview session. A follow-up is essential if one is to clarify misunderstandings and gain useful extra data on interesting lines of enquiry that emerge following transcription of the interview recording.

Interview consent form – English version

Consent to participate in research

Researcher: Jim KING   Email: abcd@efg.ac.uk

The University of Leicester, UK   Tel: 0123 456 789

Thank you for agreeing to take part in this research project which considers aspects related to classroom discourse in university L2 environments. This form briefly outlines the nature of the study and sets out your rights as a participant.

Participation in this research is entirely voluntary. You may withdraw or refuse to participate at any time without penalty. If you are happy to participate, please sign/stamp and date the bottom of this form.

Our interview will last for about 1 hour and will be recorded. All information collected during the research is confidential and will only be used for the purposes of research. This means your identity will be kept strictly anonymous and I will not divulge your name to any outside parties. Your name will not be revealed in any publications which may result from this research.

Participating in this research will not affect your grade. Your teachers will not find out your responses. Please speak openly and honestly.

If you have any questions about the research, please feel free to contact Jim KING using the contact details set out above.

I have read and understood the information in this consent form and I voluntarily agree to participate in this research project. I can confirm I have received a 1000 yen gift card recompense for this interview.

Your signature/stamp _____   Date _____

Your name (PRINT) _____

Japanese version

研究協力同意書への署名のお願い

この度は、研究プロジェクト「外国語の授業内における大学生のコミュニケーション」にご協力くださりありがとうございます。以下、本研究の本質と協力者側の権利について簡単に説明いたしますので、ご確認の上、ご署名をお願いいたします。

(研究者)

氏　名　キング　ジム

所属大学　レスター大学（英国）

E-mail アドレス　abcd@efg.ac.uk　　　電　話　0123 456 789

記

本研究への協力は完全任意です。途中、インタビューを中断することや、回答を拒否することは、いつでも可能です。また、それらにおけるペナルティーなどはございません。

インタビューは約1時間程度で、音声を録音させていただきます。

研究中に収集した全ての情報は研究以外の目的に使用されることはなく、その秘密を保持します。個人情報は厳密に扱いますので、個人名が外部に漏れることも、本研究の成果報告書等の出版物で個人名が公開されることもございません。

また、本研究への協力が、あなたの大学の成績に反映したり、大学の先生方があなたのインタビューの回答内容を後に知るようなこともありませんので、素直に率直な意見をお話しください。

本研究において質問がございましたら、上記のキング・ジム連絡先までいつでもご連絡ください。

以上

研究協力同意書

私は上記の内容を十分理解し、自らの意思に基づき本研究プロジェクトに協力することに同意します。

また、協力のお礼としてギフトカード（1000円）を受け取ったことをここに署名いたします。

平成　　　年　　　月　　　日

(協力者)

氏　名 (漢字) _____　㊞

氏　名 (ローマ字) _____

Appendix 3: The stimulated recall protocol: a step-by-step guide

Conducting a stimulated recall study in a naturalistic context (rather than in the more predictable environment of a linguistics laboratory) can be a rather hit and miss affair. A silence researcher may spend hours performing classroom observations until a suitable silent episode occurs involving a student who is willing to cooperate in a subsequent retrospective interview. To be successful at this method, you need to be patient, able to react quickly to events in the classroom and be very organised with post-lesson research procedures. Pilot testing is essential in order to get the hang of the technique. In Chapter 7 I provided a quite detailed account of how I conducted this method in my own project, so the following is just a quick step-by-step guide to the basic concepts. Of course, stimulated recalls are not limited to just student participants (as described below), they may equally be used with instructors. The following steps discuss strategies for data collection in the field. For a good overview of stimulated recall data analysis, I recommend Gass and Mackey (2000).

1. It sounds rather tautological, but every stimulated recall interview needs a stimulus. This is in order to help the participant remember an event that he/she experienced and to recollect his/her thoughts or feelings which related to it. In our case, there are two primary stimuli: the completed COPS sheet from the lesson the participant attended, and the relevant audio recording.
2. As you perform your classroom observation, be on the lookout for any silences that one of the three individually tracked students either produces or experiences directly. In the left-hand column of the COPS, make a note of the time the incident occurred so that later on you will be able to locate it easily on the recording device.
3. As soon as the lesson ends, approach the student to ask whether he/she will consent to a stimulated recall interview. You will have to be quick because learners tend to be very keen to disappear once the class ends! Only approach the student if you do not intend to observe the class again because participating in recall session focusing on silence may influence the student's subsequent classroom behaviour.
4. You should have a consent form handy and an interview room ready on the off-chance that the learner is free immediately. Although immediate recalls are best, if this is not possible, arrange for the session to take place no more than 24 hours later.
5. If your participant is free immediately, walk with him/her to the interview room and do everything in your power on your journey to put the student at ease.
6. I strongly recommend that the stimulated recall is conducted in the participant's L1. Talking about one's thoughts and feelings and discussing issues that one has perhaps not been conscious of before is a challenge enough in one's own mother tongue, let alone in a foreign language.

Appendix 3: The stimulated recall protocol: a step-by-step guide 199

7. After the consent form has been signed and the recording device switched on, describe to the student the part of the lesson where the silence took place. Describe what task or activity was taking place in as much detail as possible. After a brief explanation of the scheme's features, you can point to the event on the relevant section of the completed COPS coding sheet. You can also play the audio recording of the lesson immediately prior, during and after the silence event. If the student was using a textbook/handout at the time of the silence, use this material to jog the person's memory.
8. In reality, if interviews are conducted promptly, many students will recall incidents purely from the verbal description that you provide, particularly if the silence involved them not answering a question that was posed directly to them by the instructor. Even so, it does not hurt to employ the stimuli that you have available.
9. Ask the participant, 'What were you thinking just prior/during/after the silence?' Stress that you want to know what was going through the participant's head at that time of the incident, not what the person is thinking now. It may be necessary to repeatedly reassure the participant that everything is fine, that they have done nothing wrong and that you would just like him/her to answer your questions honestly.
10. Be ready to ask suitable follow-up questions and to employ prompting techniques if necessary but be careful not to lead the participant into giving an account that you want to hear. Remember to ask about how the student perceived his/her co-participants. Follow-up questions do not necessarily have to be cognitively orientated.
11. Before thanking the respondent and closing the session, say something like, 'Before we finish the interview, is there anything else that you would like to add?'
12. You may need to accept the fact that, no matter how well you conduct the session or how hard you try to put the respondent at ease, some learners will remain quite defensive when you question them about their classroom behaviour and their recall interviews may not produce any viable data.
13. Aim for the recall session to last only about ten to 15 minutes. After it has concluded, I recommend transcribing the encounter in full in order to provide the best possible materials for data analysis. A further useful post-session idea is to write down in a research log your own perceptions about the interview quite soon after it has ended.

Stimulated recall consent form – English version

Consent to participate in research

Researcher: Jim KING   Email: abcd@efg.ac.uk

The University of Leicester, UK   Tel: 0123 456 789

Thank you for agreeing to take part in this research project which considers aspects related to classroom discourse in university L2 environments. This form briefly outlines the nature of the study and sets out your rights as a participant.

Participation in this research is entirely voluntary. You may withdraw or refuse to participate at any time without penalty. If you are happy to participate, please sign/stamp and date the bottom of this form.

I would like to ask you some questions about your recent foreign language class and record your answers. You may choose to speak in either English or Japanese. All information collected during the research is confidential and will only be used for the purposes of research. This means your identity will be kept strictly anonymous and I will not divulge your name to any outside parties. Your name will not be revealed in any publications which may result from this research.

Participating in this research will not affect your grade. Your teachers will not find out your responses. Please speak openly and honestly.

If you have any questions about the research, please feel free to contact Jim KING using the contact details set out above.

I have read and understood the information in this consent form and I voluntarily agree to participate in this research project.

Your signature/stamp ....   Date ....

Your name (PRINT) ....

Stimulated recall consent form – Japanese version

研究協力同意書への署名のお願い

この度は、研究プロジェクト「外国語の授業内における大学生のコミュニケーション」にご協力くださりありがとうございます。以下、本研究の本質と協力者側の権利について簡単に説明いたしますので、ご確認の上、ご署名をお願いいたします。

(研究者)

氏　名　キング　ジム

所属大学　レスター大学 (英国)

E-mailアドレス　abcd@efg.ac.uk　　　電　話　　0123 456 789

記

本研究への協力は完全任意です。みなさんには、最近あった外国語の授業に関していくつか質問をしたいと思っています。音声は録音させていただきます。質問は英語・日本語のどちらを選んでいただいても構いません。途中で中断することや、回答を拒否することは、いつでも可能です。また、それらにおけるペナルティーなどはございません。

なお、研究中に収集した全ての情報は研究以外の目的に使用されることはなく、その秘密を保持します。個人情報は厳密に扱いますので、個人名が外部に漏れることも、本研究の成果報告書等の出版物で個人名が公開されることもございません。

また、本研究への協力が、あなたの大学の成績に反映したり、大学の先生方があなたのインタビューの回答内容を後に知るようなこともありませんので、素直に率直な意見をお話しください。

本研究において質問がございましたら、上記のキング・ジム連絡先までいつでもご連絡ください。

以上

研究協力同意書

私は上記の内容を十分理解し、自らの意思に基づき本研究プロジェクトに協力することに同意します。

平成　　　年　　　月　　　日

(協力者)

氏　名 (漢字) _____　㊞

氏　名 (ローマ字) _____

Author Index

Adams, R. S., 89
Agyekum, K., 13, 83
Akasu, K., 35, 36
Alberti, L., 18
Alderson, J. C., 71
Allwright, D., 90, 134, 146, 161
Anderson, F. E., 1, 42, 148
Anstey, M. E., 108
Asao, K., 35–6
Aspinall, R. W., 66, 69–72, 77, 79, 126
Auerbach, E. R., 168

Babin, P. A., 131
Bailey, K. M., 90, 134, 146, 161
Barnlund, D. C., 9, 39, 105, 137
Basso, K., 13, 23–5, 83
Befu, H., 37, 39, 47, 79
BenDebba, M., 18
Benwell, B., 148
Bernstein, B., 38
Bishop, J., 12
Blimes, J., 28
Blum-Kulka, S., 54
Bond, M. H., 39, 105
Bosher, S., 129
Braithwaite, C. A., 25–6, 141
Brislin, R. W., 136
Britzman, D. P., 18
Brown, J. D., 69–71, 73, 95
Brown, P., 35, 53–5, 63, 75
Browne, C., 73
Bruneau, T. J., 14, 19, 41, 44, 107, 139
Butefish, W. L., 129
Butler, Y. G., 68

CLAIR, 75, 77
Calderhead, J., 129
Cameron, L., 84–5, 96, 99, 101, 112, 116, 131, 142, 166
Camras, L. A., 45

Canale, M., 3
Carlsen, W. S., 141
Cathcart, D., 36–7, 116
Cathcart, R., 36–7, 116
Caudill, W., 45, 48
Cave, P., 65, 98,
Chafe, W. L., 60–1, 97
Chen, J., 51
Cheng, X., 40, 59
Clancy, P. M., 107, 115, 151
Clark, C. M., 129
Clayton, T., 91, 111
Clément, R., 131
Cohen, L., 2, 136, 161, 163
Cominos, A., 76
Coon, H. M., 39
Cope, J., 114
Coulthard, M., 96, 111
Crabtree, B. F., 10
Crown, C. L., 18–19

DaSilva Iddings, C., 4
Dale, P. N., 37–8, 47, 162
Dauenhauer, B. P., 13
Daulton, F. E., 79
de Bot, K., 2, 83–4, 99, 113, 131, 142, 156
De Mente, B. L., 34
Dinnel, D. L., 51
Djigunovlč, M. J., 67
Doi, T., 46–8
Dollinger, M. J., 34
Dore, R., 71
Dörnyei, Z., 2, 4, 17, 46, 50–1, 67, 84, 91, 97–8, 101, 106, 111, 114, 119, 131, 136, 163–5, 168
Doyon, P., 48, 70, 86, 95

Edwards, J., 148
Ehrman, M. E., 4, 17, 46, 50

Ellis, N. C., 84, 131
Ellis, R., 2, 83, 130, 167
Enninger, W., 53, 58, 107
Ephratt, M., 12, 20
Ericsson, K. A., 136
Essau, C. A., 51

Falout, J., 67
Fassnacht, C, 91
Feldstein, S., 18–19
Fennelly, M., 67
Fischer, J. L., 41–3
Flynn, C., 77
Fogel, A., 45
Ford, C., 91
Ford, K., 168
Forsyth, D. R., 117, 119
Foss, K. A., 38
Foster, P., 164
Fotos, S., 3
Fox-Turnbull, W., 129
Franks, P. H., 36, 54
Freeman, W., 115
Fröhlich, M., 8, 87, 89

Gardner, R. C., 114
Gass, S. M., 2, 10, 83, 128–30, 132, 135–7, 155, 161, 198
Gielen, U. P., 77
Gilbert, J. B., 60
Gilbert, R., 43
Gilmore, A., 167
Gilmore, P. 26–7, 92, 110
Goffman, E., 53, 75
Gomm, R., 164
Goodman, R., 71
Gorsuch, G. J., 72–4, 76, 96
Gow, L., 40
Granger, C. A., 17–18, 25, 122
Greer, D. L., 49–50, 53, 115, 156
Gudykunst, W. B., 9, 36–7, 39, 49, 54, 98, 105, 118, 122, 137
Guest, M., 29, 40, 68–9

Hall, E. T., 40
Hammersley, M., 164
Hamp-Lyons, L., 71
Hane, M., 35

Harumi, S. 52, 59–60
Hato, Y., 29, 68, 73, 124
Helgesen, M., 71
Hendry, J., 39, 44, 46, 65, 105, 137
Henrichsen, L. E., 72
Hino, N., 72–4, 96, 124
Hofstede, G., 39
Holliday, A., 3
Hokari, K., 43
Horwitz, E. K., 114
Horwitz, M. B., 114
Hudson, R. A., 41
Hymes, D., 22–3

Ide, R., 121
Iino, M., 68
Inoguchi, T., 109
Ishii, S., 19, 41, 44, 107
Iwashita, N., 2, 83
Izumi, S., 2, 83

Jacobs, G. M., 4
Jandt, F. E., 34, 36, 39–40
Jaworski, A., 6, 13–14, 17, 20, 28–9, 32, 36, 41, 43–4, 53, 56–7, 75, 92, 94, 107, 125, 133, 139
Jefferson, G., 56, 160
Johnson, D. W., 4
Johnson, K. E., 129
Johnson, R. T., 4
Jones, J. F., 95
Julé, A., 117

Kamada, L. D., 79
Kamiya, S., 64
Kanno, Y., 78, 92, 147
Kasahara, Y., 51–2
Katayama, H., 41
Kawai, M., 45
Kember, D., 40
Kemmelmeier, M., 39
Kerr, A., 78
Kikuchi, K., 70, 111
King, J., 90, 96
Kinmonth, E. H., 64, 68–9
Kleinknecht, E. E., 51
Kleinknecht, R. A., 51
Knapp, K., 75

Author Index 205

Kobayashi, C., 76
Kobayashi, Y., 72, 126
Koetting, M. G., 12
Kojima, N., 75
Kormos, J., 131
Korst, T. J., 1, 95
Kotloff, L. J., 66
Kowner, R., 37, 75, 105, 135
Kramsch, C., 37, 40, 55
Kubota, R., 40, 59, 80, 124
Kurzon, D., 14–17, 25, 51–2, 75, 110, 142
Kuwayama, T., 49

Labov, W., 9
Lane, R. C., 12
Lapkin, S., 2
Larsen-Freeman, D., 84–5, 96, 99, 101, 112, 116, 131, 142, 156, 166
Law, G., 73
Lawrie, A., 60
Lebra, T. S., 9, 19, 21, 36, 38, 48–9, 98, 105, 107, 115, 118, 137, 151
Lee-Cunin, M., 35, 68
Legatto, J. J., 131–2
Levelt, W. J. M., 131
Levinson, S., 35, 53–6, 63, 75
Lewis, C. C., 66
Li, H., 83, 135
Lincicome, M., 77
Lind, S. L., 96
Littlejohn, S. W., 38
Littlewood, W., 40, 59, 167
Long, M. H., 2, 83
Loveday, L., 35–6
Lowie, W., 84, 99, 113, 142
Luxton, R., 67
Lyle, J., 132

MEXT, 65–8, 85, 169
MacIntyre, P. D., 114, 131–2
Mackey, A., 2, 10, 83, 129–32, 135–7, 155, 161, 198
Maeda, R., 78
Mahoney, S., 76
Maki, H., 109
Malinowski, B., 32
Manion, L., 2, 136, 161

Maruyama, M., 67
Mattys, S. L., 160
McCafferty, S. G., 4
McCarthy, M., 97
McConnell, D. L., 75–7
McDaniel, E. R., 19, 34–6, 52, 98, 105, 107, 118, 142
McDonough, K., 2, 83, 130
McKay, S., 80, 124
McPake, J., 38
McVeigh, B. J., 35, 50, 70–2, 76, 86, 91, 97, 109, 111, 115, 143
Melhorn, J. F., 160
Miller, W. L., 106
Mitchell, R. G., 91
Miyake, K., 51
Miyanaga, K., 49
Miyazato, K., 74–7
Moeran, B., 36, 116
Morita, N., 148
Morrison, K., 2, 136, 161
Moskowitz, G., 8, 87
Mulligan, C., 29, 73, 75
Mulvey, B., 71
Murphey, T., 69, 71, 97, 168
Murphy, J. M., 91

Naito, T., 77
Nakane, C., 142
Nakane, I., 36–7, 40, 52, 55, 61, 97–8, 109, 129–30, 161
Nakatani, A., 45
Nasukawa, T., 66
National Center for University Entrance Exams, 69
Negishi, H., 70
Nikolov, M., 67
Nishida, T., 9, 36, 49, 54, 98, 105, 118, 137
Nishino, T., 68, 72–3, 124
Nunan, D., 129
Nwoye, G., 13

O'Brien, J., 129
O'Donnell, K., 68, 72–3
Oxford, R. L., 4, 114
Oyserman, D., 39

Paribakht, T. S., 129
Peak, L., 66, 116
Pederson, A., 104
Peterson, P. L., 129
Philips, S. U., 13, 83
Pleydell-Pearce, C. W., 160
Poland, B., 104
Poole, G. S., 29, 72, 94, 124
Porter, R. E., 41
Powney, J., 38
Pritchard, R. M. O., 44, 46, 109

Rebuck, M., 111
Reda, M. M., 83, 135
Reischauer, E. O., 34
Richards, K., xii, 89, 106, 148, 163, 194
Robinson, M. A., 129
Rogerson, P., 60
Rose, K., 43
Rovine, H., 43
Rowe, M. B., 147, 167
Ryan, S., 74, 110

Sachdev, I., 14, 28–9, 41, 92
Sacks, H., 56, 160
Sakai, H., 111
Sakamaki, S. 78
Sakano, Y., 51
Sakui, K., 29, 68, 73, 124
Sakuragi, T., 48, 51
Samimy, K. K., 76
Samovar, L. A., 41
San Antonio, P., 37, 39
Sapir, E., 20
Sasagawa, S., 51
Sato, C. J., 57, 95
Sato, M., 130
Saunders, G. R., 27, 38, 110
Saville-Troike, M., 13, 17, 21–3, 41–5, 53, 116, 141
Schegloff, E., 56, 160
Scheidecker, D., 115
Scollon, R., 19, 53–4, 57–9, 107
Scollon, S. W., 53–4, 57–9, 107
Seargeant, P., 79
Segal, M. W., 116
Sekeres, A., 77
Seki, A., 79

Shiraishi, D., 105
Shrum, J. L., 60, 147, 167
Sifianou, M., 7, 36, 53–4, 57, 107, 144
Simon, H. A., 136
Sinclair, J., 96, 111
Sloan, B., 18
Smith, L., 144, 159
Sobkowiak, W., 28, 44, 108, 139
Spada, N., 8, 87, 89
Spratt, M., 71
Stake, R., 164
Stapleton, P., 34, 37
Steger, B., 66, 96, 139
Stokoe, E. H., 148
Susser, B., 43
Suzuki, M., 66
Suzuki, T., 79–80, 107
Swain, M., 2–3, 83
Swann, J., 117

Taguchi, N., 68, 74
Takahashi, M., 66
Takatoku, S., 78
Tanabe, Y., 68
Tanaka, Y., 130
Tannen, D., 20–1, 36, 43, 53–4, 57, 107, 146
Taylor, J., 36
Tedeschi, J. T., 115
Terao, Y., 66
Thelan, E., 144, 159
Thorp, D., 60
Tobin, K. G., 147, 167
Toda, S., 45
Trompenaars, F., 57–8
Tsuda, Y., 79–80
Tsui, A. B. M., 114, 146, 162
Tsunoda, T., 38

Ukai Russell, N., 66
Ushioda, E., 98, 148

van Geert, P., 84, 131
van Lier, L., 164
Verspoor, M., 84, 99, 113, 142
Vogel, E., 45–6

Wada, M., 73, 76
Walsh, S., 146, 166
Watanabe, M., 68, 72-3, 124
Watanabe, Y., 71, 74
Watts, R. J., 56
Weiner, M., 38
Weinstein, H., 45, 48
Wesche, M., 129
Whitecross, S. E., 160
Williams, H., 44
Wilson, T. P., 161
Woodring, A. A., 39
Woods, D., 129

Yamada, H., 34, 44, 47, 49, 57-8, 79, 107, 151
Yamashita, S. O., 70, 95

Yamazaki, A., 130
Yamazaki, K., 51
Yashima, T., 92, 99, 119
Yohena, S. O., 47
Yokoyama, A., 66
Yoneoka, J., 43
Yoneyama, S., 71, 78, 95
Yoshida, K., 124
Yoshida, T., 41-3
Yule, G., 41
Yum, J. O., 34-5, 46

Zenuk-Nishide, L., 119
Zimbardo, P., 48
Zimmerman, D. H., 148-9, 160-1
Zimmerman, M. A., 34
Zuengler, J., 91

Subject Index

aisatsu, 121, 187
amae (see dependency), 46–9, 51, 60, 187
ambiguity, 12–13, 20, 24–5, 30, 44, 47, 52–5, 62
Amish, 58
Anglo-American, 14, 24, 58–9
Anglophone, 70
anxiety, 10, 15, 18, 24, 51, 55, 62, 90, 114, 132, 162
apathy, 95, 101, 118, 124, 128, 139–40, 143, 153, 158–9
assistant language teacher (ALT), 8, 64, 75–6
Athabaskan, 59
attendance, 86, 91, 111–12, 139, 142, 156
attractor, 9, 84–5, 95, 99–100, 111, 113, 116, 118–22, 126–7, 131, 140, 143, 150, 154, 156–8, 164–5
attractor basin, 85, 100, 112, 120, 126
attractor state, 9, 84–5, 98–9, 109, 119, 121, 124–8, 132, 140, 142, 147, 149, 154, 159, 162, 164
Australia, 61, 104, 130
authentic materials, 111, 167

back-translation, 106, 136
Brazil, 80
British, 103, 28–9, 38, 52
bullying (see *ijime*), 65, 77–8, 82, 87

California, 21
CANCODE corpus, 97
Center Test, 68–9, 71, 187
child-rearing, 7, 33, 44–5, 51
China, 34, 80
class credits, 112, 188

class size, 86, 118, 122, 125, 143
cliques, 10, 97–8, 116–20, 127, 144, 157, 168
coding, 8, 29, 61, 84, 87–9, 91, 97, 100, 106, 152–3, 161, 191
cognitive processing, 34, 58, 60–1, 63, 73, 97, 131, 136, 138, 147, 167
collectivism, 39, 116
COLT (Communicative Orientation of Language Teaching), 8, 87
communicative competence, 3, 64, 68, 166, 187
communicative language teaching (CLT), 3, 29, 50, 68, 71, 76, 100, 108, 124, 140, 166, 169
conflict, 4, 18, 28–9, 53–4
confrontation, 24, 27, 36, 52
Confucianism, 33–7, 46, 62
cooperative learning, 4
COPS (Classroom Oral Participation Scheme), 8–9, 84, 87–9, 91–2, 95, 97, 100–1, 134, 146, 152–4, 157, 160–2, 189–91, 198–9
cram school (see *juku*), 66, 187

deference, 23, 54
delusional social phobia (see *taijin-kyoufu*), 51
demotivation, 10, 67, 111
dependency (see *amae*), 46, 48, 187
discussion, 4, 37, 61, 88, 140–2, 147–50, 160
disengagement, 95–6, 112, 118, 124, 128, 139–40, 143, 158–9, 169
drilling, 73, 88, 133, 137–40, 143–4, 150, 158–9
dyadic interaction, 15, 17, 56, 130

Subject Index

dynamic systems theory (DST), 5, 9, 84–5, 95, 98–9, 102, 109, 113, 116–17, 119, 126–7, 131, 140, 142, 144, 146–8, 151, 153–4, 156–7, 164
dysfluency, 56

ego, 7, 27
elementary school, 65–7
ellipsis, 43, 47
embarrassment, 15, 23, 35, 49–52, 55, 62, 75, 98, 113–16, 122–3, 127, 135, 139, 156, 167, 187
emotional defence, 6, 30
empathy (see *sasshi*), 21, 33, 47–9, 51, 55, 152, 188
England, 21
examination, 3, 8, 43, 64–6, 68–72, 74, 76, 81, 90, 95, 110, 126, 143, 168–9, 187–8
examocracy, 71, 143
eye contact, 40, 52, 102, 121, 191

face, 7, 27, 32, 35, 53–6, 63, 75, 82, 98, 110, 127, 142, 156, 167, 192
face threatening act (FTA), 54–5
feedback, 2, 4, 87
FLint (Foreign Language interaction analysis system), 8, 87
fluency, 3, 36, 65, 79, 82, 167

gaijin (see foreigner), 49, 79, 187
gender, 45, 86, 117
grammar-translation (see *yakudoku*), 3, 64, 72, 81, 96, 188
group dynamics, 51, 97, 117–18, 167–8, 192, 195
group membership, 7, 22, 33, 36, 62, 98, 105, 168
group work, 88, 94, 123, 125, 142

hāfu, 79, 187
haiku (see poetry), 43, 187
haragei, 47, 187
hesitation, 23, 32, 34, 60–2, 97, 100, 160

hierarchy, 22, 33–4, 36–7, 105, 166, 194
homogeneity, 37–9, 79
Hong Kong, 162
Honshu, 86, 145
Hungarian, 14, 131
hyper-sensitivity, 48–51, 53, 63, 115, 127, 152

identity, 4, 17–18, 79–80, 82, 122, 148–50, 160, 196, 200
ijime (see bullying), 65, 77–8, 82, 187
implicit communication (see also *haragei*), 35, 38, 41–2, 45, 47–8, 63, 107, 151, 187
implicit knowledge/belief 136, 158
impression management, 115
individualism, 37, 39, 78, 116
infants, 44–6, 63
in-group, 33, 35–6, 98, 144, 168
inhibition, 6–7, 15–16, 33, 81, 97–9, 105, 113, 115–16, 118, 122, 152, 156, 167, 190, 194
input, 2, 67, 88, 97, 131, 146–7, 159, 166
Interaction Hypothesis, 2
intercultural communication, 6, 92, 99, 105, 123, 129, 135
IRF (Initiation Response Feedback), 96, 111, 166
Italian, 38

Japanese teacher of English (JTE), 3, 64, 74–7, 80, 82, 168
JET Programme, 75–7, 82
juken eigo, 72, 81, 187
juku (see cram school), 66, 187
junior high school, 65, 68, 70, 74, 86, 117, 122, 128, 134

kikokushijo (see returnees), 78–9, 92, 99, 147, 187
kindergarten, 39, 65
Korea, 57, 69, 80

language planning, 11, 165, 168
listening, 69, 74, 88–9, 94, 97, 100, 113, 130, 138–9, 145–6, 153, 191
literature, 7, 14, 33, 43–4, 62, 152

markedness theory, 28
memory, 10, 132, 135, 163, 199
MEXT (Ministry of Education, Culture, Sport, Science and Technology), 64, 66–9, 74, 78, 81, 169
miscommunication, 47, 59
mourning, 18, 24

nationalism, 65, 79
New York Jewish, 21
nihonjinron, 37–40, 48, 62, 80, 162, 187–8
niji shiken, 68–9, 71, 188
norm, 13, 40–1, 44, 51, 55, 59–60, 64, 99, 118–19, 145, 157
nursery school, 65–7, 70, 188

observer's paradox, 9
oral participation, 2–4, 6, 9, 50, 81, 87–8, 91–2, 94, 97, 100, 113, 116, 119, 127, 134, 144, 152–3, 156, 161–2, 165, 169, 190, 195
out-group, 35–6, 98, 118, 122, 168
output, 2–3, 130–1
outsourcing, 77
overlap, 6, 14, 21, 30, 57

pairwork, 71, 88, 94, 123–5, 128
pause, 7, 18–19, 23, 26, 30, 32–3, 43, 53, 57–61, 63, 73, 100, 107, 131, 139, 146–7, 160, 167
phatic silence, 20, 23
poetry (see *haiku*), 7, 33, 43, 62, 152, 187
Polish, 14
politeness, 7, 33, 36, 40, 53–5, 63, 144, 192, 195
power, 12, 22, 25–8, 30, 51, 57, 63, 92, 97, 105, 118, 137, 141–2, 146
proficiency, 10, 63, 67–8, 72, 78, 81–2, 86, 102–3, 110, 127, 136, 145, 147, 155–6, 168
propinquity, 116
proverbs, 7, 33, 41–4, 62, 152, 187
psychoanalysis, 12, 17, 51
psychoanalytic theory, 17–18, 30, 47, 48, 63

rapport, 4, 20–1, 54–5, 90, 105, 135, 154, 194
reactivity, 9, 90, 100, 134, 161
reading, 70, 73, 89, 97, 153
reform, 8, 64–5, 67–8, 72, 80–1, 169
reliability, 90, 100, 134, 136, 161
repeller, 119–20, 125
repeller state, 109, 132
restricted codes, 38
retrodictive modelling, 164–5
returnees (see *kikokushijo*), 78–9, 92, 99, 147, 187
rōnin, 69, 188

sampling, 9, 85–6, 88, 91, 103, 190, 194
sasshi (see empathy), 48–9, 58, 188
seating, 91, 105, 118, 122, 135, 168
seken, 49–51, 188
self/selves, 2, 7, 17–18, 36, 38–9, 49, 62, 105, 119, 121–2, 125, 152
self-concept, 18, 30, 148, 160
self-disclosure, 9, 42, 105
self-esteem, 50, 113, 132
self-monitoring, 33, 115
senior high school, 3, 65, 67–8, 70–1, 74, 81
Shakespeare, 145
shame, 42, 49–51, 113, 115
shyness, 15, 23, 48, 51, 95
silence –
  and awkwardness, 107, 109, 123
  and illocutionary force, 22, 53, 116
  and intentionality, 14–16, 30, 110, 136, 142
  and irritation, 107
  as a defensive strategy, 27, 50, 114–15, 142
  attitudes to, 7, 13–14, 28–9, 32–3, 40–1, 43–4, 57, 62
  beliefs about, 6, 9, 13–14, 28–9, 40–1, 44, 62, 103, 106, 126, 128, 149, 154, 158, 162, 194
  macro-level, 7–9, 32, 100, 152, 160, 165, 169
  micro-level, 7, 18, 23, 33, 56, 100, 131, 160–1
  of confusion, 97

silence – *(continued)*
  of disengagement, 95–6
  of non-verbal activities, 96
  of salient cliques (see also cliques), 97
  of teacher-centred methods, 96
silent period, 17–18, 30
sleeping in class, 89, 96, 139–40
social relationships, 7, 24–5, 46, 130, 142
socialisation, 7, 33, 44–5, 48, 63, 65, 81, 151
solidarity, 39, 54–5, 144
SOPIG (Silence and Oral Participation Interview Guide), 103, 106, 154, 192–7
speech tempo, 18–19
status, 13, 22–3, 25–7, 35, 38, 56, 76, 100, 105, 110, 113, 137, 141–2, 146, 166, 188
stereotyping, 21, 29, 37, 40, 59–60, 62–3, 159
student-initiated talk, 87, 92, 98, 100, 152, 159
student modality, 88–9, 91–2, 96, 100, 153, 161, 190–1
study abroad, 55, 94, 104, 108, 110, 119–20, 130, 140, 161
sulking, 19, 26–7, 110

superiority, 23

taijin-kyoufu (see delusional social phobia), 51
tatamae, 105, 137
teacher-initiated talk, 87, 92, 153
teacher talking time (TTT), 77, 146, 166
TOEFL (Test of English as a Foreign Language), 104, 109, 147
tolerance of silence, 4, 14, 20–1, 32–3, 57–8, 63, 97, 107–8, 155
turn-taking, 7, 33, 53, 56–8, 60–3, 95, 108, 130

UCAS (University and Colleges Admissions System), 29

validity, 87, 89, 91, 100, 135
video, 59, 91, 130–2, 190

wait-time, 60, 147, 167
washback, 70–1, 74, 95
Western Apache, 13, 23–5
writing, 34, 43, 74, 89, 97, 191

yakudoku (see grammar-translation), 8, 64, 72–4, 81, 96, 188

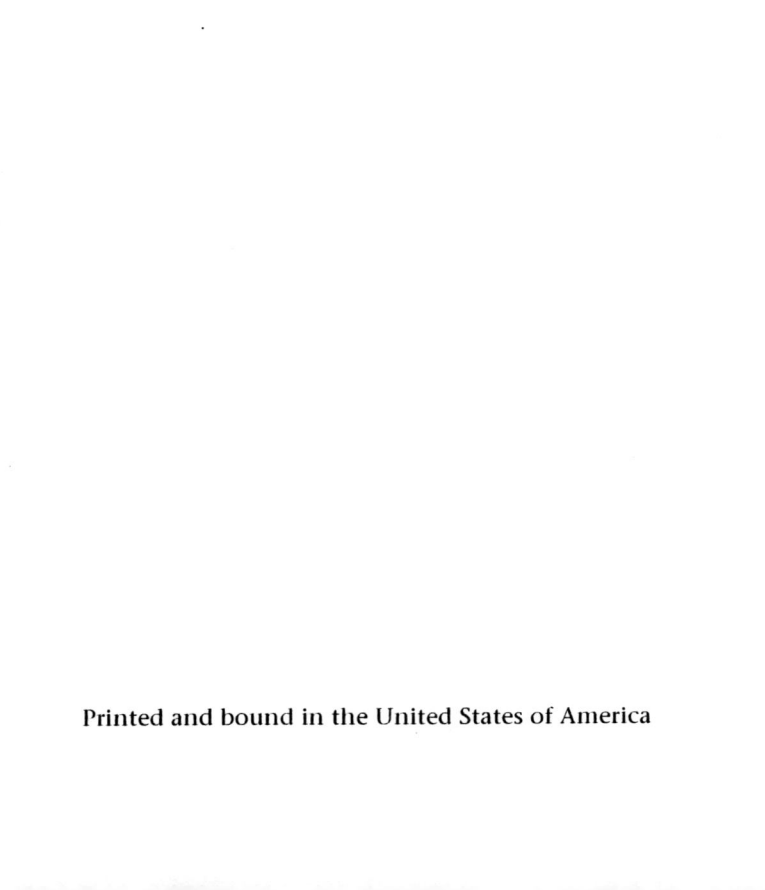

Printed and bound in the United States of America